DISASTERS at SEA

Copyright © 2009 Langenscheidt Publishing Group and Moseley Road Inc.

Published in the United States and its territories and Canada by
HAMMOND WORLD ATLAS CORPORATION
Part of the Langenscheidt Publishing Group
36-36 33rd Street, Long Island City, NY 11106

Produced for Hammond World Atlas Corporation by

MOSELEY ROAD INC.
129 MAIN STREET
IRVINGTON, NY 10533
WWW.MOSELEYROAD.COM

MOSELEY ROAD INC.
PUBLISHER Sean Moore
ART DIRECTOR Brian MacMullen
EDITORIAL DIRECTOR Lisa Purcell

SENIOR EDITOR Amber Rose
CONTRIBUTING WRITER Chris Carroll
PRODUCTION DESIGNERS Terasa Bernard, Joanne Flynn, Paul O'Brien
CARTOGRAPHY Neil Dvorak, Paul O'Brien
PHOTO RESEARCHER Ben DeWalt
EDITORIAL ASSISTANTS Rachael Lanicci, Jon Derengowski, Monica Pfister
COVER DESIGNER Jeffrey Beebe

Cover image courtesy of National Maritime Muesum, UK. *A Mediterranean Brigantine Drifting Onto a Rocky Coast in a Storm* by Willem van de Velde, the Younger, c. 1700.

Printed and bound in Canada

ISBN-13: 978-0843-708547

DISASTERS at SEA

A VISUAL HISTORY OF INFAMOUS SHIPWRECKS

LIZ MECHEM

HAMMOND World Atlas
Part of the Langenscheidt Publishing Group

▲ *Miranda - The Tempest* by John William Waterhouse, 1916

O, I have suffered
With those that I saw suffer! a brave vessel
(Who had no doubt some noble creature in her)
Dashed all to pieces! O, the cry did knock
Against my very heart! Poor souls, they perished!

—WILLIAM SHAKESPEARE, *The Tempest*

Contents

CONTENTS

HMS *Erebus* and
HMS *Terror*

SS *Princess Sophia*

RMS *Laurentic*
Spanish Armada

RMS *Lusitania*
Mary Rose

SS *Tonquin*

RMS *Empress of Ireland*

SS *Edmund Fitzgerald*

KMS *Bismarck*

SS *Andaste*   "*Great Shippe*"   Mont-Blanc
SS *Eastland*   *General Slocum*   Whydah
                  Golden Venture   Andrea Doria   Titanic
San Augustin   USS *Princeton*

Prestige

Mary Celeste

                              SS *Metropolis*
                           SS *Carroll A. Deering*
SS *Sultana*   USS *Monitor*
                         Queen Anne's Revenge

Trinidad

                        1715 Treasure Fleet

USS *Arizona*   Henrietta Marie
          Nuestra Señora de Atocha
                                USS *Maine*
                                        Santa Maria
                                            RMS *Rhone*

Medusa

MV *Le Joola*

Essex

Monongahela

USS *Wateree*

HMS *Bounty*

Shipwrecks around the World

◆ **known location
   of shipwreck**

◆ **exact location of
   shipwreck unknown**

ARA *General Belgrano*

Endurance

Vasa ◆ ◆ MS *Estonia*

Skuldelev Ships ◆
◆ MV *Wilhelm Gustloff*

◆ SS *Tubantia*

Noah's Ark

HMHS *Britannic* ◆

◆ Apostle Paul

◆ Kublai Khan's Fleet

L'Orient ◆

MS *al-Salam Boccaccio 98* ◆

MV *Doña Paz* ◆   ◆ USS *Indianapolis*

Tek Sing ◆

Batavia ◆

SS *Waratah* ◆
◆ HMS *Birkenhead*
Flying Dutchman

General Grant ◆

DOWN INTO THE DEPTHS

▲ A raging storm and rough seas batter the man-o'-war *Ridderschap* (right) and the *Hollandia* (left) against menacing rocks in the Strait of Gibraltar. The ships left Gibraltar in February 1694, never to be seen again.

Whenever a ship departs from shore, its crew members must fear that they will not return—it has always been so. Yet, whatever treasures the journey promises, whatever glory awaits in battle or discovery, these possible rewards always seem to outweigh the real risks. The sea itself is a charming companion, and, in the Age of Sail—and even beyond—it was a common conceit for sea captains to call it (or their ships) "mistress."

DANGER AHEAD

Most ships return safely to port. Yet, unfortunately, many do not. Storms, shoals, currents, human errors and arrogance, warfare, and piracy have brought down ships for millennia. Many shipwrecks vanished into the depths, never to be found again. Undoubtedly, we do not even know where to look for quite a few of these. Some famous ships—among them Christopher Columbus's most famous vessel, the *Santa Maria*—have eluded discovery despite centuries of investigation. Others, such as the *Mary Celeste* and the *Carroll A. Deering*, did not wreck at all, but their inexplicable reappearances, bereft of crew, have given rise to mysteries as yet unsolved in the ocean's vastness.

Some shipwrecks rank among history's greatest and most famous tragedies. The *Titanic* assuredly leads in this, but the *Andrea Doria*, the USS *Indianapolis*, and the *Lusitania* join the famously doomed ocean liner. Others have not received the attention that they deserve, such as the *Wilhelm Gustloff*, sunk at the end of World War II, taking with it 9,000 lives. The circumstances of some shipwrecks, notably the HMS *Birkenhead* and its self-sacrificing crew and passengers, inspire us, while others, particularly the *Medusa* and the brutality shown aboard its raft, only evoke revulsion. Some shipwrecks are remarkable for the perseverance of their crews, such as the aptly named *Endurance*, while others, such as the equally aptly named *Erebus* and *Terror*, are notable primarily for the tragedies that befell their crews after they sank.

▲ Some shipwrecks, such as the sinking of the *Vasa* in Stockholm Harbor in 1628 or the capsizing of the SS *Eastland* in the Chicago River in 1915 (above), happen before the eyes of horrified witnesses, who are unable to stop the disaster.

FROM MOTHER NATURE TO THE SUPERNATURAL

This book delves into some of the world's most amazing shipwrecks, exploring their histories and, in turn, what has happened to their remains. Chapter 1 covers the tragedies caused by Mother Nature, whether her wrath descended in the form of a hurricane, tidal wave, or crushing ice. Chapter 2 reveals the tragedies of human error, and chapter 3 continues in the same vein with tales of terrible collisions, be they with massive icebergs, hidden rocks, or other ships. Chapters 4 and 5 also concern shipwrecks fated by human design, tracing the thrilling exploits of the piracy age and the glories and horrors of war on the high seas. Shipwrecks with stranger tales to tell can be found in chapter 6, with all the haunting mysteries of the sea—from ghost ships to sea serpents to outright disappearances. Chapter 7 covers the ships lost to one of sailors' most persistent—and justifiable—fears, that of fire at sea, while chapter 8 moves out of modern history and into legend, myth, and the ancient world.

All shipwrecks, whether for their stories, their drama, or the ancient treasures that they promise, draw us to them as markers of watery graves, pointed history lessons, or curious mysteries. Their ghostly silence cannot still our fascination with their rotting decks or rusting turrets, once trod and manned by unlucky sailors. Nor, perhaps, should it: for as long as we travel the unconquerable sea, it will claim both ships and lives. Our best hope for survival on the waves is to learn the lessons they bequeath, and the only honor we can give to the lives they have claimed is a promise to never forget them.

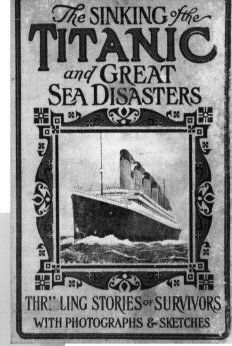

▲ Shipwrecks have long captured the human imagination, and many writers have taken up the task of chronicling the countless tales of downed ships throughout history. Although many remain obscure, certain ships have an immediate lure, as demonstrated by *The Sinking of the Titanic and Great Sea Disasters*, published in 1912, the very year the famously "unsinkable" ship sank in the North Atlantic.

◄ Some ships, such as the HMS *Rhone*, which sank in the waters off the British Virgin Islands during a hurricane in 1867, leave long-lasting skeletons that prove irresistible to both amateur and professional wreck divers.

1 · NATURE'S FURY

▲ *The Shipwreck* by Hendrik Kobell, 1775

The *San Agustin* | SPANISH TREASURE OFF THE CALIFORNIA COAST

Sixteenth-century Spanish traders did a brisk business navigating between two colonial outposts on the Pacific Ocean. In the Philippines, they traded East Asian goods, such as silk and porcelain, and in New Spain (Mexico), they bartered for silver and gold. The *San Agustin*, a three-masted, 80-foot (24 m) Manila galleon, was one such treasure ship. She holds the distinction of being the oldest known shipwreck off the coast of California.

The *San Agustin* departed Manila in July 1595. Bound for Acapulco, she carried treasure from her home port in the Philippines. King Philip II of Spain had ordered Captain Sebastian Rodriguez Cermeño to chart the coast of California, in hope of finding a safe harbor. The galleon

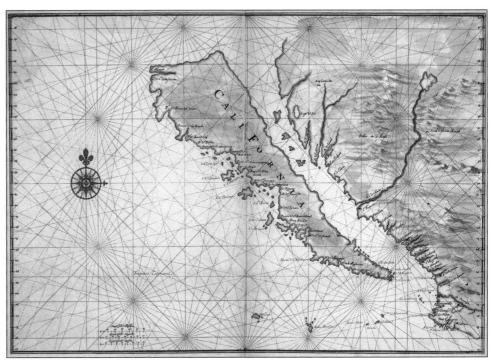

▲ Early explorers believed California to be an island, as shown on this c. 1650 European map.

▲ The rocky, often fogbound, California coast proved treacherous for ships unfamiliar with its waters. Even today, with far more advanced tracking systems, rogue waves and strange currents still regularly claim ships and lives.

reached Cape Mendocino, near the Oregon border, and from there she continued south along the foggy coast. Coming around the treacherous waters of Point Reyes in November 1595, the *San Agustin* put in at Drake's Bay, just north of San Francisco. With the *San Agustin* safely moored in the bay, Captain Cermeño took most of his crew on shore to explore.

Three weeks after the *San Agustin* dropped anchor, though, a fierce southeaster blew in, dashing apart the ship and killing two crewmen. The storm left Captain Cermeño and his men stranded on an unfamiliar shore, their 150 tons (136 metric tons) of treasure sunk to the bottom of the Pacific. The wreck of the *San Agustin* has never been found, but bits of blue Chinese porcelain and other artifacts likely from the lost galleon have washed ashore in Drake's Bay. Archaeologists and federal agencies renewed the active search for the *San Agustin* in 1997, and she remains a shipwreck ripe for discovery.

▲ Between 1565 and 1815, so-called Manila galleons (galleons that traveled between Manila and Acapulco, Mexico) brought Filipino and East Asian goods to the rest of the Spanish Empire for profits of from 100 to 300 percent.

FLOTSAM & JETSAM

Drake's Bay in California is named for the swashbuckling English privateer Sir Francis Drake (1540–95), who roamed the seas plundering Spanish ships.

TO MEXICO IN A PLANK BOAT

AFTER THE WRECK OF HIS SHIP, Captain Cermeño was faced with a near-mutinous crew of 76 men, stranded on a beach some 2,000 miles (3,200 km) from their destination in New Spain. Crew members' letters and journals and the captain's own log document their incredible passage to safety.

Cermeño decided to press on toward Acapulco by any means necessary. During their three weeks ashore, the crew members of the *San Agustin* had been assembling a small plank boat, called a *vicoro*, intended for inland exploration. Captain, crew, and one dog piled into the rickety craft and headed south. Navigating out to sea, they would have drifted past the perennially fogbound San Francisco Bay, one of the world's safest natural harbors. Two months later, in January 1596, the *vicoro* arrived safely in Acapulco. Cermeño had lost the king's ship and a fortune in goods, and he had failed to discover the sought-for safe harbor, but his fortitude had saved his crew.

▲ A 1628 relief map of Acapulco's port. Now a major tourist city in Mexico, Acapulco was New Spain's primary western port for centuries.

Nuestra Señora de Atocha

SUNKEN TREASURE IN THE FLORIDA KEYS

Guns and cannons can protect against pirates and buccaneers, but they are no match for a ferocious hurricane. The hundreds who perished on the Spanish galleon *Nuestra Señora de Atocha* learned this bitter lesson. The *Atocha* was one of a fleet of 28 ships to leave Havana in 1622, laden with precious metals and other bounty of the New World destined for the coffers of the Spanish crown.

The voyage across the Atlantic to Spain was perilous, but never more so than in the initial stretch. Pirates, who roamed the Caribbean, frequently targeted treasure-laden galleons, so armed escort boats accompanied each fleet. The 112-foot (34 m), three-masted *Atocha* served her fleet as *almiranta*, or heavily armed rear guard. Because she was so well protected by firepower—including 20 bronze cannons—she carried a ransom in treasure. Experts believe that the *Atocha* carried some 24 tons (22 metric tons) of silver bullion, 125 gold bars and coins, and huge measures of copper, tobacco, indigo, and jewels.

On September 4, 1622, the fleet set sail, weeks later than it intended. That night and the following morning, the wind began to rise, and the flotilla made for the calm waters of the Gulf of Mexico. The *Atocha*, along with two other ships in the rear guard, didn't make it. High winds and monstrous waves drove the *Santa Margarita*, the *Nuestra Señora del Rosario*, and the *Atocha* onto a coral reef near the Dry Tortugas. With 260 souls and tons of treasure aboard, the *Atocha*, her hull badly damaged, sank in only 55 feet (17 m) of water. Five men who clung to the mizzenmast survived to tell the tale.

FLOTSAM & JETSAM

"Once you have seen the ocean bottom paved with gold, you'll never forget it."

—Mel Fisher
(1922–98)

▲ Gold doubloons and silver *reales*. The *Atocha* would have carried a fortune in such Spanish coins.

THE SALVAGE OF THE *ATOCHA*

Days after the *Atocha* sank, rescue teams attempted to salvage her sunken treasure. But another hurricane blew in, tearing the standing masts and sterncastle from the hull, and obliterating any trace of her whereabouts. Searchers found her sister ship, the *Santa Margarita*, in 1626, and salvaged much of her treasure. But the *Atocha* faded from memory, too far submerged to hope for recovery.

Three centuries later, though, hope drove wreck diver Mel Fisher to search for the *Atocha*. Fisher and his crew had already helped discover the 1715 Spanish treasure fleet (see pages 18–21), and his success now led him to a greater challenge: the *Atocha*. Most rescue efforts had focused on

▲ Violent storms on the open sea, even more so than pirates, made sailing dangerous. Here, a painting of ships in a rising storm by Willem van de Velde the Younger (1633–1707) highlights the danger of tall waves.

"the last key of the Matecumbes," the location noted by seventeenth-century records. In 1985, after nearly 16 years of searching, Fisher discovered the *Atocha* and her sunken treasure near Florida's remote Marquesas Keys. A legal battle ensued, with both the United States government and the State of Florida laying claim to the bounty. Finally, the court ruled in favor of Mel Fisher. Many of the *Atocha's* treasures are now housed in a museum in Key West, Florida.

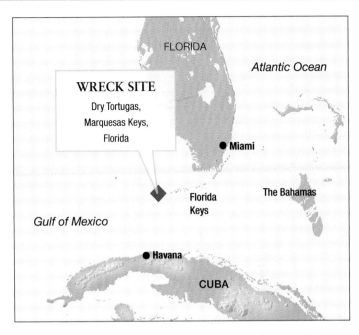

WRECK SITE
Dry Tortugas, Marquesas Keys, Florida

FLORIDA

Atlantic Ocean

● Miami

The Bahamas

Florida Keys

Gulf of Mexico

● Havana

CUBA

▲ The Dry Tortugas, now a United States national park, change constantly under the pressures of wind and water, making them difficult to chart and safely navigate.

▼ The Mel Fisher Maritime Museum in Key West, Florida, houses artifacts from several shipwrecks, including the *Henrietta Marie* and the *Atocha*.

TOOLS OF THE TRADE

MEL FISHER HAD PERSISTENCE, SKILL, AND DRIVE, but he also had the right tools for the job. He invented a device he called a "mailbox," which sent a stream of clear water down to the ocean floor, enabling treasure hunters to spot their quarry. Fisher also used a proton magnetometer, a highly sensitive form of magnetometer. These devices are commonly used in archaeology; they measure variations in the earth's magnetic field, indicating the presence of ferrous objects, or metals.

▶ An old-fashioned proton magnetometer

THE WRECK OF THE WEALTH OF THE INDIES

The 1715 Treasure Fleet

Spanish treasure ships had been lost before, but none so dramatically, or with the loss of so many men and so much wealth, as the treasure fleet of 1715. The new king of Spain, Philip V (1683–1746), inherited a nearly bankrupt realm, ravaged from the long War of Spanish Succession (1701–14). He desperately needed the bounty of this fleet. But instead of bringing home a fortune, the 1715 treasure fleet was wrecked off the coast of Florida. Its sunken treasure became one of the most spectacular salvage discoveries in modern maritime history.

The fleet of 11 ships—primarily galleons—had been lying in port in Havana, Cuba, for two years, held up by political strife back home in Spain. As July approached, the impatient captains, Antonio de Escheverz y Zubiza and Juan Esteban de Ubilla, must have been well aware that hurricane season was already underway. But the date for departure was set. The 1715 fleet intended to follow a well-traveled route to Europe, riding the Gulf Stream. The fleet included a French frigate, the *Grifón*. Historians differ as to whether the *Grifón* was a 12th ship, or counted among the 11. In either case, she was to become the sole surviving ship on the disastrous voyage.

▲ A ship goes down in a hurricane near St. Thomas island in the Caribbean Sea. Without modern technology to track such storms, ships in the Age of Sail bore the full brunt of nature's fury.

◄ The same ship, shown before the storm, gliding on smooth waters

Laden with precious metals, jewels, porcelain, and other goods, the fleet sailed from Havana on July 24, 1715. Historians believe that the total worth of the registered cargo was around $86 million in modern currency, mostly in the form of silver and gold. Hundreds of trunks were filled with cobs, crude chunks of precious metal, and close to seven million of the famed Spanish coins, pieces of eight. Treasure fleets are often called "plate fleets," after the Spanish word for silver, *plata*.

On July 31, 1715, a violent hurricane swept north from the Gulf. Those ships in the front of the fleet were wrecked in deep water and lost their entire crews and treasure. Some crew and passengers in the rear guard, whose ships were closer to land, managed to survive, but an estimated 1,000 men were lost in the powerful storm.

THE BATTLE OF VIGO BAY

ARRIVING HOME FROM THE NEW WORLD, the Spanish plate fleet of 1702 met with a disastrous fate. The flotilla entered Vigo Bay on the west coast of Spain and dropped anchor. On October 23, English and Dutch ships—enemy combatants in the War of Spanish Succession—attacked. Spanish and French ships, carrying millions of pesos in gold and silver, constituted the treasure fleet. Some of the treasure had already been off-loaded, but the Anglo-Dutch forces captured several of the ships—and a small fortune along with them. Under orders from the French commander, the crews of the remaining ships set fire to them in order to avoid capture or pillage. The sunken treasure in Vigo Bay has eluded centuries of salvage operations.

▲ A Dutch image of the Battle of Vigo Bay, with Dutch and English ships in the foreground. The engagement cost Spain and France a fortune in lost treasure and ships. They also lost an ally: Portugal broke its treaty and joined the Dutch and English side.

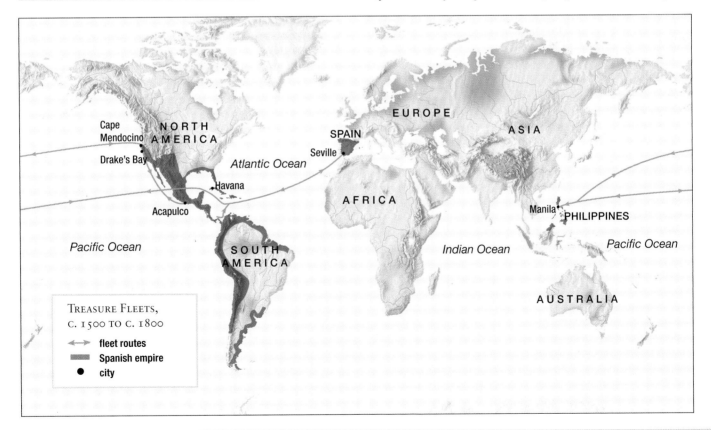

TREASURE FLEETS, C. 1500 TO C. 1800

←→ fleet routes

▬ Spanish empire

● city

The 1715 Treasure Fleet | CONTINUED

▲ A nineteenth-century illustration shows crewmen desperately rowing away from the sinking *Urca de Lima*. Rediscovered in 1928, the wreck became Florida's first Underwater Archaeological Preserve.

SALVAGE—THEN AND NOW

When news of the wreck reached Havana, the Spanish governor had but one concern—immediate salvage of what treasure could be found. It is thought that nearly half of the fleet's precious cargo was recovered from these salvage operations. Not all of this wealth was restored to the Spanish, however. With such riches at stake, the wreck of the 1715 fleet became a prime target for pirates and privateers. A feeding frenzy of treasure hunters and pillagers descended on the site. Others lay in wait for ships carrying salvaged goods. Among these was the notorious English privateer Henry Jennings, who made off with about 400,000 pesos from a salvage fleet.

Two and a half centuries later, in the 1950s, a Florida man named Kip Wagner stumbled on a gold coin while walking on the beach. Wagner devoted years to the pursuit of the coin's source. Teaming up with treasure diver Mel Fisher, Wagner and his associates discovered numerous wreck sites from the 1715 treasure fleet and the precious goods that had gone down with the ships. Many of these treasures are on view in museums; others are traded on the active numismatic, or coin collecting, market.

One of the ships that sank in shallow water, the *Urca de Lima*, survived both storm and salvage nearly intact. Today, the *Urca de Lima* is a favorite site for divers. The Florida shoreline where the 1715 ships sank—the counties of Martin, Indian River, and St. Lucie—is known as "Treasure Coast." Both long-term professional wreck divers and casual day divers continue to unearth the sunken wealth of the Indies.

FLOTSAM & JETSAM

The nickname "two bits" for the U.S. quarter derives from the Spanish dollar—the peso or *real de a ocho* ("piece of eight"). The *real* was sometimes cut into eight pie-shaped pieces to make smaller change.

▲ Spain built Morro Castle at the mouth of the harbor in Havana, a major Spanish port in the New World and starting point for most treasure fleets. First built in 1589, the castle was captured by the British in 1762 and returned to Spain in 1763. The lighthouse was built in 1846.

▼ A Spanish galleon

▲ Above and right, Spanish silver dollars, minted in 1739, during the reign of King Philip V

THE SPANISH GALLEON

THE GALLEON WAS THE WORKHORSE of Spanish treasure fleets from the sixteenth to the eighteenth centuries. Distinguished by a high forecastle and an even higher sterncastle built onto a high, flat stern, the galleon also featured a prominent beak and bowsprit. Galleons carried from three to five masts. These were square-rigged on the fore- and mainmasts; the mizzenmast and bonaventure mizzen (the third and fourth masts) were lateen-rigged, or fitted with triangular sails. These powerful ships were commonly armed with a battery of cannons for protection and could engage as readily in war as in trade.

The *Essex* RENDEZVOUS WITH THE LEVIATHAN

If truth is stranger than fiction, the story of the whaleship *Essex* is a case in point. Widely regarded as inspiration for Herman Melville's classic novel *Moby Dick*, the *Essex,* an 87-foot (27 m) long ship, was smashed by a whale in 1820. Eight men out of a crew of 20 survived, 5 in open boats on the sea, 3 others on an uninhabited Pacific island. All 8 were eventually rescued, but not until those adrift had resorted to cannibalism—even drawing lots on who was to survive and who was to become fodder for his fellow castaways.

One of the survivors, first mate Owen Chase, wrote an account of the ordeal, published in 1821 to wide acclaim. In 1980, experts authenticated another account of the disaster, this one written by then 14-year-old cabin boy Thomas Nickerson. From these two narratives, historians have pieced together a detailed picture of the horror and despair that followed the wreck of the *Essex*.

"WE HAVE BEEN STOVE BY A WHALE"

Whaling had become big business on Nantucket Island by 1819, when the *Essex* set sail for the last time. The trade in whale blubber, which furnished lamp oil, had enriched the close-knit Quaker community. The quarry of choice was the massive sperm whale, named for the highly prized waxy liquid, or spermaceti, carried in its protruding forehead.

After hunting the sperm whale nearly to oblivion in the Atlantic Ocean, whaling crews were obliged to sail around Cape Horn and into the Pacific to track their bounty. It was here, on November 20, 1820, that a huge sperm whale attacked the *Essex.* Chase's narrative puts the whale at close to 85 feet (26 m) in length, although few sperm whales have been recorded longer than 60 feet (18.2 m). The whale rammed the *Essex* twice—the second time, as Chase describes it, "with tenfold fury and vengeance in his aspect." With scant supplies, the crew set off in three whaleboats to find land that they knew to be more than 1,000 miles (1,600 km) away.

CAST ADRIFT

Chase and Nickerson manned one rickety whaleboat, along with four other crewmen. Seven men each piled into the remaining two boats, but three put off at uninhabited Henderson Island to await their fates.

The captain and one other crewman were the sole survivors of their boat; a passing ship discovered them 90 days later. The desperate men had survived by eating their dead, including Owen Coffin, the captain's young cousin. Faced with certain starvation, the men had drawn lots for who would sacrifice his life for the others; Coffin chose the black spot. Chase, Nickerson, and boatsteerer Benjamin Lawrence, who likewise had eaten their dead, were picked up 93 days after the wreck of the *Essex*. Rescue arrived for the men on the island soon after. The third boat has never been found.

FLOTSAM & JETSAM

Harpooned whales could drag whaleboats at speeds up to 23 miles per hour (37 km/h). Sailors called this a "Nantucket sleighride."

▲ Sperm whales, though hunted extensively for centuries, are today protected worldwide and are significantly less endangered than some of their cousins.

▲ A harpooned whale attempts to flee the surrounding boats. After a harpoon caught in a whale's flesh, sailors would "play" the whale from whaleboats up to 30 feet (9 m) long. Male sperm whales can weigh as much as 45 tons (41 metric tons), so this pursuit risked life and limb.

THE WHITE WHALE

HERMAN MELVILLE'S 1851 novel *Moby Dick* owes a direct debt to Owen Chase's narrative. Melville's dramatic, biblical prose, rendered in first-person narration, tells of a captain's relentless quest for vengeance on a white whale that had wrecked his boat years before. In 1841, on board the whaler *Acushnet,* Melville met Chase's son William, whose ship had paused for a "gam," or meeting, with Melville's boat. William Chase gave Melville his own copy of his father's narrative.

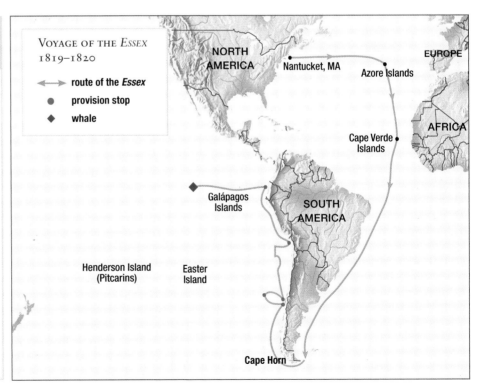

VOYAGE OF THE *ESSEX*
1819–1820

⟷ route of the *Essex*
● provision stop
◆ whale

NORTH AMERICA

Nantucket, MA

EUROPE

Azore Islands

AFRICA

Cape Verde Islands

Galápagos Islands

SOUTH AMERICA

Henderson Island (Pitcarins)

Easter Island

Cape Horn

THE ILL-FATED IRONCLAD

USS *Monitor*

Built for battle, the USS *Monitor* was cheated out of her promised military glory when she met with an untimely end. The *Monitor* was the first ironclad warship in the U.S. Navy's fleet and served as a prototype for dozens of similar vessels. The brainchild of Swedish engineer John Ericsson, the *Monitor* was built in 1862 in just over 100 days, part of a Civil War arms race. She was to be the answer to the Confederacy's own ironclad, the CSS *Virginia*. The two ships would soon stand off in the hallmark naval battle of the Civil War, the Battle of Hampton Roads. Neither ship survived her first year.

With a length of 172 feet (52 m), the *Monitor* carried an innovative revolving gun turret on her deck, providing 8-inch (20 cm) thick walls of iron protection for the gunners inside. Two 11-foot (3.5 m)

Dahlgren smoothbore cannons could fire and retract through gun ports fitted with hinged doors. The 9-foot (2.9 m) high, 22-foot (6.7 m) wide gun turret, along with the deck, the smokestack, and the pilothouse, were the only portions of the ship that sat above the waterline. The remainder lay below water, making her a semisubmerged ship. A steam-driven propeller, or marine screw, powered the *Monitor* at a steady but slow pace; her maximum speed was 5.5 knots.

The *Monitor*'s first military engagement, the Battle of Hampton Roads, was also her last. She served her duty to the Union army on March 9, 1862, holding off her Confederate ironclad rival, the CSS *Virginia,* and maintaining the Union blockade of the Virginia port. The four-hour battle was a draw. But the *Monitor* never fought again; eight months later, less than a year after her launch, she sank in high waves off the coast of North Carolina.

▲ Sixteen men died when the *Monitor* went down, but the United States continued to build ships of her design—called "monitors"—through World War I.

▲ Although the battle did not affect the course of the Civil War, the engagement of the *Virginia* and the *Monitor* marked the beginning of a new age in naval warfare, one which made wooden warships obsolete.

▶ John Lorimer Worden commanded the USS *Monitor* in her historic battle with the CSS *Virginia*.

VIRGINIA, NÉE MERRIMACK

THE *MONITOR'S* IRONCLAD rival in battle, the CSS *Virginia*, was built from the charred remains of a wooden Union ship named the USS *Merrimack*. Just two months after the Battle of Hampton Roads, Union forces surrounded the *Virginia*. Rather than allow capture, her commanders ordered the *Virginia* to be blown up. She met her fiery end on the night of May 10, 1862.

▶ The *Virginia* explodes into flaming debris. Her builders had used the remains of the USS *Merrimack* to build this Confederate ironclad.

USS *Monitor* CONTINUED

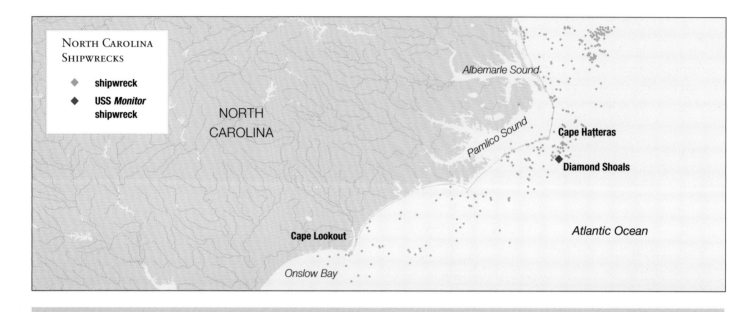

NORTH CAROLINA
SHIPWRECKS

◆ shipwreck

◆ USS *Monitor*
shipwreck

NORTH
CAROLINA

Albemarle Sound

Pamlico Sound

Cape Hatteras

Diamond Shoals

Atlantic Ocean

Cape Lookout

Onslow Bay

THE GRAVEYARD OF THE ATLANTIC

THE *MONITOR* WAS NEITHER THE FIRST SHIP nor the last to sink in the waters off Cape Hatteras, North Carolina. The area is so rife with shipwrecks that it has earned the nickname "Graveyard of the Atlantic." By some estimates, more than 2,000 ships have been wrecked here, from the earliest English brig recorded in 1585 to the present day.

In geographic terms, the Outer Banks of North Carolina are really barrier islands. Two strong ocean currents meet here—the cold Labrador Current, which flows south from Labrador and Newfoundland, and the warm Gulf Stream, which originates in the Caribbean Sea. This confluence creates turbulent waters and unpredictable currents and has carved a series of shifting undersea sandbars known as the Diamond Shoals. These sandbars extend from the point of Cape Hatteras as far as 14 miles (22 m) offshore. If this treacherous

geography isn't enough, the Outer Banks is also one of the most hurricane-prone regions in the Atlantic.

The list of ships wrecked here tantalizes wreck divers and romantics alike. But it is also a pointed history lesson, as the staggering variety of craft buried here attests. The Outer Banks have long been critical points along many shipping routes, serving vessels bound on widely diverse errands. Pirate galleons harboring pieces of eight, four-masted schooners, luxury liners, coal barges, oil tankers, battleships, submarines, and hundreds of small craft have all met the same fate off these shores. In the powerful San Ciriaco hurricane of 1899 alone, nine ships were lost in the course of two days. Locals claim that the feral horses that roam the Outer Banks are the remains of a herd brought on board a Spanish galleon. Many such mysteries remain unsolved in the Graveyard of the Atlantic.

SWEPT UNDER

The *Monitor*'s great advantage in battle—her low profile and fully submerged hull—was also her Achilles' heel as a seagoing craft. Built for the calmer waters of rivers and inlets, the *Monitor* was unable to hold her own in the open sea. She also lacked sufficient buoyancy, for reasons that experts have been debating since her demise.

After the *Monitor*'s historic battle, the navy sent her to Washington Navy Yard for refitting. The side-steamer *Rhode Island* towed her on the return trip. On December 31, 1862, the two ships encountered heavy waves off Cape Hatteras, North Carolina, and gale winds of an estimated Force 7 on the Beaufort scale—wind speeds up to 38 miles per hour (61 km/h). Powerful waves easily broke over the *Monitor*'s low deck, overwhelming it until the deck was nearly flush with water. The *Rhode Island*'s crew and lifeboats saved many of those aboard the *Monitor*, but the flat deck of the ironclad offered little purchase with waves breaking over the turret. The pounding waves relentlessly swept overboard those unable to reach the lifeboats.

Letters from surviving *Monitor* crew members describe the horror of the sinking. Many watched from the deck of the *Rhode Island* as their iron "home" tossed helplessly in the storm. Paymaster William Keeler wrote, "What the fire of the enemy failed to do, the elements have accomplished." The tossing waters claimed not only the ship, but also 16 men out of the 62 aboard the USS *Monitor*.

FLOTSAM & JETSAM

The *Monitor*'s low profile and protruding turret gave her the nickname "cheese box on a raft."

RECLAIMING THE *MONITOR*

Just over a century later, a 1973 expedition from Duke University discovered the remains of the *Monitor*. Lying 16 miles (26 km) off the coast of Cape Hatteras, she was submerged about 230 feet (70 m) deep, lying upside down on the ocean floor. In 1975, the area around the wreck was designated a National Marine Sanctuary. Considered an artificial reef, the *Monitor* wreck sustains numerous marine life forms, from corals and sponges to sea bass and barracuda.

Scientists have been studying the *Monitor* and her undersea environment since her discovery. In the 1990s, when experts found that she was deteriorating at an accelerated rate, they began to raise pieces of the ship, one by one. First came the propeller, raised in 1998, followed by the steam engine. The massive gun turret, along with its two Dahlgren cannons, was raised in 2001. The *Monitor*'s relics are housed in a museum, while her wreck lies protected below.

▲ A brass signal lantern from the *Monitor*. Before the age of radio or electronic communication, ships communicated by flashing lights from signal lanterns, not unlike Morse code.

▶ A school of amberjack swims about the wreck of the *Monitor*.

The *General Grant*

GOLD, CASTAWAYS, AND SEALSKIN SUITS

Gold was discovered in the sheep country of Australia in 1851, triggering a fevered gold rush that lasted more than a decade. By the 1860s, prospectors from all reaches of the British colonies had amassed small fortunes. On May 4, 1866, the American clipper ship *General Grant* left Melbourne for London, laden with wool and sheepskins. Also on board were a number of gold miners and their families, carrying home their new wealth in the form of 2,567 ounces (73 kg) of gold bullion. Most of them never made it home. On May 13, the *General Grant*, a victim of drift, tide, and bizarre bad luck, was shipwrecked on the forlorn Auckland Islands.

▲ A contemporary picture of the *General Grant*'s slow demise, with survivors pulling desperately away in lifeboats

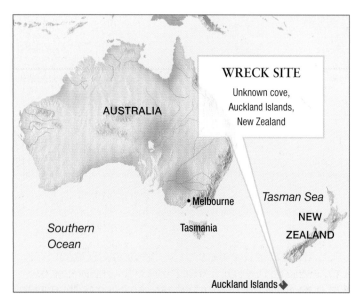

WRECK SITE
Unknown cove, Auckland Islands, New Zealand

AUSTRALIA

• Melbourne

Tasman Sea

NEW ZEALAND

Southern Ocean

Tasmania

Auckland Islands ◆

BETWEEN A ROCK AND A TIDAL PLACE

The *General Grant* was a three-masted clipper ship, measuring 179.5 feet (55 m) long, with a beam of 34.5 feet (10.5 m). On May 11, only a week out from port, heavy fog, dead winds, and near zero visibility overcame the *General Grant*. She began to drift, pulled by a strong current toward the treacherous Auckland Islands, which lie between New Zealand and Antarctica. When the ship emerged from the fog, she was face to face with a cliff of jagged black rock, towering some 400 feet (122 m) above the sea.

Survivors of the *General Grant* later told of the slow, unfolding horror as the ship drifted into an ever-narrower cove. Overhanging rocks tore asunder first the foremast and then the mainmast. Soon it was clear: the *General Grant* had been sucked into a cave. What remained of the mainmast struck the roof of the cave, staying the ship.

Toward dawn the tide began to rise, and with it, the ship. The mast, stuck fast against the rock ceiling, was now forced down through the wooden hull, piercing a hole in the keel. As water rushed in, the panicked crew and passengers scrambled for lifeboats. Only 14 men and 1 woman survived, out of the 83 souls aboard the *General Grant*.

LOST

The 15 survivors of the *General Grant* were now left to fend for themselves on these uninhabited, barren islands. One of the men, Irish gold miner James Teer, found he had a single dry match. The survivors kept the fire that he lit burning for the entire 18 months of their sojourn. As winter set in, the castaways made coats, trousers, moccasins, vests, skirts, and hats of sealskin to fend off the cold. They subsisted on a diet of seal meat, fish, wild pigs, and goat.

In January, after eight months on the islands, a breakaway crew of four men decided to risk the rough waters in an effort to seek help. Carrying a small store of supplies, the men launched one of the two 22-foot (6.7 m) lifeboats; they were

▲ Sea lions and seals shelter on the remote and unforgiving Auckland Islands. Not only did these animals feed and clothe the *General Grant*'s survivors, but they also attracted the sealing ship that eventually rescued the surviving 10 castaways.

never heard from again. An elderly man among the group died a few months later, and the remaining 10 castaways kept a steady watch for passing ships.

Finally their wait was over—a sealing expedition arrived on November 21, 1867. Instead of accepting the offer of transport to New Zealand, though, the castaways chose to stay on the islands and help with the sealing, prolonging their stay by six additional weeks. The world was fascinated by the trials of these 10 survivors and by the lure of the *General Grant*'s sunken gold, which no one has yet recovered.

▲ Mary Ann and Joseph Jewell, two of the *General Grant* survivors, pose for a news photograph in the sealskin clothing that had warmed them during their ordeal.

▲ Two nineteenth-century attempts to settle on the Auckland Islands failed. None of the six islands have arable soil, and the shrubby growth supports little animal life.

RMS *Rhone*

HAUNTED WRECK OF THE CARIBBEAN

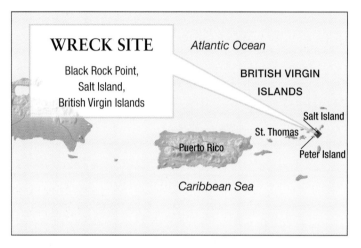

WRECK SITE

Black Rock Point, Salt Island, British Virgin Islands

Atlantic Ocean

BRITISH VIRGIN ISLANDS

Salt Island

St. Thomas

Puerto Rico

Peter Island

Caribbean Sea

▼ The wreck of the RMS *Rhone*. Although most of the wooden decks have long since rotted, much of her bow remains. The hull, encrusted with coral, is home to scores of sea creatures, including groupers, barracudas, eels, lobster, and octopi.

The RMS *Rhone* has led at least two lives. First she plied the seas as one of a storied duo of iron-hulled ships considered "unsinkable"—the British navy bestowed this honorific on both the *Rhone* and the *Titanic*. As a cargo ship and passenger liner, the RMS *Rhone* sailed between Great Britain, the Caribbean, and South America, and later into the seas of the West Indies. For a second act, she has lain in state at the bottom of the sea, her curious underwater visitors numbering in the thousands.

Strong, fast, and luxurious, the *Rhone* was a thoroughly modern craft when she was christened in 1865. Measuring 310 feet (94 m) bow-to-stern, with a beam of 40 feet (12 m) and two masts, the *Rhone* also boasted a steam-powered bronze propeller, accounting for her great speed of 14 knots. Sadly, her tenure as the jewel of the Royal Mail Steam Packet Company was brief. Only two years later, the *Rhone* entered her second life. Wrecked in a fierce hurricane in 1867, the *Rhone* sank in the shallow waters off Salt Island in the British Virgin Islands. Her remains have become one of the top wreck-diving sites in the world. Now, eerie stories are adding new life to the legend of the *Rhone*, with some divers reporting strange sensations and unearthly sounds.

THE UNSINKABLE *RHONE*

Captain Robert F. Wooley commanded the *Rhone* on her 10th sailing. On October 19, 1867, Wooley learned from another ship, the RMS *Conway*, that his usual coaling station on the then-Danish island of St. Thomas was closed—a precaution against a yellow fever outbreak. Wooley and the captain of the *Conway* dropped anchor in Great Harbour on St. Peter to commiserate, both men keeping a steady eye on the falling barometer. Experts have surmised that the veteran sailors decided that it was too late in the season for a hurricane and wrote off the approaching storm as a nor'easter. Just in case, though, the *Conway* off-loaded her passengers onto the *Rhone*. After all, she was unsinkable.

The hurricane struck with ferocity on October 29. Meteorologists now label this as a Category 5 storm, the worst to ever strike the Virgin Islands. As the *Rhone* set sail and steam to the maximum, her massive anchor stuck, separating from the ship with a great, shuddering jolt. Wooley and his crew tried to make for the open sea, navigating between Salt Island and Dead Chest Island. The *Rhone* had almost cleared Black Rock Point on Salt Island, when the wind suddenly changed direction. Strong gusts violently dashed the grand, unsinkable *Rhone* against the jagged rocks. Cold seawater met the hot boilers, setting off an explosion that tore the ship apart, separating bow from stern. A towering wave, it is said, swept Robert F. Wooley from the bridge.

The captain went down with his ship; nonetheless, Wooley had taken precautions for his passengers' safety. As the storm intensified, he had ordered all passengers to be tied to their beds, for their own protection. Twenty-three survivors emerged from the wreck out of the original 146 people on board; of these, only one was a passenger. The *Conway*, meanwhile, was cast ashore at Baughers Bay, Tortola. All on board were saved.

FLOTSAM & JETSAM

The phrase "Good night, sleep tight" comes from the formerly common practice of strapping passengers and crew into their bunks, to prevent injury as the ship tossed through the night.

▲ Curious divers explore the ship's remains. Despite rumors of ghostly groaning sounds, the wreck of the *Rhone* is a popular dive site, and the area around it was turned into a national park in 1967.

▲ Salt Island, shown above. The wreck of the *Rhone* lies off Black Rock Point on the west coast of this small island in the British Virgin Islands.

STRANGE NOISES ON THE *RHONE*

SWIMMING THROUGH the peaceful undersea landscape of the *Rhone*, divers have felt mysterious taps on the shoulder and have heard eerie moaning sounds. *National Geographic* investigated, filming a segment at the wreck of the *Rhone* for their *Is It Real?* series. Debunkers point out that, underwater, sound travels in unexpected ways. Distant whale calls, for example, could easily be mistaken for ghostly moans. The sounds could have even have come from the 500-pound (225 kg) goliath grouper that once made the wreck its home. Still, legends of the haunting continue to mount. Grouper or ghost? The *Rhone* holds her secrets close.

| USS *Wateree* | # SHIPWRECK ON LAND |

Shipwreck hunters usually have to dive for their quarry. To find the wreck of the side-paddle warship USS *Wateree*, though, an explorer would have to trek inland. The *Wateree* holds the distinction of having wrecked on terra firma—more than 400 yards (366 m) above the high-water line. While in port in Peru in 1868, an 8.5 magnitude earthquake triggered tidal waves that swept the *Wateree* off her anchor chains and left her high and dry. Salvage costs proved so high that the U.S. Navy deemed the *Wateree* a total loss.

Built in Chester, Pennsylvania, the USS *Wateree* was a side-paddle-wheeled steamer, 205 feet (62 m) long, with a hull of iron. Though commissioned in Philadelphia in 1864, her maiden voyage around Cape Horn to the West Coast was so lengthy and difficult that she required dry dock and repairs in San Francisco. The *Wateree* then spent two years patrolling the west coasts of Central and South America, defending U.S. interests as part of the navy's South Pacific squadron.

EARTHQUAKE AND TSUNAMI

At 5:05 PM on August 13, 1868, the USS *Wateree* was anchored in the harbor of the sleepy Peruvian town of Arica (now in Chile). A low rumbling noise caused her commander, James H. Gillis, to look ashore. To his horror, the buildings in the little town began to crumble before his eyes. He raced to the bridge and calmly began issuing orders. Hatches were battened down, anchor chains made ready to veer away, arms tied down securely. Commander Gillis led a party ashore to help with any rescue efforts, including the recovery of bodies. Lieutenant

Commander M. S. Stuyvesant braced himself and the ship for the inevitable, as aftershocks continued to rumble through harbor and ship alike.

Twenty-seven minutes after the original quake, the sea in the harbor began to rise. As the onshore current grew ever more violent, the ship began dragging her anchors. Four men wrestled the ship's wheel, while the rest of the crew frantically veered out anchor chains, straining to keep ahead of the rushing torrent. Suddenly, and with barely a pause, the great inrushing reversed, and the ship swung around 180 degrees as the water flowed out as violently as it had entered. The anchors held. Ships around the *Wateree* began to succumb, yet still she held fast.

Several more cycles of violent tidal shifts battered the warship. Just before 7:00 PM, the biggest tidal wave yet lifted

▲ The *Wateree* sees her last minutes afloat as an enormous tidal wave prepares to lift her onto dry land.

and turned the iron hulk, driving the *Wateree* nearly onto her beam ends and snapping both her anchor chains. All of the other boats in the harbor were lost. But a colossal tsunami lifted the *Wateree* and drove her onward past the beach, over the now-engulfed town, until finally she bottomed out, 430 yards (393 m) inland from the last high-water mark. The *Wateree* had only one casualty, but the tsunami devastated Arica, with estimates of up to 25,000 dead.

1868 EARTHQUAKE OF ARICA

affected area
● city

▲ The USS *Wateree* rests high and dry after her remarkable ordeal.

ROOM FOR RENT

SEVERAL MONTHS after the navy determined that the *Wateree* was a loss, it sold her to a developer, who converted her to an inn. For years after, she was used as living space, as a makeshift hospital, and as a barn for livestock, until finally she decayed into total disrepair. The only remains of the *Wateree* still extant are her rusting boilers, which are displayed outside Arica as a memorial to the ship that sank on land.

▶ Time and weather managed what the sea could not, and the *Wateree*'s boilers are all that remain of the ship wrecked on land.

HMS *Erebus* and HMS *Terror* VANISHED

▲ Crewmen from the HMS *Erebus* and the HMS *Terror*, in happier days, complete the first modern sounding in deep water.

In spring 1845, the HMS *Erebus* and the HMS *Terror*, under the command of Sir John Franklin, set off from London to explore the arctic wastes in search of the Northwest Passage. Two months later, the two ships' expedition mark—a distinctive yellow stripe—was sighted as they sailed past Lancaster Sound in Baffin Bay. Neither ship was ever seen again. Later investigations proved that arctic ice crushed the *Erebus* and the *Terror*, though their fate wasn't known for years after they seemingly vanished from the face of the earth.

The *Erebus* and the *Terror* were originally built as bomb ships. Not only did the mortars that passed for naval armament in the early nineteenth century weigh 6,000 pounds (2,722 kg) each, they also kicked like mules when fired. Ships designed to carry and brace those gigantic cannons therefore passed the prerequisite for polar exploration—bulldog strength. In preparation for the rigors of the Arctic, the British government fitted out the *Erebus* and the *Terror* with the best state-of-the-art technology it could command. Admiralty shipyards refitted both ships fore and aft with additional oak beams, double planking on the hulls, and waterproof fabric between reinforced decking layers. Additional measures made these ships even stronger and faster—extra-thick copper plate on the bottom, triple-thick sails on the top, and steam-driven propellers completed the polar outfitting.

DARKNESS AND TERROR

Sir John Franklin turned the *Erebus* and the *Terror* north out of the Thames in spring 1845. Within two years, Franklin himself was dead, his men marooned, and his ships entrapped in the ice of Victoria Strait. By spring 1848, scurvy or starvation had killed 23 more crewmen. Those remaining had a terrible choice. The ships were holding off the ice better than expected, but supplies were running out and sickness ran rampant. All the remaining crewmen of the *Erebus* and the *Terror* set out to walk across the ice to Fort Resolution, 600 miles (966 km) to the southwest. Every single one of them died of exposure, starvation, or disease. The two ships were lost to the ice and never found.

By 1849, four years after his departure, shipping circles in London began to ponder Franklin's fate. During the next decade more than 30 search parties set out, over sea and land. Through the years, searchers found tantalizing clues to the outcome, including the site where the expedition had wintered its first year out. Three graves and a massive pile of lead-tainted food tins indicated that the expedition had landed in trouble even before the ice entrapped the ships.

Dozens of twentieth-century searches for the remains of Franklin's crew yielded additional clues, as scientists exhumed numerous corpses, well-preserved by the frigid conditions. Autopsies confirmed earlier theories of lead poisoning as a contributing factor in the deaths of the crewmen. Likely resorting to cannibalism, the crew would have been driven mad by lead poisoning, frozen with cold, and tortured by hunger, as they wandered to their anonymous doom on the vast, empty ice.

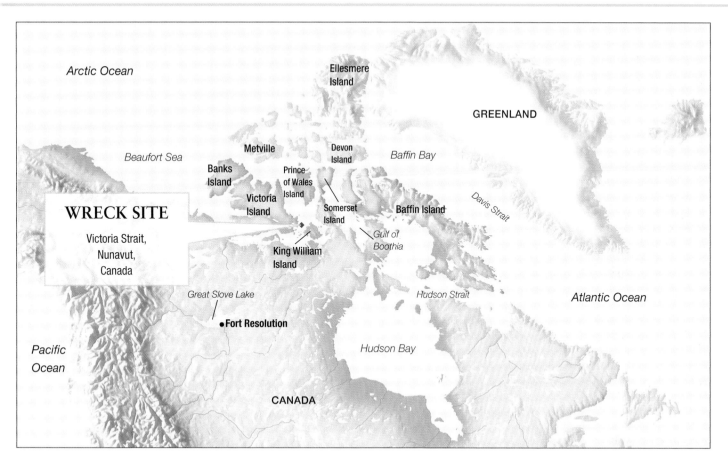

WRECK SITE

Victoria Strait,
Nunavut,
Canada

Arctic Ocean

Beaufort Sea

Ellesmere
Island

GREENLAND

Metville

Banks
Island

Prince
of Wales
Island

Victoria
Island

Devon
Island

Baffin Bay

Somerset
Island

Baffin Island

Davis Strait

King William
Island

Gulf of
Boothia

Great Slove Lake

Hudson Strait

Atlantic Ocean

Pacific
Ocean

●Fort Resolution

Hudson Bay

CANADA

▲ Native Inuit peoples provided searchers with important clues to the fate of
the Franklin party, including the information that ice had claimed the ships.

THE WIDOW FRANKLIN

JANE FRANKLIN, Sir John's disconsolate wife, spent the better energies of her widowhood on organizing and financing expeditions to determine her husband's fate. Even when the government gave up hope and called off the search for Sir John, Lady Franklin persevered. In 1854, a search party found the first relics from the expedition and gathered stories of the disaster from the native Inuit. Five years later, another search party found a rock cairn on King William Island that contained a note recounting the tragic end of the *Erebus* and the *Terror*. These contemporary searches yielded another unlooked-for result—a detailed mapping of thousands of miles of Arctic coastline.

The *Endurance*

THE GREATEST ANTARCTIC RESCUE OF ALL TIME

The *Endurance* was built to challenge an implacable foe—ice. The Irish explorer Ernest Shackleton (1874–1922) purchased and outfitted her for polar operations, and promptly headed south, intending to become the first to cross the continent of Antarctica on foot. Sadly, the *Endurance*'s first voyage was also her last. She encountered ice floes that solidified as the wind forced them into a dense mass. Marooned in pack ice in January 1915, she was crushed beneath the ice of the Weddell Sea by November.

The *Endurance*'s 144-foot (43.9 m) length and 25-foot (7.6 m) beam sat atop a keel constructed of four interlocking pieces of solid oak, built up to a thickness of more than 7 feet (2.1 m). Interconnected joints and fittings reinforced one another and supported sides up to 30 inches (76.2 cm) thick. The bows, designed to meet the ice head on, were 4.5 feet (1.4 m) of solid oak, hewn from trees selected to match the curve of the prow. Twice the normal number of frames supported the Norwegian fir, oak, and greenheart sheathing. The *Endurance* carried three masts of sail and a coal-fired steam-propulsion engine. All of these features added up to one of the strongest ships ever constructed. Yet all that strength counted for naught when tested against the inexorable force of wind-packed ice.

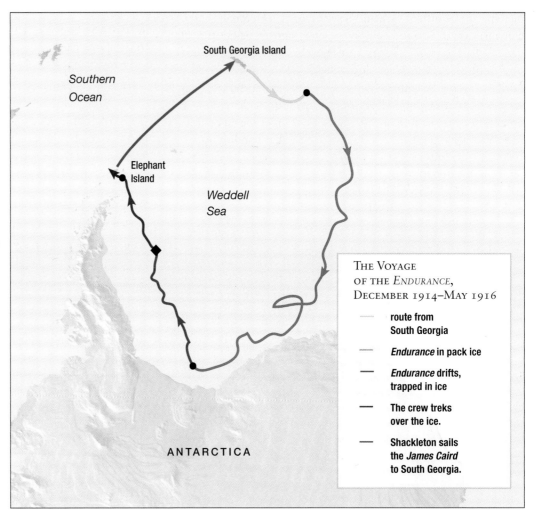

THE VOYAGE OF THE *ENDURANCE*, DECEMBER 1914–MAY 1916

- route from South Georgia
- *Endurance* in pack ice
- *Endurance* drifts, trapped in ice
- The crew treks over the ice.
- Shackleton sails the *James Caird* to South Georgia.

THE CREW OF THE *ENDURANCE* ENDURES

Perhaps no other shipwreck meets a fate as gentle, and as cruel, as a vessel entombed in ice. Gentle because the wreck takes place over a span of months, and cruel because there is little doubt of the final result as, ever so slowly, glittering ice inexorably crushes the trapped vessel. The crew of the *Endurance* could only wait with horror as each passing day brought another snap of timber or another tearing creak, as their ship lost her 10-month struggle with the ice.

Shackleton's crew of 28 men could not know that the sinking of the *Endurance* was only the beginning of their adventure. They abandoned ship and spent the next five months camping and trekking over the ice. Upon reaching open water, the company took to small, open boats and managed to gain Elephant Island—a mere spit of rock boldly piercing the Southern Ocean. From there, Shackleton and five crewmen undertook and completed what many consider the greatest feat of small-boat navigation in history: they sailed an open boat more than 800 miles (1,287.5 km), from Elephant Island to safety. Seventeen days at sea saw them at the whaling station of South Georgia Island. Shackleton immediately organized a rescue mission to return to Elephant Island for the rest of his crew, but he was thwarted by weather conditions. It would take him four attempts before he at last succeeded in returning and rescuing the bulk of his crew. Amazingly, every single crewman of the *Endurance* survived the wreck—and the epic privation and hardship that followed.

ETCHED IN SILVER

THE WRECK of the *Endurance* became one of the most chronicled of all time. The fact that all aboard survived the horrendous conditions certainly contributed,

▲ One of Hurley's photographs, showing the *Endurance* lying helpless in the Antarctic ice

but the presence of Frank Hurley, ship photographer, rendered the wreck of the *Endurance* unique. Hurley documented everything from everyday morale-building football games to the terrifying sight of *Endurance* finally slipping beneath the ice. Hurley's gripping photographs, made on large-format glass negatives, illustrate both the humanity and the awesome forces of nature encountered on that ill-fated expedition.

▲ In 1921, Shackleton returned to the Antarctic for what proved to be his final journey. He died on South Georgia island, where his previous journey had ended.

FLOTSAM & JETSAM

"Pack-ice might be described as a gigantic and interminable jigsaw-puzzle devised by nature."

—Sir Ernest Shackleton

▶ Sir Ernest Shackleton

SHIPPING IN THE ARCTIC

Marine travel between the Pacific and Atlantic Oceans was once a long and treacherous prospect. Before the Panama Canal opened in 1914, ships had to round Cape Horn, the southern tip of South America, in order to bridge the American continents. Small wonder, then, that as early as the fifteenth century, colonial powers sought an alternate

▲ *The Sea of Ice*, by Caspar David Friedrich, c. 1823. The sorry remains of a ship can be seen to the right, crushed under the inexorable force of a frozen ocean.

route for ships—one that passed through the Arctic Circle. The Northwest Passage, as it came to be called, took on near-mythic proportions; many expeditions were lost in ice and unnavigable frigid waters seeking the fabled route. Sir John Franklin's doomed 1845 *Erebus* and *Terror* expedition was one of many such attempts.

Arctic shipping became a reality after Norwegian explorer Roald Amundsen became the first to navigate the Northwest Passage in 1906. Since then, commercial freighters, cruise ships, and even small sailboats have made their way through the chain of seas and islands that dot the Arctic Circle north of Canada and Russia. One helpful innovation is the icebreaker, a ship specially designed to crush ice with its

protruding bow and then guide the ice safely away from the ship's propellers and engines

Despite advances in maritime technology, Arctic routes are still too treacherous for major commercial shipping. Furthermore, the governments whose lands border the Arctic Ocean—the United States, Canada, Russia, Norway, and Greenland (Denmark)—are embroiled in territory disputes that complicate easy shipping in the Arctic.

THE ICE IS MELTING

SCIENTISTS AND EXPERTS ARE NEARLY UNANIMOUS in their misgivings about global climate change, which is seen as profoundly impacting the balance of life on Earth. The shipping industry sees a silver lining, however, because melting Arctic ice opens previously impassable shipping routes. Scientists estimate that the Arctic ice shelf has retreated up to 40 percent in the last four decades. Some experts predict that by 2030, the summer months will find the Arctic Ocean completely free of ice. Environmentalists counter with concern, though—increased shipping could wreak great damage to waters, wildlife, and native people in the already fragile Arctic ecosystem.

▲ This satellite image of the Arctic Circle shows record ice loss. In 2007, the ice sheet coverage in this once-frozen land measured 38 percent below average.

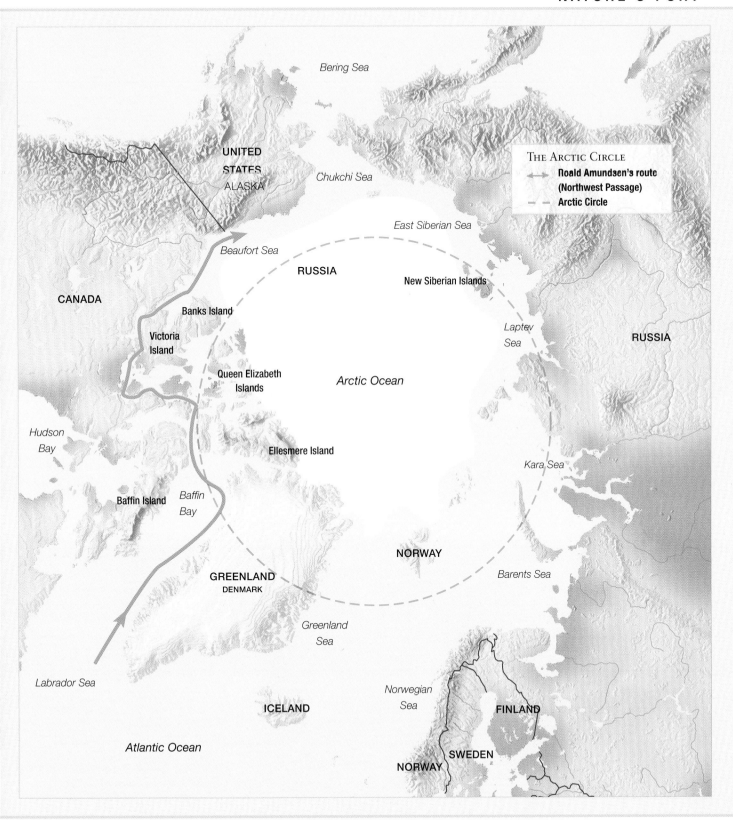

Bering Sea

UNITED
STATES
ALASKA

Chukchi Sea

East Siberian Sea

THE ARCTIC CIRCLE

Roald Amundsen's route
(Northwest Passage)

Arctic Circle

Beaufort Sea

RUSSIA

New Siberian Islands

CANADA

Banks Island

Laptev
Sea

RUSSIA

Victoria
Island

Queen Elizabeth
Islands

Arctic Ocean

Hudson
Bay

Ellesmere Island

Kara Sea

Baffin Island

Baffin
Bay

NORWAY

GREENLAND
DENMARK

Barents Sea

Greenland
Sea

Labrador Sea

Norwegian
Sea

FINLAND

ICELAND

SWEDEN

NORWAY

Atlantic Ocean

SS *Edmund Fitzgerald* | TRAGEDY ON LAKE SUPERIOR

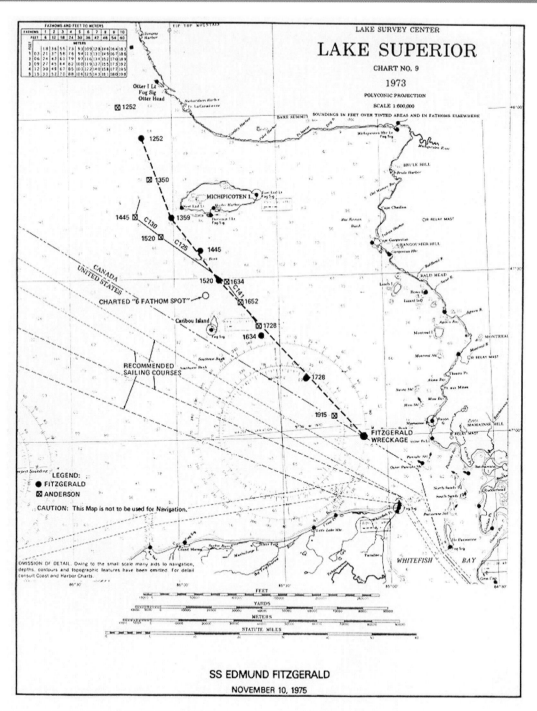

SS EDMUND FITZGERALD
NOVEMBER 10, 1975

Great Lakes ore carrier the SS *Edmund Fitzgerald* disappeared in a violent November storm in 1975. The ship went down so suddenly that she had no time even for a distress call. On November 10, within sight of a sister ship not 10 miles (16 km) behind, the SS *Edmund Fitzgerald* sank with the loss of all 29 hands aboard.

The *Edmund Fitzgerald* was built to be the biggest carrier on the Great Lakes. At 729 feet (222 m), she held that title from her launching in 1958 until 1971. Her cargo that fall, loaded through vast hatches in the deck, was taconite—small pellets of iron ore that would be forged into steel for the auto industry.

DIRE STRAITS

Captain Ernest McSorley of the *Fitzgerald* hugged the northern shore of Lake Superior as long as possible, while the storm swept across the plains onto the Great Lakes. The "Mighty Fitz" took the lead on the SS *Arthur M. Anderson* as both ships left the relative safety of the lee shore and struck off to the southeast, aiming for the shelter of Whitefish Bay. By

◀ Despite rapid rescue efforts and detailed mapping, the causes of the *Edmund Fitzgerald* wreck were never discovered.

early evening, conditions had deteriorated from bad to terrible. McSorley reported over the radio that he was having trouble in the heavy waters. He had lost both of his radars and was slowing his speed to compensate for a pronounced list. The *Anderson* stayed 10 miles (16 km) behind the *Fitzgerald*, her crew relaying radar information via ship-to-ship radio. At about 7:10 PM the ships passed one final bit of radio traffic:

"*Fitzgerald*, how are you making out with your problems?"

"We are holding our own," came the optimistic reply.

But they were not holding their own. Fifteen minutes later, the *Fitzgerald* disappeared from the *Anderson*'s radar screen. The *Anderson* immediately hailed the *Fitzgerald*, but to no avail. The Mighty Fitz was gone.

Searchers found the great ship within days; she had broken in two, 17 miles (27 km) off Whitefish Bay. The Coast Guard reported that crew negligence had caused the sinking: hatch covers had not been properly closed, allowing water to rush in. The Lake Carriers' Association issued its own report, blaming poor navigation. The crew of the *Anderson* bolstered the latter report; they had seen radar views of the *Fitzgerald* passing over the dangerous Six Fathom Shoals, which could easily have grounded her. Other theories involve pairs of waves—either fore and aft waves that raised the ship and allowed her heavy cargo to break her in two, or an abaft wave (near the rear of the ship) that lifted the stern, plunged the bow into another wave, and sent her straight down to the lake floor.

The tragedy of the *Fitzgerald* has inspired story and song, notably the ballad "The Wreck of the Edmund Fitzgerald" by Gordon Lightfoot. The mystery of the powerful ship's sudden demise only adds to her tragic allure.

FLOTSAM & JETSAM

Great Lakes seamen have a fitting name for the fierce autumn winds responsible for so many of the lakes' shipwrecks—the "Witch of November."

▶ The anchor of the *Edmund Fitzgerald*

SEAMAN'S HONOR

CAPTAIN BERNIE COOPER, of the SS *Arthur M. Anderson*, proved himself a real hero that terrible night. Cooper was the first to know that the *Edmund Fitzgerald* was in trouble. In addition to immediately alerting the Coast Guard when the *Fitzgerald*'s lights and radar track went black, Cooper took his ship back out of the shelter of Whitefish Bay to search for the missing ship during the height of the storm.

▼ The region between Grand Marais and Whitefish Point on Lake Superior is so shipwreck prone that it is called the "Graveyard of the Great Lakes."

2 · THE FATAL FLAW

▲ *Shipwreck on a Rocky Coast* by Wijnand Nuijen, 1837

The *Vasa*   ROYAL SWEDEN'S VAINGLORIOUS JEWEL

▲ Despite his failure with the *Vasa*, Gustavus Adolphus of Sweden was a highly successful king, leaving a major European legacy and enacting widespread domestic reforms.

The customer is always right, especially when the customer is King Gustavus Adolphus of Sweden (1611–32). The powerful monarch wanted a warship worthy of his military and naval might, one that would garner him victory in the Thirty Years' War (1618–48). He ordered the magnificent *Vasa*, named for his royal house, to be fitted with 64 cannons and bedecked with hundreds of ornate carvings. Engineers protested; the ship would be top-heavy, they said, and poorly ballasted. But the royal order held.

On her maiden voyage on August 10, 1628, the *Vasa* sailed out of port and into Stockholm's harbor. Less than a mile out, her sails filled with wind, and she fired a salute. A cheer went up from the assembled onlookers. Suddenly, she heeled sharply onto her port side. She righted herself briefly before heeling again. This time, water rushed into her gun ports, and she promptly sank to the bottom of the harbor. Sweden lost 50 lives that day, and the crown lost a fortune. The *Vasa*'s guns, carvings, and majestic trappings plummeted into 110 feet (33 m) of cold, Baltic water. In the decades following the disaster, searchers salvaged a number of the valuable cannons from the *Vasa*'s wreckage. But nothing could be done to raise the grand warship, a victim of her monarch's pride.

▲ The *Vasa*. Every year, thousands of visitors flock to the Vasa Museum on the island of Djurgården in Stockholm. The Swedish government had the museum specially built to display the nearly fully intact seventeenth-century warship.

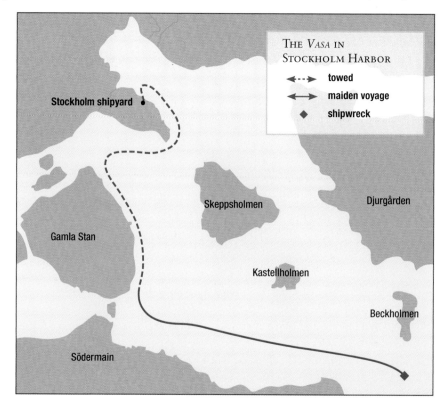

THE *VASA* IN STOCKHOLM HARBOR

‹- - -› towed
‹——› maiden voyage
◆ shipwreck

Stockholm shipyard
Skeppsholmen
Djurgården
Gamla Stan
Kastellholmen
Beckholmen
Södermain

RECOVERING THE *VASA*

For more than three centuries, the *Vasa* lay where she had fallen. Then, in 1956, an amateur archaeologist discovered the sunken ship. A consortium headed by the Swedish navy went to work uncovering and preparing to raise the wreck. In 1961, after five painstaking years of dangerous underwater work, divers raised the *Vasa*, a near-intact seventeenth-century warship. The frigid waters of the Baltic, the low salinity, and the absence of shipworms had combined to preserve the *Vasa*, her carvings, and myriad treasures. The rescuers found about 25 human skeletons in the ship, along with stores of clothing, plates, coins, and everyday objects—a virtual time capsule of seventeenth-century Sweden.

Conservators went to work immediately to restore the *Vasa* and prevent further deterioration. Restorers sprayed the ship with polyethylene glycol to preserve the wood, which otherwise would have disintegrated upon exposure to the air. Housed now in a dedicated museum in Stockholm, the *Vasa* displays her once-bright sculptures arrayed in their former positions on the gunwales and stern. A scale-model replica of the *Vasa* shows her in all her gilded and painted glory—the gods, demons, mermaids, and golden Swedish royal crest shining forth once more.

▲ A model of the *Vasa* at the Vasa Museum. Her bold, bright colors and 700 carvings served to aggrandize Sweden and disparage her enemies.

THE DIVING BELL AND THE CANNONS

IMAGINE SITTING INSIDE a huge iron bell, open at the bottom. A massive chain attached to the bell's top lowers you and the bell into the water. Although submerged, you can still breathe—the water pressure outside the bell has trapped air inside the bell chamber.

This is a diving bell, sometimes called a wet bell. This device was in use as early as the fourth century CE in ancient Greece. Until diving helmets appeared in the nineteenth century, it was the sole means of descending far underwater, and the only hope of rescuing lost fortune from shipwrecks. In 1664, two German divers descended 100 feet (30 m) in a diving bell to the wreck of the *Vasa*. With enormous effort and personal risk, they retrieved some 55 of the ship's 64 cannons.

▲ A diving bell on display at the Marinmuseum in Karlskrona, Sweden

► A backgammon game board recovered from the sunken *Vasa*

The *Medusa* | BETRAYAL AND BRUTALITY

▲ *The Raft of the Medusa* by Théodore Géricault

Some stories of shipwreck and survival remind us of the grandeur of the human spirit under the most abject of conditions. The wreck of the *Medusa* (*La Méduse*) is not one of them. It is, in fact, among the most brutal and horrifying stories in maritime history. From an incompetent captain to a murderous band of survivors, the events surrounding the 1816 wreck of the French frigate are a study in the despicable.

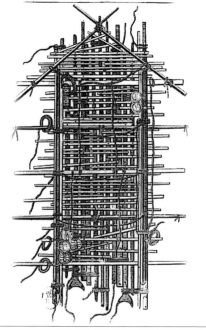

▲ A plan of the raft of the *Medusa*, from an 1818 history of the shipwreck, shows the hasty assemblage that doomed most of the 147 passengers and crewmen forced to refuge on the flimsy craft.

THE RAFT OF THE MEDUSA

The *Medusa* tragedy fascinated the young French painter Théodore Géricault (1791–1824). Géricault even talked with two of the survivors as he made preparatory sketches for a large-scale painting of the event. First exhibited at the Paris Salon of 1819, *The Raft of the Medusa* (*Le Radeau de la Méduse*) shows the desperate survivors crowding heedlessly over the bodies of the dead and dying as they spot a ship in the distance. The painting uncompromisingly highlighted the brutality of survival, and it had its intended effect: scandal. Viewers directed a good measure of their disgust at the Bourbon monarchy, which was blamed for the lax oversight onboard the *Medusa* and the horrors that ensued.

MONSTROUS *MEDUSA*

The *Medusa* sailed for Senegal on June 17, 1816, in convoy with three other ships. She left a France that was deeply divided between supporters of Napoleon and those loyal to the newly reinstalled monarchy. Among the 400 men, women, and children aboard was the new governor of French Senegal, Julien-Désiré Schmaltz, along with his wife. The crew of 160 was under the loose command of the inept monarchist Hugues Duroy de Chaumareys, who had last sailed some two decades earlier.

The speediest way to travel southeast along the coast of West Africa is to hug the shore, profiting from the dominant winds. It is also the most dangerous: the coastal geography includes shifting shoals and sandbars. De Chaumareys chose the dangerous route. Breaking away from her three-ship escort, the *Medusa* made good time, especially because her captain neglected to slow for regular soundings. Soon she ran aground on the notorious Arguin Bank, approximately 31 miles (50 km) off the coast of present-day Mauritania. The crew constructed a crude raft out of the ship's masts and crossbeams. The captain, governor, and other notables seated themselves in six lifeboats, while 147 crewmen and passengers—many of them Napoleon supporters—crowded onto the 65-by-23-foot (20 x 7 m) raft. Seventeen men refused to even board the raft, and stayed with the ship. When rescuers located the *Medusa* 40 days later, only 3 remained alive.

ANARCHY ADRIFT

Setting off for shore, the lifeboats towed the raft, whose desperate passengers clung on for their lives. Within hours, towing became untenable, and those aboard the lifeboats simply cut the raft loose, to cries of *"Nous les abandonnes!"* ("We are abandoning them!"). Some sources claim that Governor Schmaltz himself wielded the knife.

With no means of steering, no sails, and only wine and sodden biscuits for provision, the raft turned into a scene of pandemonium. Many drowned in the first few hours, when a scramble ensued for the center of the raft—the only portion above water. There was no command and no mercy, as the strong cast the weak overboard. Each day the numbers of the living dwindled; some perished by drowning, some by suicide, some by murder. By the third day, those alive were cannibalizing the dead, and, by the fifth day, only 30 remained alive. When rescuers finally recovered the raft, 17 days after it had set adrift, only 15 of its 147 original passengers remained.

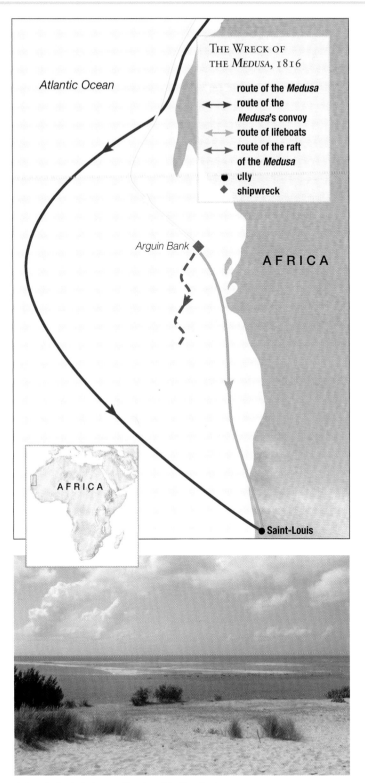

THE WRECK OF
THE *MEDUSA*, 1816

route of the *Medusa*
route of the
Medusa's convoy
route of lifeboats
route of the raft
of the *Medusa*
● city
◆ shipwreck

Atlantic Ocean

Arguin Bank

AFRICA

AFRICA

● Saint-Louis

▲ Arguin Bank, today a national park in Mauritania

SS *Metropolis*

A PITIFUL RUIN ON THE OUTER BANKS

All was not well as the steamship *Metropolis* left Philadelphia in late January 1878, bound for Brazil with 248 passengers and a load of iron rail. A leak near the rudder got steadily worse, to the point where the pumps couldn't keep up and water started to fill the bilges. The captain ordered coal dumped overboard to lighten the ship, a prudent and effective action. Not prudent, however, was his decision to continue the voyage and steam past the nearby port of Hampton Bays, Virginia, where he could have put in for repairs. Instead, the *Metropolis* continued south into the troubled waters off Cape Hatteras, North Carolina. By then, the heavy cargo had begun to shift, pounding the ship from within with every wave.

ROUTE OF THE SS *METROPOLIS*, JANUARY 1878

⟷ route of the SS *Metropolis*
● city
◆ shipwreck

PENNSYLVANIA
NEW JERSEY
● Philadelphia
● Baltimore
◆ Washington, D.C.
DELAWARE
WEST VIRGINIA
MARYLAND
● Richmond
VIRGINIA
Hampton ●
Virginia Beach ●
◆ Currituck Beach
Atlantic Ocean
NORTH CAROLINA
Outer Banks

As the *Metropolis* approached the light at Currituck Beach, a rogue wave overtook her, tearing away most of her superstructure and half of her lifeboats and dousing the fires in her boilers. She proceeded under sail, but failed to make the beach. Within hours, her hull was battered and smashed against the sands of the Outer Banks, and the Atlantic had taken 85 souls to their final rest.

FAILED RESCUE

Lighthouse keeper John G. Chappell and the men of the Currituck Lifesaving Station had been patrolling the storm-tossed beach all night. They were back at the station recuperating when the report came in that the *Metropolis* had gone aground and was breaking up. Quickly deciding that they didn't have time to drag their huge surfboat several miles to the wreck site, Chappell immediately

▲ The Currituck Beach Lighthouse, constructed only three years before the tragic loss of the SS *Metropolis*

strapped the first-aid kit to his back and set off on the station's only horse. His exhausted men followed behind, dragging the half-ton cart of rescue gear across the soft sand.

Upon arriving at the wreck site, Chappell found the *Metropolis* foundering offshore, under siege from the pounding breakers. Rescuers on the beach clearly heard the screams of her passengers. Many had already jumped into the sea. Chappell offered aid to those who made it to the beach as his crew arrived and began setting up their state-of-the-art rescue equipment. A mortar fired a projectile, trying to attach a rope to the stricken ship, but missed. The second shot was perfectly on target, but an inexperienced seaman on the *Metropolis* rigged the rope improperly, and it parted. Further attempts to land a line failed. Though many passengers made it to shore, those who remained on board perished when the ship broke up. They, along with unlucky swimmers, were lost to the waves. The wreck lived in infamy, with contemporary reports denouncing the captain's fatefully bad decision.

FLOTSAM & JETSAM

According to eyewitnesses, a large Newfoundland dog dragged one half-drowned *Metropolis* survivor from the pounding surf.

▶ A contemporary illustration of the foundering *Metropolis* and the merciless onslaught of the waves

▼ Illustrations of a Merriman suit from 1875

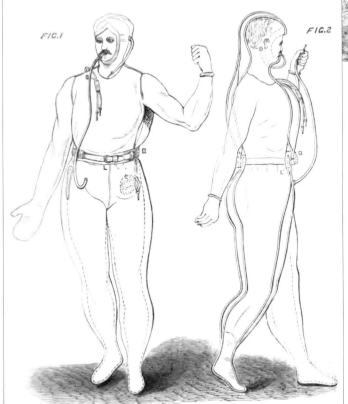

CUTTING-EDGE RESCUE ATTEMPT

BECAUSE THE *METROPOLIS* had the good fortune to go aground adjacent to the lifesaving station at Currituck Beach, she was treated to the most modern rescue techniques of the day. These techniques were almost—but not quite—up to the task. Failing to land a rope onto the ship from shore, the rescuers were forced to give up from lack of powder. If they had landed a line, they could have deployed rigging and brand-new "Merriman suits," which were the precursors to today's survival suits. After the wrecks of the *Metropolis* and her predecessor, the *Huron*, which had wrecked nearby two months earlier, Congress appropriated funds for increased lifesaving operations along the East Coast.

| SS *Eastland* | # SUMMER OUTING TURNED TO RUIN |

Saturday morning, July 24, 1915, dawned unseasonably cool in downtown Chicago. For its annual all-company picnic, Western Electric had engaged three steamships to take employees to Michigan City, Indiana, for the day. At 6:30 AM, passengers began streaming onto the SS *Eastland*, docked on the Chicago River at the Clark Street Bridge. A total of 2,752 people jammed onto the liner for the short trip across Lake Michigan. Many of the picnic-goers stood on deck, wanting to watch the departure from outside.

Their festive mood was soon shattered. At 7:10, the *Eastland* began to list to her port side, and, for the next 15 minutes, passengers grew increasingly alarmed. As the ship continued to list, the portside gangways began to admit water. At 7:28, the great ship groaned and rolled gently, but inexorably, onto her side, coming to rest abreast of the dock. In the confusion that ensued, a third of those aboard perished that terrible day in Chicago, in only 20 feet (6 m) of water.

A SINISTER FLAW

The steamship *Eastland* was built in 1903 to ferry tourists around the Great Lakes. Touted as the "Speed Queen of the Great Lakes," she nevertheless exhibited serious design flaws. From her earliest voyages, the *Eastland* had a propensity

▲ A rowboat filled with survivors of the *Eastland* disaster makes its way to safety. Other survivors are seen standing on the foundered boat in the background.

to list, or tilt to one side. The condition could generally be corrected by flooding the ballast tanks in the bilge of the ship, though listing was a particularly perilous flaw for a touring ship that frequently saw legions of passengers congregating on the upper decks, unpredictably shifting the ship's weight.

The sinking of the *Titanic* in 1912 had inspired the passage of the Seaman's Act in 1915, which stipulated the addition

▲ The *Eastland* lies on her side, with her top deck facing the photographer. Behind, onlookers watch resuce efforts underway from the safety of the adjacent pier.

of lifeboats to all vessels. The addition of lifeboats and deck strengthening reinforcement to the *Eastland* added weight on top—these "improvements" raised an already dangerously high center of gravity even higher.

FROM PICNIC TO PANIC

As passengers boarded that morning, the engineers had even more trouble than usual keeping the ship balanced. Her ballast tanks were at first ineffective at countering her list, so much so that the chief engineer sent someone topside to check if perhaps the ship had hung up on the pier. The ship eventually righted herself, and preparations to cast off continued. As her engines began to slowly push the *Eastland*'s stern away from the pier, the portside list returned, and it quickly worsened. Passengers panicked as furniture, dishes, cutlery, and bottles crashed over to the port side. As water poured in through open portside gangways, terrified people leapt off the starboard side deck. The weight shift increased, propelling the ship ever farther off her lines until, with a crack, the shore lines parted, and the ship rolled clean over to her side.

The rolling ship threw many passengers clear; others managed to escape to the adjacent pier, a mere 20 feet (6 m) from the *Eastland*, or to rescue ships that quickly appeared on the scene. One nearby ship, the *Kenosha*, came alongside the *Eastland*'s hull, which enabled many people left stranded on the capsized vessel to leap to safety. But too many didn't make it. On that black day, one originally meant for fun and laughter, 841 passengers and 4 crew members were killed in the shallow waters alongside a pier in downtown Chicago.

WORKING-CLASS HEROES

STEVEDORES AND OTHER WORKERS on the docks that cool July Saturday watched in horror as the *Eastland* rolled over. Several of them immediately responded with torches in hand to the cries and hammering coming from the overturned hull and began cutting their way through the solid steel. Though hindered by the ship's crew, who objected to the destruction of their hull, the shore party nonetheless rescued more than 40 passengers.

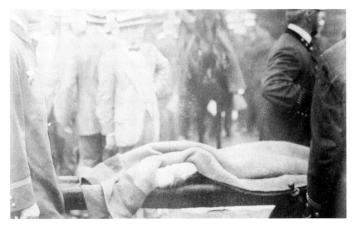

▲ Rescuers carry an *Eastland* victim away from the disaster.

▲ Rescuers wrap a man's jacket around a young survivor. The tragedy left the children of 19 families orphans, and it entirely wiped out 22 families.

▲ Cranes on a barge right the toppled ship. After the disaster, the *Eastland* lived a second life as the USS *Willmette*, an Illinois Naval Reserve gunboat.

SS *Princess Sophia*

ALASKA'S GREATEST TRAGEDY

History can be an unreliable teacher. Captain Leonard Locke commanded the SS *Princess Sophia* for her last journey in 1918. A Canadian Pacific Railroad coastal ferry, the *Princess Sophia* foundered on a reef in a narrow channel during an intense snowstorm, 30 miles (48 km) north of Juneau, Alaska. Two ships had met a similar fate within recent memory. The captain of one had made the fatal decision to evacuate in rough conditions, with the loss of all lifeboats. The other captain had safely evacuated all passengers. With these two shipwrecks in mind, Captain Locke erred on the side of caution and kept his passengers onboard. Forty hours after foundering, and with a flotilla of rescue ships nearby, the *Princess Sophia* was swept away in raging waves and a deadly boiler explosion. All 343 aboard were lost in Alaska's worst maritime disaster.

Launched in 1911, the *Princess Sophia* boasted double-hulled steel construction. She was more than fit for her customary route through the Inland Passage, a protected waterway through the narrow channels and fjords of coastal British Columbia and Alaska. On her final journey, the *Princess Sophia* carried many families returning from the Yukon Territory. After the wreck, recovery workers told of the heartbreaking sight of children's toys floating in the icy water.

A FATAL GAMBLE

The *Princess Sophia* departed Skagway, Alaska, at 10:00 PM on October 23. A blinding snowstorm quickly beset her as she entered Lynn Canal. The ship drifted slightly off course in the dangerous channel—a mistake that cost her dearly. Unable to right her course, at 2:00 AM on October 24, the *Princess Sophia* struck Vanderbilt Reef—a flat, rocky surface in the middle of the channel. A radio distress call reached Juneau, and a flotilla of rescue ships made for the *Princess Sophia*. A large American lighthouse ship, the USLHS *Cedar*, only reached the site at 10:00 PM, some 20 hours after the *Princess Sophia* foundered. No ship could approach the reef itself, or the foundering *Princess Sophia*, in the storm-tossed waters.

The captains of the *Cedar* and the *Princess Sophia* maintained near-steady radio contact. What to do? A rescue attempt in the rough water, with limited visibility, could doom the rescue ships. Launching lifeboats could doom the *Princess Sophia*'s passengers. Captain Locke decided to wait for clearer weather, calmer seas, and a favorable tide—the *Princess Sophia* wasn't moving off the reef, nor taking on water. But the storm worsened instead of abating. The afternoon of the third day—October 25—the radio operator sent out a call: "Ship foundering on reef. Come at once!" Thirty minutes later, at 5:20, came the final signal from the *Princess Sophia*: "For God's sake, hurry—the water is in my room!" Historians believe the boiler exploded shortly after this, dashing apart the ship. Nearly all the watches found on the dead had stopped at 5:50 PM.

▲ The *Princess Sophia* lay in sight of land, but freezing waters, rough waves, and rocks surrounding the reef prevented the launch of lifeboats and thwarted rescue.

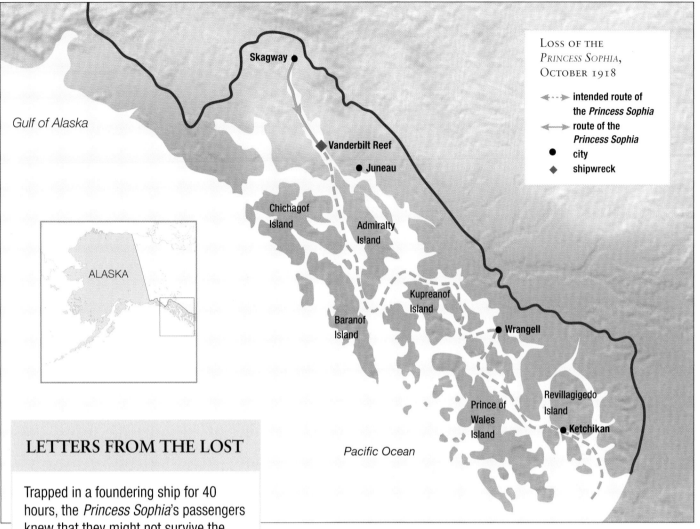

LOSS OF THE
PRINCESS SOPHIA,
OCTOBER 1918

◄- - -► intended route of
the *Princess Sophia*
◄——► route of the
Princess Sophia
● city
◆ shipwreck

Gulf of Alaska

Skagway ●

Vanderbilt Reef ◆

Juneau ●

Chichagof
Island

Admiralty
Island

ALASKA

Kupreanof
Island

Baranof
Island

Wrangell ●

Revillagigedo
Island

Prince of
Wales
Island

Ketchikan ●

Pacific Ocean

LETTERS FROM THE LOST

Trapped in a foundering ship for 40 hours, the *Princess Sophia*'s passengers knew that they might not survive the ordeal. Some wrote letters, later found on their recovered bodies, to loved ones. One letter in particular, from Englishman John R. Mastell and addressed to his fiancée, was widely reprinted in newspapers. It began, "My own dear sweetheart, I am writing this my dear girl while the boat is in grave danger." The letter includes a hastily jotted will.

▶ The *Princess May*, grounded on Sentinenal Island (near Vanderbilt Reef) in 1910, had safely evacuated all of her passengers. One year later, the *Princess May* participated in the ill-fated rescue attempt of the *Princess Sophia*.

MS *Estonia* | DEATH IN THE BALTIC

Built in Germany in 1980, the MS *Estonia* was more than 500 feet (155 m) of modern steel cruise ferry, with every safety appliance and innovation the late twentieth century had to offer. The *Estonia* plied ferry routes under various names and owners in Scandinavia and Europe throughout the 1980s and had gained a reputation as a good ship to handle in rough weather. Her sudden and violent sinking in 1994, in an unremarkable storm in the Baltic Sea, shocked the world, especially because it resulted in the loss of 852 lives.

The MS *Estonia* regularly made the run between Tallinn, Estonia, and Stockholm, Sweden. On September 27, 1994, after loading her passengers and cargo, the *Estonia*'s crew locked and sealed her double-bow door for an on-time departure of 7:00 PM. All seemed normal onboard as she headed into the Baltic Sea, into the typical autumn gales. Seas were 10 to 13 feet (3–4 m), with winds of Gale Force 7–8 on the Beaufort scale. Rough conditions, but nothing the *Estonia* hadn't weathered many times before.

▲ A model of the doomed ferry in a Tallinn, Estonia, museum

CAPSIZED!

At around 1:00 AM the next morning, crew members heard a loud bang, followed by the sound of grinding metal. The crew immediately inspected the bow loading doors—particularly the "visor" outer door that met the waves head on—but could find nothing amiss. Yet, not 15 minutes later, a wave tore the visor off completely, allowing the sea to reach the inner ramp that protected the car deck. The cascade of events quickly went from bad to worse, as water rushed into the open car deck, with a force compounded by *Estonia*'s fast passage into oncoming seas. Within minutes, the ship became increasingly unstable from the water sloshing around the open car deck. Free surface effect, a phenomenon that can quickly make it impossible for a ship to right itself, took over. The modern steel ship rolled over and sank to the bottom of the Baltic Sea.

Many of those who made it to the deck survived, but some 750 people trapped inside perished. Lifeboats and rafts were launched, and the luckier passengers clambered aboard. The shipping lanes of the Baltic are crowded, and rescue arrived fairly quickly to the stricken *Estonia*. An investigative commission following the disaster blamed passive and ineffective crew members, interior announcements in the Estonian language only, and other communication problems for the high death toll. The commission also called for new standards of training and ferry regulation, in hopes of preventing a repeat of the terrible events of September 28, 1994, in the Baltic Sea.

▲ The MS *Estonia* boasted all the usual precations, including life preservers, but to shockingly little avail.

CONSPIRACY ON THE SEA?

THE SHOCKING LOSS OF A MODERN, well-maintained steel passenger ferry in normally heavy seas might be expected to encourage speculation about causes. In the case of the *Estonia*, a number of factors emerged after the sinking that caused observers to question the official account of events. Rumors of an explosion and a corresponding hole in the hull took on additional credence when it was revealed that the *Estonia* had twice borne classified military shipments on previous runs. Charges surfaced that the Russian Secret Service was involved. The Swedish and Estonian governments accused each other of covering up secrets, and each launched private investigations. The Swedish government's failed attempt to entomb the wreck in concrete—an act that would have prevented further investigation— lent additional fuel to the conspiracists' fire.

▲ A monument to the MS *Estonia*'s victims in Stockholm

▶ Tallinn erected its own tribute to the lost ferry crew and passengers, called the *Katkenud liin* (Broken Line), right.

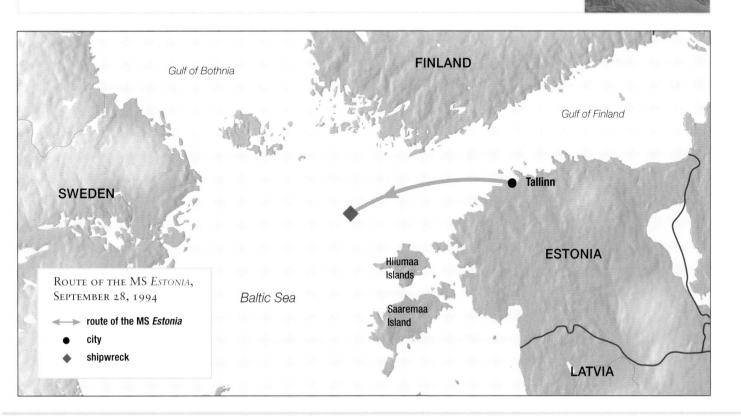

Gulf of Bothnia

FINLAND

Gulf of Finland

SWEDEN

Tallinn

ESTONIA

Baltic Sea

Hiiumaa Islands

Saaremaa Island

ROUTE OF THE MS ESTONIA, SEPTEMBER 28, 1994

←→ route of the MS *Estonia*
● city
◆ shipwreck

LATVIA

MV *Le Joola* — A Modern African Tragedy

▲ The *Le Joola*, upside down, slowly succumbs to the waves. A French navy raft floats beside the ferry, but rescue efforts proved largely ineffective.

MV *Le Joola*, a modern German-built ferry, plied the busy African West Coast trade routes. She capsized in a sudden squall off Gambia on September 22, 2002. There were 64 survivors, but as many as 1,863 souls perished. The loss of *Le Joola* is considered one of the worst nonmilitary maritime disasters, second only to the *Doña Paz*.

The MV *Le Joola* was a 261-foot (79.5 m) long multi-ferry, purpose-built for the unique demands of coastal Africa. Though designed for about 536 passengers, nearly three times that many were on board for *Le Joola*'s final journey. To make

matters worse, many passengers were merchants bearing huge amounts of luggage, heading for the markets of Dakar. Reports that *Le Joola* was listing upon departure that final night indicate possible mishandling of cargo.

BROADSIDE SQUALL

Weather was good as *Le Joola* boarded her final passengers and freight at Ziguinchor, Senegal, but the ferry was dangerously overloaded, overbooked, and poorly maintained. After reporting via radio that all was well at the beginning of her voyage, she ran into a squall one hour into the journey. Some 17 miles (27 km) off Gambia, a gale erupted, striking *Le Joola* broadside. Conditions belowdecks were stiflingly hot, so the deck was crowded with passengers, who rushed to the lee side to escape the gale's violent onslaught. That shift of weight, combined with the intense cross force of wind and water, caused the huge ship to suddenly capsize. Many passengers on deck were thrown into the water, but the speed of the roll was such that anyone inside the ship was doomed. The upside-down ship remained afloat for 15 hours, during which time survivors could hear banging and yelling from inside the ship, yet were helpless to effect a rescue. Around 3:00 PM the following day, the MV *Le Joola* slipped beneath the waves.

The squall that beset *Le Joola* was indeed severe, yet there seems little doubt that the overcrowding, poor maintenance, and inept cargo loading contributed to the disaster. The actual number of dead will never be known, but most experts

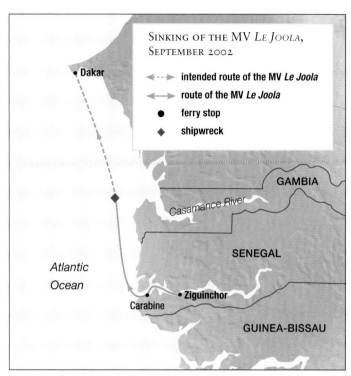

▲ The ferry *Aline Sitoé Diatta* now runs the Dakar–Ziguinchor route. Despite *Le Joola*, many West African ferries still sail while dangerously overcrowded.

believe the death toll from *Le Joola* is higher than that of the *Titanic*. Only about 1,000 people had tickets for *Le Joola*, but in that region of Africa passengers without tickets or money to pay are often allowed to board anyway, resulting in severe overcrowding. National politics and bureaucracy also worsened the calamity, because it took nearly 12 hours for any rescue, other than local fishermen on pirogues, to arrive.

The loss of the MV *Le Joola* stunned the region and the world. Inquests into the tragedy resulted in a few politicians losing their jobs but failed to turn up conclusive blame for the tragedy. Unfortunately, not much has changed, and vessels in the area remain dangerously overcrowded even now.

WHAT'S IN A NAME?

LE JOOLA WAS NAMED in honor of the Djula people of South Senegal. These tribesmen were early traders on the routes between Western Africa and the Sahara region. Sadly, many Djula probably perished that terrible night off Gambia.

▲ A monument in Ziguinchor remembers the victims of the MV *Le Joola* tragedy.

The *Prestige* | EUROPE'S DEADLIEST OIL SPILL

The *Prestige* oil spill illustrates the disastrous consequences of negligence and self-interest. The Greek-owned oil tanker *Prestige* was aging and structurally deficient when she departed St. Petersburg, Russia, in November 2002. The single-hulled, 26-year-old ship was loaded with 77,000 tons (66,850 metric tons) of crude oil. As she made her way down the west coast of Europe, she was caught in a fierce storm on November 13.

When the crew discovered that one of the ballast tanks was taking on water, they requested leave to enter a port on Spain's northwest coast. Spanish authorities refused, fearing that the tanker would begin to leak oil onto their coastline. France and Portugal followed suit, each country hoping to avert a disaster on its own shores. With no safe port, the *Prestige* was forced to ride out the storm, an attempt that would lead to the worst oil spill to ever strike the shores of Europe.

▲ Oil from the *Prestige* coated rocks black for miles of shoreline.

BLACK TIDE

Soon after the *Prestige*'s distress call, the dreaded spill began. While the *Prestige* endured a pounding in the waves off Spain's Galician coast, a 40-foot (12 m) gash opened in the hull. Oil began to leak from the rapidly deteriorating tanker, and the Spanish government dispatched ships to tow her into deeper water. There, authorities claimed, the colder water would isolate the inevitable oil spill. While being towed—six days after her initial storm damage—the *Prestige* split in two and sank about 150 miles (250 km) from the coast, releasing thousands of tons of her toxic cargo. Her crew had earlier been evacuated, and authorities now took her captain into custody as the catastrophic effects of the spill became clear.

▲ A video captures the *Prestige* as she breaks in two some 150 miles (250 km) off Spain's coast in the Atlantic Ocean.

NUNCA MAIS

CLEANUP OF THE *PRESTIGE* OIL SPILL began immediately, both on land and at sea. Workers in white coveralls smeared with the black oil soon dotted the Galician coastline as they attempted to remove the oil. Many were volunteers, part of a massive grassroots movement known as *Nunca Mais,* or "Never Again," in the Galician dialect.

At sea, dredging and salvage ships arrived from far and wide. A Dutch dredger was able to collect 1,500 tons (1,360 metric tons) of oil in one salvage operation. Other ships erected long barriers to try to contain the oil and prevent it from reaching shore. Meanwhile, investigation into the disaster revealed that the *Prestige* had failed inspections in several ports, and that its former captain had been forced to resign when he protested the shoddy state of the tanker.

▲ Volunteers donned white Tyvek overalls to clean the beach at Nemiña, Spain.

The rocky coastline of Galicia, Spain, is home to numerous species of seabirds, and it is an important fishery center. As the oil spill reached the coast, residents described the horrific sight of the so-called black tide—rocks and water coated with a slick black sheen, millions of fish and birds washed up dead, and a stench compared to a gasoline station. A six-month ban on fishing cost the local industry dearly, but the devastation is still not contained, even today. An estimated 80 percent of the oil in the tanker was spilled, or close to 63,000 tons (57,150 metric tons). Environmentalists predict that the effects of the spill on marine life will continue for about 10 years. Furthermore, the hull of the *Prestige* still lies below the sea. Undersea robotic pods sealed some of its seams, but thousands of tons of oil still remain in the submerged tanker, a second disaster waiting to happen.

▲ The damage done to wildlife by oil spills is tremendous. Rescuing affected birds is painstaking for humans and traumatic for the animals, many of which—even if they survive—have no safe habitat to return to.

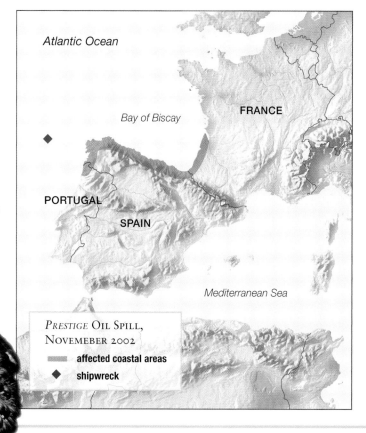

Atlantic Ocean

Bay of Biscay

FRANCE

PORTUGAL

SPAIN

Mediterranean Sea

PRESTIGE OIL SPILL,
NOVEMEBER 2002

▬▬ affected coastal areas
◆ shipwreck

ECOSYSTEM WRECKS

Accidents involving oil tankers occur with about the same regularity as other kinds of shipping accidents, which run the gamut from unfortunate to tragic. The results of tanker mishaps, though, range from devastating to catastrophic. For shipping and oil companies, such losses can total billions of dollars, especially when lawsuits and cleanup costs are factored in.

From an environmental point of view, though, the loss is measured in terms of life and death—mostly death for the myriad species affected by an oil spill. Birds, fish, and marine mammals such as otters, seals, dolphins, and whales die immediately, as their bodies are coated with toxic oil. Later generations of these animals often have increased mortality, because their food supply and habitat remain contaminated.

▲ The *Prestige* was not the only tanker to spill off Europe's shores. In 1978, the *Amoco Cadiz*, a single-hulled tanker, wrecked off the coast of France, splitting into two.

There is a human cost as well, especially in regions that rely heavily on local fishery. With their prime source of income cut off, such communities can simply vanish.

The worst marine oil spills in history—measured in gallons of oil spilled—were not the results of shipping accidents. The 1991 Gulf War oil spill and the 1980 Ixtoc I oil well spill in the Gulf of Mexico claim this distinction. But shipping disasters account for the bulk of oil spills worldwide. Among the most notorious of these, and still the worst oil spill in U.S. history, is the 1989 *Exxon Valdez* oil spill in Prince William Sound, Alaska. Still, the total oil released (about 10 million gallons, or 38 million liters) from the *Valdez* pales in comparison with at least a dozen other oil tanker wrecks since the mid-twentieth century. The Greek tanker *Atlantic Empress,* which wrecked off the coast of Trinidad and Tobago in 1979, for example, spilled nine times that much oil.

▲ From June 3, 1979, to March 23, 1980, the Ixtoc I oil well exuded the equivalent of 10 to 30 thousand barrels of toxic crude oil per day into the Gulf of Mexico.

▲ Scores of volunteers participated in cleanup efforts after the *Exxon Valdez* oil spill, which contaminated 700 miles (1,125 km) of coastline with crude oil.

IN THE LONG TERM

SCIENTISTS HAVE WIDELY STUDIED the short- and long-term consequences of marine oil spills. The National Oceanographic and Atmospheric Administration (NOAA) estimates that the area affected by the *Exxon Valdez* may take up to three decades to recover from the devastating spill. The International Maritime Organization (IMO) has instituted regulations that attempt to abate future oil spills, such as a ban on single-hulled tankers that will take effect in 2012. The IMO and other organizations are also focusing attention on reducing greenhouse gas emissions from the shipping industry, in an effort to strike a balance between the commercial needs met by shipping and the environmental health of the planet.

MS *al-Salam Boccaccio 98*

BETRAYAL ON THE RED SEA

Design flaws, severe overcrowding, poor maintenance, and large, open cargo bays: a recipe for disaster. And so it was when the MS *al-Salam Boccaccio 98* caught fire, capsized, and sank in the Red Sea on February 3, 2006. The death toll was close to 1,000 people.

The MS *al-Salam Boccaccio 98* had been built in 1970, but, in 1991, the owners added two additional passenger decks on top, while the cargo area was enlarged to hold 320 automobiles. Some 1,300 passengers could now travel in the *Boccaccio 98*, but the additional height of her superstructure made her more vulnerable to wind and waves. As a RO/RO (roll-on/roll-off) ferry, *Boccaccio 98* had an open deck that ran the entire length of the ship, was close to the waterline to ease boarding and egress of automotive cargo, and hosted doors large enough to admit enough water to destabilize the ship.

▲ Many ferries ply the waters of the Red Sea and her canals. Unfortunately, poor maintenance, uncertain politics, and piracy threaten all too many of these ships.

HUMAN ERROR WRIT LARGE

The MS *al-Salam Boccaccio 98* departed Duba, Saudi Arabia, en route to Safaga, Egypt, on schedule at 7:00 PM. Within two hours, a fire broke out in a storeroom. The crew brought the fire under control, but noticed a list to the ship, perhaps induced by the failure of pumps to eliminate the seawater used to douse the fire. Over the next several hours, crews repeatedly got the fire under control only to have it reignite. Passengers were instructed to move to the top of the ship and crowd to the port side to try to counteract the ever-worsening list. As the captain turned the ship back toward its port of origin, the *Boccaccio 98* heeled over farther still, until she suddenly rolled completely to starboard.

As horrible as the accident was, the aftermath was worse. No SOS was ever sent out, and rescue didn't arrive for many hours after the *Boccaccio 98* capsized. Though most passengers had donned life jackets before the sinking, they had been given no instructions on how to inflate rubber rafts, nor were any of the 10 large lifeboats (which held 100 people each) launched. The ship's crew reportedly saved themselves first, leaving the passengers to fend for themselves. Arriving rescuers found more dead bodies than people to save.

Experts cited several possible causes for the disaster: an overbuilt superstructure; water from firefighting sloshing around the huge void of the auto deck; or a possible tie-down that failed, allowing a car to fly across the deck and pierce the hull. Whatever the cause, human error was certainly at the root. The MS *al-Salam Boccaccio 98* did not have to sink that dark February night on the Red Sea.

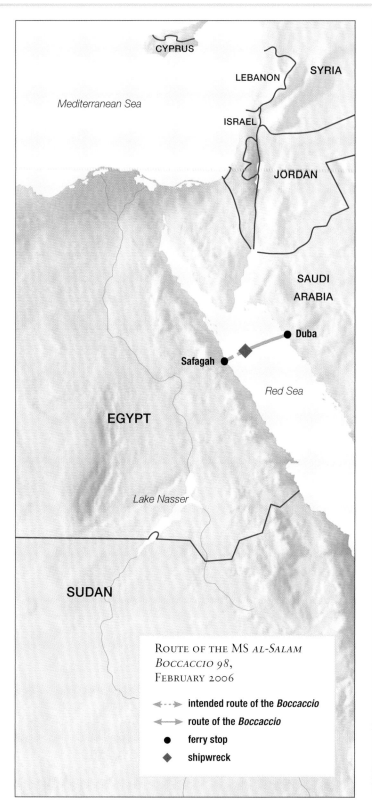

▲ Numerous shipwrecks and extensive reefs make the Red Sea a wreck diver's mecca. Shown above is the wreck of the *Salem Express*, a roll-on/roll-off ferry that sank during a violent storm in the Red Sea December 1995, killing at least 470.

ROUTE OF THE MS *AL-SALAM BOCCACCIO 98*, FEBRUARY 2006

‹‑‑‑› intended route of the *Boccaccio*
‹—› route of the *Boccaccio*
● ferry stop
◆ shipwreck

CYPRUS
LEBANON
SYRIA
Mediterranean Sea
ISRAEL
JORDAN
SAUDI ARABIA
Duba
Safagah
Red Sea
EGYPT
Lake Nasser
SUDAN

LORD JIM REDUX?

ONE OF THE MOST MEMORABLE SCENES of Joseph Conrad's novel *Lord Jim* is a fire aboard ship. The crew conceals the fire so they can flee, leaving the passengers to their doom. The captain and crew of the *Boccaccio 98* made comparisons to Conrad's tale only too easy. Captain Sayed Omar was not only derelict in his duties, but besmirched the honor of generations of sea captains when he was witnessed leaping into one of the first life rafts launched. Captain Omar's crew followed his lead, reportedly instructing passengers on the sinking ship to "just relax; go back to your cabin," all the while donning their own life jackets.

3 · COLLISION COURSE

▲ *Marine* by Carl Wilhelm Barth, 1885

The *Tek Sing* | THE ILL-FATED *TRUE STAR*

▲ Junks date back at least as far as the Han Dynasty (220 BCE–200 CE). Contrary to popular belief, they are not just small harbor boats, but also world travelers. Here, the *Keying*, a three-masted junk similiar to the *Tek Sing*, draws a crowd at the Battery in Manhattan. The *Keying* was the first ship from China to visit New York.

Many modern observers picture Chinese junks as small square-rigged ships capable of nothing more than creeping along the shore, barely venturing beyond sight of land, heading only downwind. In fact, junks sailed all over the world, battling high seas, bad weather, and contrary winds along China's widespread trade routes. The *Tek Sing*, or *True Star*, was huge for her time, a 164-foot (50 m) three-masted oceangoing junk of more than 1,000 tons (900 metric tons) displacement.

On her final voyage in February 1822, the *Tek Sing* carried a vast cargo of goods: ink pads, iron and brass cannons, padlocks, candlesticks, and pocket watches. But all that was nothing compared to the prodigious cache of porcelain—some 350,000 pieces comprising several tons of plates, cups, utensils, and figurines, both contemporary and ancient. At the time, porcelain was so highly prized that it was more valuable than gold.

The *Tek Sing* may have been loaded down with cargo, but she was even more heavily laden with humans. In cabins and even on the open deck, the junk carried between 1,400 and 1,600 passengers, mostly laborers headed for work in the cane fields of Indonesia. The vast majority of them would never arrive.

SHORT CUT TO DISASTER

Sailing out of Amoy (present-day Xiamen), China, and bound for Jakarta, Indonesia, the *Tek Sing* had sailed uneventfully at sea for several weeks. But the overwhelming number of passengers onboard strained the ship's reserves. Captain Io Tauko made the fateful decision to try to take a shortcut through the Gaspar Strait. Had he steered but 100 yards (94 m) to either side, he would have cleared the Belvidere Shoals, but whitecaps concealed the shallow reef, and the *Tek Sing* hit ground hard, splintering apart almost at once. Within minutes, she had sunk in 100 feet (30 m) of water, leaving at least 1,600 dead bodies floating in her wreckage.

The high death toll has led modern observers to christen the *Tek Sing* "The *Titanic* of the East." A day after the wreck, Captain James Pearl, commanding the HMS *Indiana*, came upon an area of rocks not on his charts. To his crew's amazement, as the "rocks" drew closer, they turned out to be wood, bamboo, and all manner of flotsam and jetsam. And on each piece of floating debris lay one or more dead or dying man. "I discovered the sea covered with humans for many miles," reported Captain Pearl, as he immediately lowered boats and set about rescuing as many survivors as he could. He was able to rescue only 190, while other boats in the area saved another 18. The rest died there, on the Belvidere Shoals of the South China Sea.

BLUE AND WHITE GOLD

THE *TEK SING* IS PERHAPS BEST KNOWN due to events that took place almost 200 years after the sinking, when treasure hunter Mike Hatcher and his boat, the *Restless M*, tracked down the wreck in 1999. Following the faintest of sonar traces, Hatcher and his team first located huge iron rings, which had once strengthened a gargantuan mast. Following the rings' trail, the divers zeroed in on a coral-covered mound approximately the reported size and shape of the lost *Tek Sing*. Standing perfectly packed where the ship had virtually decayed around them were towers of porcelain—row upon row of precious blue and white, celadon, and monochrome pieces. Historians estimate that the oldest of these date from the 1660s. The haul of the *Restless M* turned out to be the largest amount of porcelain ever obtained from a single shipwreck.

◀ In January 2001, Mike Hatcher took a dive in a display tank at a boat show in Düsseldorf, Germany, to display a porcelain vase and a blue and white plate that were both part of his huge find on the wreck of the *Tek Sing*. Just a couple of months earlier, a nine-day auction of 350,000 of the antique pieces had taken place in Stuttgart.

| HMS *Birkenhead* | # CHIVALRY TO THE LAST MAN |

The HMS *Birkenhead* was a three-masted sailing frigate fitted with two steam-driven paddle wheels. Built in 1845 as the *Vulcan*, an iron-hulled warship, the *Birkenhead* was renamed and reclassified as a troopship before her first commission. When she departed Ireland on January 7, 1852, the *Birkenhead* carried soldiers bound for the Xhosa wars in South Africa. She was never to make land, but the stoic bravery of the men aboard the sinking *Birkenhead* profoundly impacted both naval protocol and British cultural identity.

◀ In the only known contemporary image of the frigate HMS *Birkenhead,* she takes to the sea with sails down, using her steam-driven paddle wheels.

ON THE ROCKS

Captain Robert Salmond, of a long line of Royal Navy officers, commanded the *Birkenhead* on her final voyage. Of the 634 aboard, most were soldiers, but there were a number of officers' families as well. The ship made good time to Simon's Town, close to Cape Town, where she took on cavalry horses and fresh water. On February 25, she departed for Algoa Bay on a calm sea. In the wee hours of February 26, as the ship approached Danger Point, the leadman took a sounding of 12 fathoms. Suddenly, the *Birkenhead* rammed into an uncharted rock. The huge gash in the hull allowed water to rush in, and hundreds of soldiers drowned belowdecks, barely awake for their final moments. The rest rushed to the deck, where the officers and passengers assembled. The ship was sinking fast.

WOMEN AND CHILDREN FIRST

Discipline was the order of the hour, as Captain Salmond issued clear and firm commands. Lieutenant-Colonel Alexander Seton of the 73rd Regiment of Foot, whose men made up the bulk of the troops aboard, was the commanding military officer. The men fell into orderly ranks, as sailors attempted to lower the lifeboats. Of the eight boats, only three

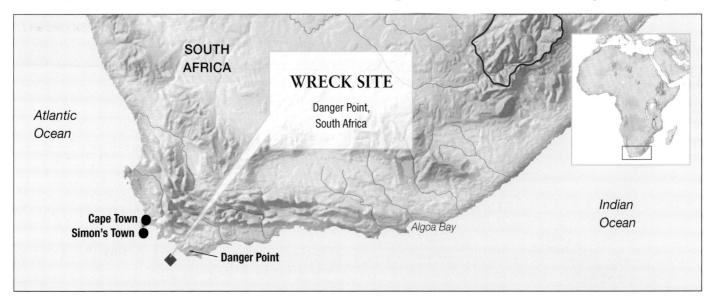

SOUTH AFRICA

WRECK SITE
Danger Point, South Africa

Atlantic Ocean

Cape Town ●
Simon's Town ●

◆ ── Danger Point

Algoa Bay

Indian Ocean

were seaworthy. Untried soldiers and decorated officers alike stood aside to allow all the women and children to board the lifeboats first.

When the boats were safely launched, Captain Salmond ordered all men who could swim to jump overboard and make for shore. Colonel Seton immediately overruled him, fearing that the men would overwhelm the lifeboats and imperil the women and children. So the men stood firm and silent, arrayed on deck as their ship broke apart and sank, 25 minutes after striking the rock. The horses, released from the hold, struggled to make shore, but many fell victim to the sharks that now swarmed to the scene.

The following morning, the British schooner *Lioness* reached the scene. After rescuing those on the lifeboats, she proceeded to the wreck of the *Birkenhead*, whose topmast just protruded above the water. About 40 men were rescued, while some 60 had made it to shore by clinging to floating wreckage and fighting off the rapacious sharks.

In all, only 193 survived the wreck of the *Birkenhead*. The memory of those who perished is burnished by their heroism, which saved every woman and child aboard the doomed ship.

▶ Erected in 1936, a plaque affixed to the Danger Point Lighthouse recalls the tragedy of the *Birkenhead*, honoring those men who bravely gave their lives so others could survive.

▲ A poignant illustration from 1887 depicts the despondency, altruism, and, ultimately, resolution, shown by the soldiers and sailors onboard the *Birkenhead*.

THE *BIRKENHEAD* DRILL

THE HEROISM OF THE MEN aboard the *Birkenhead* was immortalized by Rudyard Kipling in his poem, "Soldier an' Sailor Too," with the lines: "But stand an' be still to the Birken'ead drill/is a damn tough bullet to chew." The protocol of allowing women and children to disembark first is still recognized today. Many feel the "Birkenhead Drill" exemplifies the British world view, placing high values on stoicism, calm under fire, and death before dishonor.

RMS *Titanic*
PRIDE GOES BEFORE A FALL

▲ An artist's rendition of the RMS *Titanic* plowing into a deadly iceberg. It took 2 hours and 40 minutes for the last part of the ship to vanish into the sea after she struck the iceberg.

Any loss of life at sea is a tragedy for those involved. In general, the greater the loss, the greater the tragedy. But one shipwreck, though its casualty count is lower than some, towers above all others. The 1912 wreck of the RMS *Titanic* has all the hallmarks of tragedy in its original sense. In classical Greek drama, a tragedy depicts a noble who falls from a great height, done in by his hubris, or pride. The storied *Titanic*, the largest vehicle at the time of her launch and deemed "practically unsinkable" by the Royal Navy, embodied both greatness and hubris. Her fall to ruin from these soaring heights may help explain the unique place the *Titanic* has held in the public imagination for a century.

The *Titanic*'s maiden voyage ranked among the most anticipated events of her day. Her passenger list included legions of the rich and famous. Less celebrated were the hundreds of third-class passengers, many poor emigrants headed optimistically for America. On April 10, 1912, the *Titanic* welcomed her first passengers and the bulk of her crew at Southampton, England. Additional passengers boarded at Cherbourg, France, and at Queenstown, Ireland. On April 11, 1912, she sailed for New York. Close to midnight on April 14, the *Titanic* struck an iceberg. She sank in the wee hours of April 15 into the icy waters off Newfoundland. The total death toll from the disaster was 1,517 people.

FLOTSAM & JETSAM

Was it a bad omen? On pushing off from the pier at Southampton, the *Titanic* came within feet of striking the SS *City of New York*, which was docked nearby. The *New York* had been cast off her moorings by *Titanic*'s powerful wake.

STYLE AND SAFETY
The *Titanic* was the gem of the White Star Line, built to outdo any other passenger liner of her class. Everything about her was superlative. She was the

largest, at 882.5 feet (269 m), and displaced some 52,000 tons (47,175 metric tons). Her 11 decks and 840 staterooms could house more than 3,500 passengers and crew. Three years in the building in Belfast, Northern Ireland, she cost £1.5 million, funded by American financier J. P. Morgan. Her fittings were the most luxurious available, with hand-carved woodwork and stained glass skylights. The *Titanic*'s onboard amenities included a swimming pool, a gymnasium, Turkish baths, and a squash court. Thoroughly modern for her time, the *Titanic* came equipped with powerful generators that supplied electricity for 10,000 lamps, 50 telephones, heaters in every cabin, and elevators between decks.

But the *Titanic* had more than luxury to boast about. Her safety statistics were on par with her opulence. Chief among these was her compartmentalized hull. Fifteen bulkheads separated 16 watertight compartments, which could be sealed off by watertight doors. If water breached one or more of the compartments, the flooding would then be localized. Engineers asserted that the *Titanic* could float with as many as four flooded compartments, giving life to the "unsinkable" moniker. This theory was never tested; the iceberg tore through and flooded five compartments at once.

THE FATEFUL NIGHT

April 14 was calm and clear. During the course of the day, radio operators received messages from several other ships, warning that there were icebergs ahead. Then, at around 10:00 PM, the SS *Californian* sent a more urgent message. Instead of slowing down, though, *Titanic* Captain Edward J. Smith inexplicably ordered "full steam ahead."

▲ An artist's rendition of the sinking of the *Titanic*. With so few lifeboats, nearly 70 percent of the people she carried onboard died when she went down.

The first to spot the fatal iceberg was lookout Frederick Fleet. At 11:40 PM, he sounded the ship's bell and telephoned to the bridge. Attempts to slow, stop, or turn her proved futile, and the *Titanic* sliced hard and irrevocably against the iceberg. The towering mountain of ice slashed the fore starboard side of the *Titanic*, buckling the steel plates of her hull.

The ship was taking on water fast in her bow, and the watertight compartments proved inadequate. The unsinkable *Titanic* began to sink. First-class passengers' cabins were closest to the lifeboat decks, so they assembled first. Some third-class passengers, berthed deep in the bowels of the

SPEED QUEEN?

DESPITE HER OTHER ATTRIBUTES, the *Titanic* was not the fastest ship afloat, nor was she designed to be. Her two steam-driven and one turbine propeller (with power totaling 46,000 horsepower) enabled a maximum cruising speed of 21 knots, a figure well under the 25 knots claimed by the *Mauritania*, holder of the Blue Riband for fastest Atlantic crossing. *Titanic*'s statelier pace puts to rest notions that she was trying to set a speed record. This theory has been advanced to help explain why she plowed at full speed through the deadly field of icebergs.

▲ Although lavishly fitted, the *Titanic*, as many other White Star ocean liners, was designed to profit from the European poor flocking to America in the early twentieth century. Not all passengers enjoyed the ship's more opulent settings, and many of these would die in the bowels of the ship.

The *Titanic* Continued

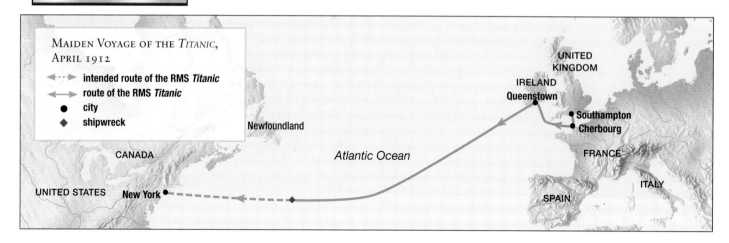

MAIDEN VOYAGE OF THE *TITANIC*, APRIL 1912

‹-‹-‹-› intended route of the RMS *Titanic*
‹—› route of the RMS *Titanic*
● city
◆ shipwreck

UNITED KINGDOM
IRELAND
Queenstown
Southampton
Cherbourg
Newfoundland
Atlantic Ocean
FRANCE
CANADA
ITALY
UNITED STATES   New York
SPAIN

boat, never even made it to the deck. The distance from the lifeboats may help explain the high proportion of first- and second-class passengers who were saved, though some have suspected that the steerage passengers were barred from the decks, or that the prosperous bribed their way to safety.

▲ A newsboy touts one of the biggest stories of the twentieth century.

▶ Upon hearing of the disaster, the passengers' and crew's families, friends, and even strangers mobbed the White Star Line offices in New York, desperate for news of the *Titanic*.

LIVES SAVED, LIVES CLAIMED

There were 2,228 passengers and crew aboard the *Titanic* on her maiden voyage, but the 20 lifeboats could hold only half this number. Surprisingly, this was in excess of the shipping regulations of the day—a statistic that bolstered the *Titanic*'s touted safety features. Nevertheless, the fact was glaring and immediate: there was not enough space aboard lifeboats for all to be saved.

First Officer William Murdoch gave the order from the lifeboat deck: women and children were to evacuate first. Husbands and fathers bade tearful farewells to their families, as the lifeboats were lowered at an average of 60 percent capacity. One officer fired shots to warn men away from storming the lifeboats. Some 74 percent of the women on board survived and 52 percent of the children, but only 20 percent of the men made it away alive. Many men feared being branded a coward were they to board the lifeboats. Such misgivings didn't plague J. Bruce Ismay, the White Star Line's president, who survived the wreck and was widely vilified for it. Captain Smith went down with his ship.

THE UNTHINKABLE SINKABLE SHIP

By 2:05 AM, the *Titanic*'s bow was completely submerged. The stern lifted frightfully high above the water, and one of the four funnels collapsed, killing many in the water. The ship broke in two, and the bow sank immediately. The stern section floated for a few moments, then plunged into the sea.

THE *TITANIC* ORPHANS

KNOWN AS THE *TITANIC* ORPHANS because they were the only children rescued without a parent or guardian, Michel and Edmond Navratil had been traveling with their father, Michel. Michel Sr. managed to place his sons on the last lifeboat to leave the sinking ship. But their troubles were not over. Michel Sr. had separated from their mother in France and registered the family under assumed names, which made it difficult for authorities to identify the French-speaking toddlers. Weeks afterward, their mother recognized newspaper photos of the boys, and she traveled to New York to be reunited with them. Michel, the elder, was the last male survivor of the *Titanic*. He died in 2001.

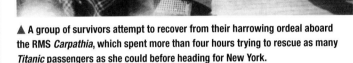

▲ A group of survivors attempt to recover from their harrowing ordeal aboard the RMS *Carpathia*, which spent more than four hours trying to rescue as many *Titanic* passengers as she could before heading for New York.

▲ ▲ Michel and Edmond Navratil (at right holding a toy ship) pose for news photos.

The RMS *Carpathia,* answering distress signals and rockets from the *Titanic*, worked her way through the dangerous ice fields and arrived on the scene two hours later. Captain Arthur Henry Rostron immediately ordered his sailors to begin picking up passengers from lifeboats. No one else survived; all those floating in the frigid water quickly fell victim to hypothermia. The *Californian*, another ship in the area, was widely blamed for not answering *Titanic*'s call immediately. She arrived some hours later to relieve the *Carpathia*, which proceeded to New York with the far-too-few survivors.

REDISCOVERY

THE WRECK OF THE *TITANIC* lay where she had fallen until 1985, when a joint French-American expedition located her remains. Using manned submersibles and remote-operated photographic equipment, the wreck has now been explored and filmed. Many artifacts have been recovered, but the American and Canadian governments—and several outside organizations—dispute the ownership of the wreck's contents.

The rediscovery of the *Titanic* led to renewed interest in the so-called shipwreck of the century; the widely popular 1997 movie was only one of many books, plays, and films about the near-legendary tragedy of the *Titanic*.

▲ Eating utensils recovered from the ship

◄ A railing of the sunken *Titanic* rusts beneath the waves, at a depth of 2.5 miles (4 km).

WRECK DIVING

From the time of the first shipwrecks, the lure of sunken treasures and undersea exploration has exerted a powerful pull. Wreck-diving enthusiasts, or those who dive to explore shipwrecks, range from casual sport divers to dedicated professionals with elaborate gear at their disposal. The advances in diving equipment in the last half century have opened the underwater landscape to numerous discoveries of lost ships.

The earliest known diving equipment was the diving bell—said to originate in Greece in the fourth century BCE—which allowed brief submersion in shallow waters. Later diving bells took various forms, mostly as enclosed chambers. By the early eighteenth century, wreck divers could stay underwater for as long as 30 minutes, certainly long enough to bring up a small bounty of treasure.

DIVING SUITS

Until the development of diving equipment, though, we could only dream of descending to the ocean floor. The enclosed diving suits introduced in the early nineteenth century made this possible. The downside was that the diver had to wear very heavy equipment, including a metal helmet, and remain tethered to a hose that delivered pumped-in air.

SCUBA AND SUBMERSIBLES

The twentieth century brought the freedom of diving with scuba equipment, initially dubbed "Aqua-Lung" by its inventor, Jacques Cousteau. Scuba, an acronym for "self-contained underwater breathing apparatus," was unveiled in 1943. It made possible deeper and longer dives—as deep as 430 feet (131 m). In 1964, scientists launched

▲ The wreck of the *Dunraven*, a British steam and sail ship that sank in 1876 in the Red Sea carrying spices, cotton, and timber from India. After hitting a reef, she sank in 100 feet (30 m) of water. She lay undisturbed for a century before a team of archaeologists found her and stripped her of her contents. She now makes a home for marine life such as corals, nudibranchs, and the very rare ghost pipe fish.

◄ A surface-supplied diving helmet, used when air is delivered from the surface. This technique is still preferred over scuba diving in certain situations—for example, when the water is polluted or possibly toxic.

▲ Although this submersible has many uses for marine scientists and oceanographers, *Alvin* may be most famous for her role in exploring the wreckage of the RMS *Titanic* in 1986. Launched from a support ship, she carried Dr. Robert Ballard and two companions to the wreckage of the sunken liner.

SEARCHING THE SEA

BEFORE DIVERS CAN INVESTIGATE A WRECK, they first have to find it. Locating wrecks involves still more technology, primarily sonar equipment and magnetometers. Sonar, or sound navigation ranging, can map a region of the undersea landscape using sound waves. Magnetometers locate metal objects, such as the metal hull of a boat, or cannons, fittings, and metal artifacts on an older wooden ship. The wreck of the *Titanic*, at 12,460 feet (3,965 m), was discovered in 1985 by a joint French-American crew. The expedition used advanced sonar equipment and an unmanned submersible equipped with video cameras, which relayed the findings back to the jubilant crew on its research boats.

the first submersible—a small submarine used for undersea archaeology. Today, wreck divers use all this equipment and more to locate wrecks and recover their treasure. Depending on the jurisdiction, strict laws usually govern the ownership of a sunken ship's treasure; some allocate a generous portion to the discoverer, some allocate none at all. Still, the thrill of wreck diving is lure enough for many.

◄ A scuba tank and breathing apparatus give a diver the most freedom and flexibility.

▲ A magnetometer searches for a lost Civil War–era vessel. Too late to effect a rescue, NOAA and the Office of Naval Research (ONR) hope to recover some history.

RMS *Empress of Ireland*

COLLISION IN THE FOG

The *Empress of Ireland* boarded 1,475 passengers and crew in Quebec City the afternoon of May 28, 1914. She was bound for Liverpool under the command of Captain Henry George Kendall, newly appointed to the post. The *Empress* stopped to take on mail before she prepared to head for the open water of the Atlantic. In the deepening fog, just after 2:00 AM on the 29th, Kendall sighted the Norwegian coal ship *Storstad* and prepared to pass port to port. Both ships entered the dense fog bank and slowed considerably to pass each other.

Later accounts would differ as to why, but instead of proceeding in a straight line, the *Storstad* took a sharp turn to starboard and rammed the *Empress of Ireland* amidships, between her two smokestacks. The collier then backed off, leaving a 14-by-25-foot (4.3 x 7.6 m) hole in the *Empress*. Within minutes, the *Empress of Ireland* had rolled over onto her side. The ship hung suspended in the still water for just 10 minutes, enough time for scores of passengers to escape

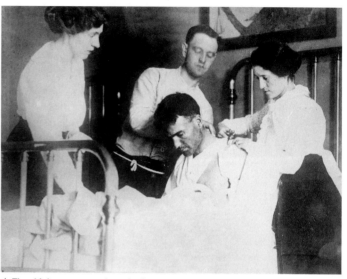

▲ The ship's surgeon and a pair of nurses work to save one of the victims of the *Empress of Ireland* tragedy. Only 42 of the ship's 279 female passengers lived.

through portholes or clamber along the vertical decks to relative safety. Finally her stern rose, and the *Empress of Ireland* slipped into the inky depths of the St. Lawrence River, taking 1,012 victims with her.

TRAGEDY STRIKES

Launched in January 1906, the *Empress of Ireland* was built as a steam liner in full turn-of-the-century style. Her 570-foot (174 m) length accommodated 780 first- and second-class passengers and an additional 750 in third class. The *Empress* made the

◀ Most ocean liners of the day featured a bow that slanted backward, as this photo of *Empress of Ireland* shows. This design feature resulted in damage below the *Empress of Ireland*'s waterline, dooming the ship and many of her passengers. Her fate quickly inspired a design shift to a forward-slanting bow.

run from Liverpool to Quebec City and back regularly and quickly, earning her Royal Mail Steamer title by carrying mail between England and the colonies.

When the Norwegian collier struck the *Empress of Ireland* square amidships, the *Storstad*'s bow, reinforced for Nordic ice, cut through the liner's skin like a can opener. As water poured in through the gaping hole, the ship rolled, exposing her starboard portholes to the river. Though regulations required all portholes to be sealed, they were nearly all wide open in an effort to ventilate the stuffy cabins below. Many victims drowned nearly instantly as water flooded their cabins. The increasingly severe list allowed the launch of only four lifeboats. Captain Kendall had been thrown from the bridge when the ship rolled, but he was rescued by one of his lifeboats and immediately began organizing rescue efforts, pulling victims from the water and shuttling them to shore.

The eventual victim count was 1,012, making the disaster the worst in Canada's history. The cause of the collision remained in dispute, with boards of inquiry in Canada and Norway each finding in favor of their respective countrymen.

FELINE INTUITION?

FOR TWO YEARS PRIOR TO HER SINKING, the *Empress of Ireland* had hosted a ship's mouser, a stout ginger tabby by the name of Emmy. A loyal crew member, she never missed a trip. Until, that is, that fateful day, when Emmy simply would not stay onboard. Repeated attempts to corral her failed, and the *Empress* sailed cat-free. It is said that Emmy watched the *Empress of Ireland* steam off on her fateful final journey from atop the building that would later house the bodies of many of the disaster's victims.

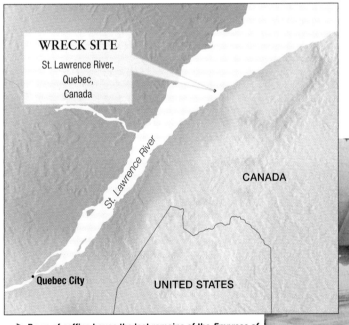

WRECK SITE
St. Lawrence River,
Quebec,
Canada

St. Lawrence River

CANADA

Quebec City

UNITED STATES

▶ Rows of coffins house the last remains of the *Empress of Ireland* victims at Rimouski, Canada, where she had last paused to load mail. Among the passengers was a large group from the Salvation Army, including members of the Canadian Salvation Army Band who were headed to London for a conference. All of them died. The death toll was also dismally high for children: only 4 of the 138 children onboard survived.

SS *Mont-Blanc* | A DISASTER FOR THE AGES

▲ The explosion, felt as far away as 186 miles (300 km), caused some soldiers to compare the immediate area to war-torn Flanders.

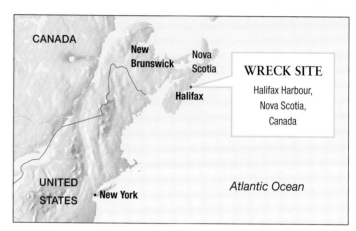

CANADA

New Brunswick

Nova Scotia

Halifax

UNITED STATES • New York

WRECK SITE

Halifax Harbour, Nova Scotia, Canada

Atlantic Ocean

The French tramp steamer *Mont-Blanc* loaded up her cargo in New York harbor in December 1917. Her load of high explosives was destined for the war in Europe. The manifest of TNT, picric acid (wet and dry), gun cotton, and benzol reads like a recipe for a bomb. German U-boats heavily patrolled the North Atlantic during World War I, making it dangerous territory for any ship—much less one loaded to the gills with explosives. Thus the SS *Mont-Blanc* headed north to Halifax, Nova Scotia, to join up with a convoy for the perilous journey across the Atlantic.

The antisubmarine nets had already been closed for the night when the *Mont-Blanc* arrived in Halifax, so the ship had to lay to for the night. The next morning, the *Mont-Blanc* steamed into the harbor, joining the flotilla of boats organizing for departure in convoys. Inside the harbor, the Belgian relief ship *Imo* had also been delayed by the submarine nets. The crew of the *Imo* was anxious to head out of the harbor as soon as the nets were lowered. The *Mont-Blanc* was the second of four ships heading up into the harbor. In her haste to depart, the *Imo* passed the *Stella Maris* on the wrong side. When the *Imo* came around into the path of the *Mont-Blanc*, the two ships began a series of frantic whistle blasts, attempting to avoid a collision. As the ships drew near, they each executed evasive actions: the *Mont-Blanc* turned hard to port, while the *Imo* reversed her engines hard astern. The last-minute attempts to avoid collision proved futile, and the two ships collided. Within 10 minutes the *Mont-Blanc* was afire, and 15 minutes after that, she exploded in a 3-kiloton (2,700 metric tons) blast that was the largest human-made explosion until the atomic bomb.

THE HALIFAX EXPLOSION

Incredibly, the crew of the *Mont-Blanc* abandoned ship when the fire broke out. All but one escaped with their lives. Other ships in the harbor and people in the surrounding towns would not be so lucky. As the fire on the *Mont-Blanc* worsened, she drifted onto a pier, which also then caught fire. Firefighters, sailors, and passersby crowded around Halifax Harbour to watch the exciting event, with no notion of the surprise that lay in store. Hundreds of spectators and rescuers were killed instantly when the fire reached the high explosives, setting them off in one gigantic cataclysm. In all, more than 2,000 people are thought to have perished, and thousands more were injured.

The blast set off a shock wave that collapsed walls, crushed buildings, and sent a roiling cloud of smoke and debris 20,000 feet (6,000 m) in the air. A gun barrel from the *Mont-Blanc* came to rest 3 miles (5 km) from the harbor, and the ship's anchor came down 2.5 miles (4 km) away. Then came the shrapnel, molten metal that rained down on the harbor, maiming, killing, and starting fires. Finally, a tsunami, a gigantic wave triggered by the massive displacement of water, rolled over the town, destroying structures, and drowning even more victims than were killed by the blast. The final indignity came in the form of a blizzard, which hit several hours after the explosion and caused additional death and misery to the anguished citizens of Halifax.

▲ Overlooking a wasteland of devastation, the *Imo* can just be seen across the harbor through the smoke from the explosion of the *Mont-Blanc*. The blast razed one ship and completely destroyed a pier.

◄ Some Halifax buildings, such as St. Joseph's Convent, took damage too heavy to repair. It took years before all buildings were restored or replaced.

▼ Antisubmarine nets stretch across a harbor in Halifax, Nova Scotia.

FLOTSAM & JETSAM

Antisubmarine nets stretched the width of Halifax Harbour during World War I. The chain-link net prevented both subs and torpedoes from entering the harbor.

The *Andrea Doria* | LAST OF THE GREAT LUXURY LINERS

The mid-twentieth century marked the end of the transatlantic luxury liner. Air travel became more affordable and widely accessible and reduced a five-days' journey to five hours. But the era of luxury liners went out with a bang. In the postwar era, many shipping companies produced jewels of the sea, notably the Italian Line with its sleek sister ships of the 1950s, the *Cristoforo Colombo* and the *Andrea Doria*. Both ships were named for famous citizens of Genoa, the latter a sixteenth-century naval hero.

The *Andrea Doria* was the Italian Line's flagship, fashioned as a seagoing work of art that showcased the height of Italian design and craftsmanship. She accommodated three classes of passengers, supplying each class with its own outdoor swimming pool. Her fittings were lavish and modern; all cabins, even those in tourist-class, were air-conditioned. At 700 feet (213 m) long, and with a speed of 23 knots, the

Andrea Doria was elegant and fast. Her one center funnel, painted with the Italian Line's signature red, white, and green colors, gave her a streamlined look.

On her 1956 final journey across the Atlantic, veteran seaman Captain Piero Calamai commanded the *Andrea Doria*. She departed Genoa for New York on July 17, 1956, and made good time across the pond. Approaching Nantucket Island, the *Andrea Doria* ran into heavy fog. The night of July 25, 1956, she collided with the Swedish-American liner *Stockholm*. Though most of her passengers were saved, the spectacular *Andrea Doria* was lost to the sea. For many, her passing marked the end of an era.

RADAR AND FOG

Just a few hours before it struck the *Andrea Doria* broadside, the Swedish-American liner MS *Stockholm* had departed New York, en route to Sweden. The ship, built for northern seas, had a bow reinforced for ice. The *Stockholm*'s captain, Harry Nordenson, retired for the night, leaving the bridge under the control of third mate Johann-Ernst Carstens, with an injunction to summon him immediately if the ship should encounter fog. The shipping lanes along the East Coast of the United States were notoriously crowded, and the area off the coast of Nantucket, Massachusetts, is notoriously foggy.

The bridge of the *Andrea Doria*, meanwhile, was under command of her master. Captain Piero Calamai was aiming for an on-time arrival in New York, and when he entered the fog zone, he reduced his speed only slightly, from 23 to just under 22 knots—still a rapid clip. At 10:40 PM, the radar screen showed a boat approaching some 17 miles (27 km) off. Calculating quickly, Calamai predicted the ships would pass about a mile (1.6 km) apart, with the

▲ The crowded shipping lanes were both bane and balm for the *Doria*, because of the availability of ships in the area that could rush to the stricken vessel's rescue.

▲ A disabled fishing ship hitches a ride from a Coast Guard ship through the Nantucket fog. Even with improved technology, the region remains hazardous.

DANGEROUS WATERS

NANTUCKET IS NICKNAMED the "Faraway Isle" for its location far out into the waters of the Atlantic. The shoals to the east and south of the island are notorious danger spots and have been the site of numerous shipwrecks over the centuries. In 1976, just 20 years after the sinking of the *Andrea Doria,* the oil tanker *Argo Merchant* ran aground on Fishing Rip Shoal. Though no lives were lost, the tanker spilled some 7.6 million gallons (28.7 million liters) of crude oil, creating an ecological disaster.

In an effort to prevent shipwrecks, in 1854 Nantucketers established a lightship station on the shoals. Since that time, a lightship has patrolled the dangerous waters, giving both light and foghorn signals to passing ships. One notable lightship, *LV 117,* was herself done in by the fog. In 1934, the RMS *Olympic,* sister ship to the *Titanic,* rammed the *LV 117.* Eleven people died in the collision.

Stockholm to starboard. Nevertheless, he guided the *Andrea Doria* slightly farther to port, to increase the margin of safety. Calamai also activated the watertight bulkheads in the hull, which closed off the 11 separate compartments.

With less than a mile visibility, the two ships were relying entirely on radar to plot their relative positions. As the ships came within sight of each other, it suddenly became clear that they were on a collision course—and only a mile (1.6 km) apart. The *Stockholm* veered about 20 degrees to starboard, while the *Andrea Doria* made a turn to port, exposing her starboard side to the oncoming ship. Historians surmise that the *Doria* was hoping to clear the Swedish liner; with several minutes' more time, this strategy would have worked. But it was not to be: at 11:10 PM, the *Stockholm* plowed into the starboard side of Italian liner, killing 46 of her passengers. Five crew members of the *Stockholm* died in the collision. Her bow was badly smashed, but she stayed afloat.

▶ The great luxury liner's namesake, Genoese admiral Andrea Doria (1466–1560), pictured here as the ancient sea-god Neptune

The *Andrea Doria* CONTINUED

▲ The damaged bow on the luxury liner *Stockholm* after its collision with the *Andrea Doria*

DISTRESS AND RESCUE

Captain Calamai sent an SOS call, while his ship reeled from the damage. The huge V-shaped gash in her starboard side allowed water to gush into the empty fuel tanks, causing her to list precariously. Water rushed over the bulkheads, flooding the other compartments. Within 20 minutes, the captain made the decision to abandon ship.

Unlike the *Titanic*, the *Andrea Doria* had more than enough lifeboats for her passengers. The increasing list, though, rendered the lifeboats on the port side inaccessible. Fortunately, help soon met the *Andrea Doria*'s distress call. The elegant French liner *Île de France* sped to the scene. Her captain, Baron Raoul de Beaudéan, was to become the hero of the hour. Steaming up to the sinking *Andrea Doria*, the French ship turned on every light aboard, to produce a sudden, gleaming presence in the midnight blackness. The *Île de France* picked up 753 passengers and crew from the *Andrea Doria*,

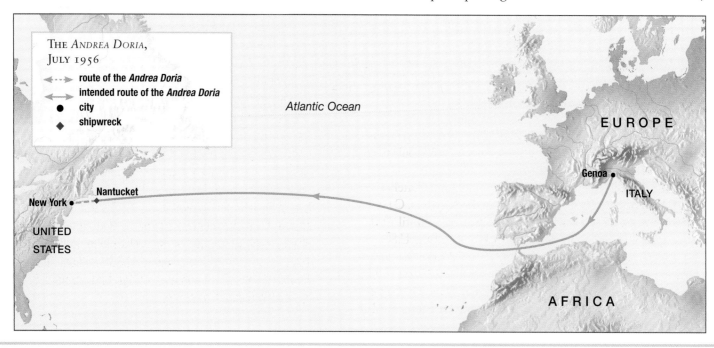

THE *ANDREA DORIA*,
JULY 1956

  route of the *Andrea Doria*
  intended route of the *Andrea Doria*
● city
◆ shipwreck

Atlantic Ocean

EUROPE

Genoa ●
ITALY

New York ● ● Nantucket

UNITED
STATES

AFRICA

▲ The *Andrea Doria* begins to list just moments before sinking

WHO WAS TO BLAME?

AN OFFICIAL INQUEST into the collision between the *Stockholm* and the *Andrea Doria* began on September 19, 1956. The *Andrea Doria*'s captain, Piero Calamai, was charged with several infractions, notably his continued speed through a hazardous fog, and his failure to observe the protocol of heavy shipping lanes by turning to port instead of starboard. Calamai had also neglected to refill his empty fuel tanks with seawater, as was proscribed for adequate ballast.

On the part of the Swedish liner, Captain Harry Nordenson of the *Stockholm* had left the bridge under dangerous conditions. In addition, the *Stockholm* was traveling some 20 miles (32 km) north of her standard shipping lane. In the end, the two shipping lines agreed to a 50-50 portion of blame, each line responsible for its own damages. The heavier burden fell on the Italian Line; it had lost the jewel of its fleet, valued at $30 million. The *Stockholm* was repaired and refitted and continued to sail for decades to come.

while the *Stockholm* rescued 542. Smaller boats nearby joined the rescue flotilla; in all, the rescuers saved 1,660 souls from the sinking *Andrea Doria*.

Both the *Stockholm* and the *Île de France* immediately returned to New York to deliver injured passengers. Captain Calamai and his officers did not leave their ship until 9:00 AM the following morning, when they boarded the U.S. Coast Guard ship *Hornbeam*. They watched from the deck of the *Hornbeam* as the *Andrea Doria* sank in 225 feet (69 m) of water, 45 miles (72 km) off the coast of Nantucket. The Atlantic Ocean claimed first her bow, then her stern, until at 10:09 AM she could be seen no more.

MV *Doña Paz*

COLLISION WITH AN INFERNO

▲ A photo claimed to show the MV *Doña Paz* while she was named the MV *Don Sulpicio*

Fire at sea has been a sailor's worst nightmare for centuries. And that nightmare has not abated with the passing of wooden vessels; modern steel ships can succumb to flames as well. When the heavily overloaded ferryboat *Doña Paz* was struck by the oil tanker *Vector* in 1987 in the Philippines, *Vector*'s cargo of various petroleum products burst into flames that engulfed both vessels. The sea itself appeared to catch fire, and victims were forced to choose between the flames and the burning, shark-infested waters of the Tablas Strait. Within four hours both vessels had sunk, leaving survivors floating among the dead and burned corpses, waiting for aid that would be many hours in coming.

Doña Paz was a 305-foot (93 m) ferryboat built in 1963 in Japan. Her original passenger capacity was just over 600 people. When she shifted to the Philippines, officials raised her capacity to more than twice that, 1,424—with no significant alterations or refitting. Official reports generated after the accident put the number of dead at 1,749, but anecdotal reports place the number of passengers actually on board closer to 4,000. No matter the exact numbers, the sinking of the *Doña Paz* was one of the worst maritime disasters in history.

THE OCEAN AFLAME

The MV *Doña Paz* steamed south from Japan and began carrying goods and people on the Philippines circuit in 1975, while still—at only 13 years old—a fairly new ship. Overloaded though she was, all seemed calm and well in hand on the bridge of the *Doña Paz* as she plied the waters off Dumali Point the night of December 20, 1987. Events were so routine that the captain retired to his cabin to watch a movie, and the two first mates left the bridge for drinks and cards, leaving only an inexperienced seaman on watch at the helm. For her part, the *Vector* was operating without a lookout, license, or qualified officer.

Around 10:30 that night, for reasons still unknown, the *Vector* slammed into the *Doña Paz*, in the open ocean, with clear conditions and choppy but moderate seas. Neither ship had altered course or given warning blasts of whistle or bell. The first sign of trouble most passengers and crew on either ship noticed was the terrifying explosion of grinding metal. The impact ignited a conflagration of 8,800 barrels of oil and gasoline, which quickly spread through both ships and spilled onto the sea itself. Though they sent distress calls, neither ship launched lifeboats, and only 24 people survived. The rest perished, killed by neglect and inattention as surely as by flame and water.

WRECK SITE

Tablas Strait,
The Philippines

▲ Oil fires are deadly even on land. On water, they are devastating. Because oil floats, the sea has no chance to extinguish the flames. Here, an oil well fire in 1991; note the enormous size of the explosion.

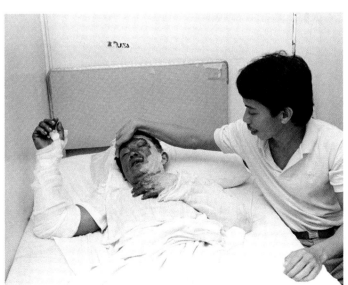

▲ A severely burned survivor, with a relative, heals in a Manila hospital.

ALL SQUEEZE ABOARD

IT IS A COMMON PRACTICE for crews of ferries in developing nations to board many more passengers than have tickets. Those crew members who don't believe in granting free passage to the poor may often be persuaded to allow passengers on board for a small consideration, usually much less than the cost of the entire fare. Aside from the obvious safety hazards, an additional downside to this practice is that when disasters occur, families of unticketed victims often have difficulty proving eligibility for benefits. In the case of the *Doña Paz*, the Philippine Supreme Court eventually ruled that even victims not on the ship's manifest were entitled to indemnity and remuneration.

4 · PIRACY, MUTINY, AND SKULLDUGGERY

▲ *An English Ship in Action with Barbary Pirates* by Willem van der Velde the Younger, c.1680

The *Batavia* STARVATION, TREACHERY, AND MURDER

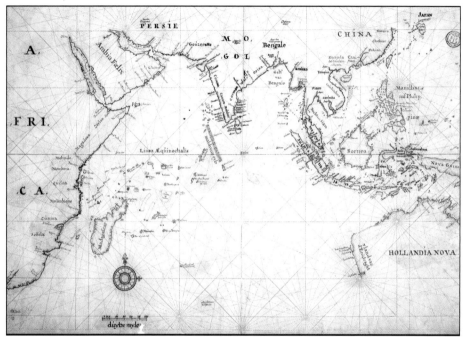

▲ A Dutch East India Company map of its trading area in 1665, including the whole of the Indian Ocean

of the ordeal for her passengers and crew: mutiny, murder, and mayhem were soon to follow.

RUN AGROUND

When the *Batavia* struck Morning Reef on June 4, 1629, she sank slowly enough that all but 40 passengers and crew were able to make their way ashore in the surviving longboat and yawl. The *Batavia*'s commander, François Pelsaert; her captain, Adrian Jacobsz; and a score of other passengers and crew set off in the yawl. The rest of the refugees remained behind, under the command of Junior Merchant Jeronimus Cornelisz.

Pelsaert and Jacobsz sailed the open boat for 32 days across the open ocean to the city of Batavia (present-day Jakarta, Indonesia). Upon their arrival, the governor immediately provided a ship, and Pelsaert and Jacobsz set sail back to their stranded cohort. Unfavorable winds slowed their return journey, and 90 days after they had left, they returned to a scene of utter horror.

Early in the seventeenth century, the Dutch East India Company (in Dutch, the *Vereenigde Oost-Indische Compagnie*, or *VOC*) commissioned the *Batavia*. A merchant ship meant for trade, the *Batavia* nonetheless carried 24 cannons. Trading in the seventeenth century meant sailing literally halfway around the world into uncharted territories. In many foreign lands, traders met with hostile natives and often had to fend off pirates and competitors from other companies and nations.

On October 29, 1628, the *Batavia* set off from the port of Texel, in the Netherlands, for her maiden voyage. She never returned. In June 1629, she foundered on a reef in the Houtman Abrolhos islands off the west coast of Australia. Her sinking, however, was only the beginning

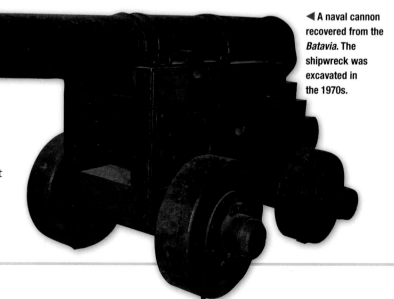

◀ A naval cannon recovered from the *Batavia*. The shipwreck was excavated in the 1970s.

MUTINY MOST FOUL

Left in command, Jeronimus Cornelisz showed his true colors. He immediately impounded all weapons and food. Next, he marooned a number of the passengers and remaining crewmen on adjacent West Wallaby Island, instructing them to search for water. Returning to his own isle of tyranny, Cornelisz gathered a small mutinous band and initiated a wild killing spree. The tyrants murdered women, children, the infirm, and the elderly—all in the name of conserving resources. They kept some women alive, but not for honorable reasons.

Meanwhile, the sailors and passengers left to die on West Wallaby unexpectedly found food and water supplies. They sent their prearranged smoke signals to alert Cornelisz of their success. After Cornelisz's dispatch failed to return any prisoners, the tyrant shipped to Wallaby Island himself, along with five men. The stranded crewmen overpowered Cornelisz, killed his companions, and took the tyrant prisoner.

At this juncture, Pelsaert dramatically arrived back on the scene. Hearing the charges of murder and mayhem from the survivors, he immediately placed the mutineers under arrest. After quick trials, Cornelisz and several of his conspirators were executed. The rest were taken back to the city of Batavia for trial and, for most, execution. Pelsaert himself was found to have acted negligently. The crown seized his assets, and he died shortly thereafter. Of the 341 souls originally aboard the *Batavia*, only 68 survived her maiden voyage.

FLOTSAM & JETSAM

Even before the *Batavia* sank, Cornelisz had conspired to mutiny and seize the ship's vast stores of gold and silver. He intended to kill most aboard and dedicate the *Batavia* to a career of piracy.

▲ Both sides of a Dutch East India Company coin, minted in 1735, with the company's VOC logo

◄ A replica of the *Batavia*. Had the ship survived, she would have carried one of her company's most valuable products: spices.

The *Henrietta Marie*
A SLAVE SHIP DISAPPEARS

Few things present as awful an image as a slave ship. Such vessels carried men, women, and children who had been kidnapped, thrown into the hold of a ship, and shackled hand and foot with unforgiving manacles. Worse yet was the arrival in a strange land, in which their captors paraded the enslaved, still shackled and naked, into the town square of a strange city. There these men, women, and children were sold into short and brutal lives of unceasing toil.

In September 1700, before the *Henrietta Marie* began her last voyage, she likely filled her holds with human cargo at the notorious Gorée Island, a slave transfer station off the coast of present-day Dakar, Senegal. Her holds could carry 300 sorry souls, but more than 20 percent of that number would perish on the Atlantic crossing. As the ship approached its destination of Port Royal, Jamaica, the slavers allowed their captives on deck for the first time since leaving Africa. The slavers prepared the captives for market, giving them increased rations, baths, haircuts, and other care; healthy-looking slaves fetched a higher price. After disembarking his "freight," Captain Thomas Chamberlain filled the now-empty holds of the *Henrietta Marie* with sugar, cotton, wood, and indigo dye, and departed for England on May 18, 1701. A month later, negotiating the treacherous Florida Straits, the *Henrietta Marie* sank off the coast of Florida under unknown circumstances. No one survived to tell the tale of her disappearance.

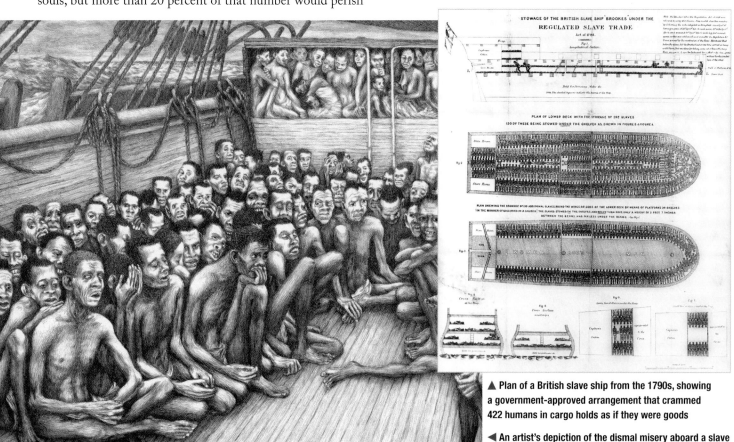

▲ Plan of a British slave ship from the 1790s, showing a government-approved arrangement that crammed 422 humans in cargo holds as if they were goods

◄ An artist's depiction of the dismal misery aboard a slave ship, including women and children stuffed onto shelves

BURIED SECRETS UNCOVERED

The *Henrietta Marie* would have been one of the numerous slave ships lost to history if treasure hunters hadn't discovered her nestled in the protective caress of the sandy bottom of the Florida Strait. In 1972, famed treasure hunter Mel Fisher and his company discovered the wreck near New Ground Reef, 34 miles (55 km) off Key West, Florida, as they searched for the sunken Spanish galleon *Nuestra Señora de Atocha* (see pages 16–17). They at first discounted their find as "the English wreck" when it became clear that there was no cache of Spanish gold hidden beneath the sands. Treasures of another sort languished in a warehouse for 10 years until divers and scholars of African American history focused their attentions on the artifacts, which included shackles salvaged from the mysterious ship. The shackles pointed the way, and then diver/archaeologist David Moore salvaged a bell. Its inscription confirmed the ship's name and the date: THE *HENRIETTA MARIE*, 1699. With the name and the date it was now possible to research the ship's past.

The oldest slave ship ever found in U.S. waters opened a window into a dark period in American history. By correlating historical records with the huge trove of artifacts found on the seafloor, historians gained new insight into the brutal human trade. The treasure hunters who initially discovered the ship's remains have donated them to a not-for-profit marine historical society, which organizes tours and displays the objects. Historians and the general public alike can study these artifacts, which help tell a vast and vitally important story.

▶ **Shackles used for restraining slaves**

WRECK SITE

Gulf of Mexico

FLORIDA

Key West

Atlantic Ocean

WRECK SITE

New Ground Reef, Florida Straits, Florida Keys

CUBA

Caribbean Sea

LINKS TO HISTORY

IN 1972, MOE MOLINAR, an African American treasure hunter working with Mel Fisher's company, rode his salvage vessel, the *Virgalona*, through a squall while anchored over a Spanish treasure galleon. Molinar figured that he had time for one more dive that stormy afternoon on the Florida Strait. Just as he had nearly depleted his oxygen supply, his hands stopped dead at an iron bar buried in the soft sand. Attached to the iron bar were shackles, something not typical on Spanish treasure galleons. Recognizing what he held, he returned to the ocean floor. By sunset, he had pulled from the wreck dozens of rusted shackles of all sizes: from large, bulky ones to fit a man's wrists down to tiny ones made to restrain a child. Although Molinar was well aware of how the shackles had once been used, they still went to a Key West warehouse. It would be 10 long years before historians realized the importance of Molinar's find.

The *Whydah* — FROM SLAVE GALLEY TO PIRATE SHIP

▲ Pirates navigate their boat (any small vessel with under three masts) toward an unfortunate ship, ready to board her and take whatever plunder they find.

The *Whydah* led a short, fast life of infamy. Her first incarnation was as a British slave ship. Launched in 1715, the three-masted galley acted in the gruesome and profitable trade in human cargo, sailing on the triangular course between Europe, Africa, and the Caribbean. In 1717, during her second voyage, the notorious pirate Samuel "Black Sam" Bellamy captured the *Whydah.*

At 100 feet (31 m), the *Whydah* was fast—she could reach 13 knots—and she was heavily armed with 18 cannons. The trade routes between Europe, Africa, and the Caribbean were dangerous, patrolled by pirates intent on seizing the costly cargo these ships carried.

From Europe to Africa, the *Whydah* carried goods like cloth and arms; from Africa to the Caribbean, on what was known as the "Middle Passage," she carried humans—enslaved Africans destined for the plantations of the Americas. On the *Whydah*'s return trip from the Caribbean to Europe, she carried the spoils of this brutal trade: gold, silver, sugar, spices, and medicinal products. These proved a tempting target for the pirate Black Sam Bellamy.

BLACK SAM BELLAMY

Samuel Bellamy was an English merchant seaman when he fell in love with a young Massachusetts woman named Maria Hallet. Hoping to bolster his fortunes and win Maria's hand, Bellamy started a new career as a treasure hunter, searching for profitable shipwrecks. He and his friend Palgrave Williams soon traveled south to Florida to cash in on the bounty of the wrecked 1715 treasure fleet. In the Caribbean, Bellamy fell in with English pirate Benjamin Hornigold, who trained him in the ways of the outlaw.

By 1717, Bellamy was known as the "Robin Hood of the Seas." He had captured some 50 boats and traveled in a small flotilla of two ships. In February of that year, he spied the *Whydah* in the Antilles and gave chase. Three days later, he won her from Captain Lawrence Prince, an experienced slave trader, after a perfunctory exchange of hostilities. Bellamy gave Prince his former ship, the *Sultana,* and the 330-ton (300 metric tons) *Whydah* became Black Sam's flagship.

But Black Sam captained her for only a few short months. Some historians believe that Bellamy was ready to cash out—to return to his ladylove a rich man, marry her, and settle down to raise a family. Whatever his intentions, Bellamy guided the *Whydah* north up the East Coast, and on April 26 ran into a fierce nor'easter off the coast of Wellfleet, Massachusetts. The *Whydah* ran aground, stern first, and then was tossed back into deep water, where she broke asunder. Only two men survived. Black Sam and the rest of his 180-man crew went down with the *Whydah*.

The *Whydah*'s survivors claimed that she was loaded with some four tons of treasure at the time of her sinking, from gold dust, jewels, and costly merchandise to the stock-in-trade of the pirate: Spanish pieces of eight. The wreck of the *Whydah*—and her bounty of treasure—lay underwater until 1984, when salvor Barry Clifford, using maps drawn up at the time of the shipwreck as his starting point, discovered them.

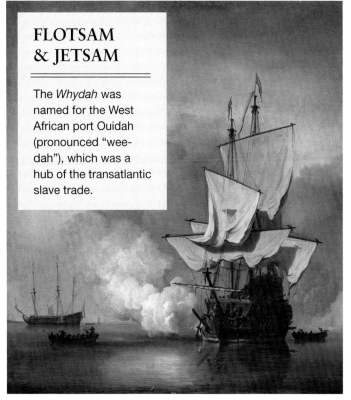

FLOTSAM & JETSAM

The *Whydah* was named for the West African port Ouidah (pronounced "wee-dah"), which was a hub of the transatlantic slave trade.

▲ The *Whydah*, like the ship pictured above, fired cannons broadside. Pirates such as Black Sam Bellamy chose their ships carefully. Ideally, a captured ship would increase the pirate's speed, firepower, or both.

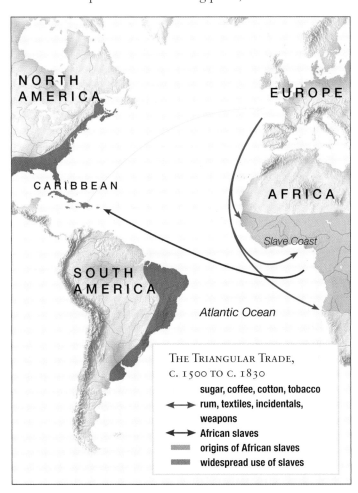

NORTH AMERICA

EUROPE

CARIBBEAN

AFRICA

Slave Coast

SOUTH AMERICA

Atlantic Ocean

THE TRIANGULAR TRADE, C. 1500 TO C. 1830

→ sugar, coffee, cotton, tobacco
← rum, textiles, incidentals, weapons
← African slaves
   origins of African slaves
   widespread use of slaves

LITTLE JOHN KING

AMONG BELLAMY'S CREW was a young boy named John King, who had joined the pirates willingly. Aged between 9 and 11, John is the youngest known pirate. His remains were positively identified after Barry Clifford discovered the *Whydah*. King's leg bone, still clad in a silk stocking, was near a small, buckled black shoe.

▶ The remains of the littlest pirate: a silk, stocking, a buckled shoe, and a fibula

The *Queen Anne's Revenge* | BLACKBEARD'S FLAGSHIP

FLOTSAM & JETSAM

Blackbeard struck terror into his victims by wearing lit cannon fuses in his hair as he stormed a ship.

▲ Mayhem aboard the *Adventure.* Blackbeard's last battle, fought against Lieutenant Robert Maynard of the Royal Navy, rid the world of the mighty pirate, but generated his enduring and apocryphal legacy: that an impressive cache of treasure lay somewhere well hidden, the location lost forever to a stroke of Maynard's sword.

Every pirate has his day. For Blackbeard (c. 1680–1718), one of the most notorious brigands of the Golden Age of Piracy, his ship had her day first. Her master followed a few months later. The *Queen Anne's Revenge,* as Blackbeard dubbed his flagship, was lost on the shoals off North Carolina's Beaufort Inlet, then known as Topsail Inlet, in 1718.

At the time of the shipwreck, Blackbeard controlled a combined crew of some 300 men, operating on at least four ships. Of these, the *Queen Anne's Revenge* was the apple of his

eye. Built in 1710, in England, and christened the *Concord,* the future pirate ship first served a stint in the grim transatlantic slave trade. One year after her launch, the French captured the *Concord,* modified her to hold even more cargo, renamed her *La Concorde,* and put her to work on the triangular trade route from Europe to Africa to the Caribbean. In 1717, *La Concorde* sailed on her third and final slave-trading voyage, when a flotilla of pirates, led by Blackbeard and Benjamin Hornigold, waylaid her in the Grenadines.

QUEEN ANNE'S PIRATES

The band of pirates—some 150-strong—easily overpowered *La Concorde*; the French ship gave up after two volleys from the pirates. Blackbeard, whose relation with the elder Hornigold was something between protégé and partner, assumed command of the 200-ton (180 metric tons) ship. Renaming her the *Queen Anne's Revenge*, he fitted her out as a 40-gun terror of the seas.

Blackbeard was born Edward Thatch, or Teach, probably in England. He turned to piracy after a stint as a privateer—essentially a state-sanctioned pirate—during the War of Spanish Succession (1701–14). Blackbeard quickly gained a reputation for ferocity and ruthlessness, though the rumors seem to outweigh documented bloodshed. A towering man, Blackbeard had the swagger, swords, and eponymous facial hair to back up the vilest rumors. With the aid of the *Queen Anne's Revenge*, Blackbeard took his brazenness a step further. Historians estimate that Blackbeard captured or pillaged up to 50 ships during his career.

In late May 1718, the *Queen Anne's Revenge* and three smaller ships sailed up to the harbor of Charleston, South Carolina. They stayed for a week, seizing ships, goods, and even hostages as they wished. The blockade continued until Blackbeard received a chest of medicine in exchange for a hostage. From Charleston, his flotilla then sailed north. Shortly thereafter, the *Queen Anne's Revenge* ran aground.

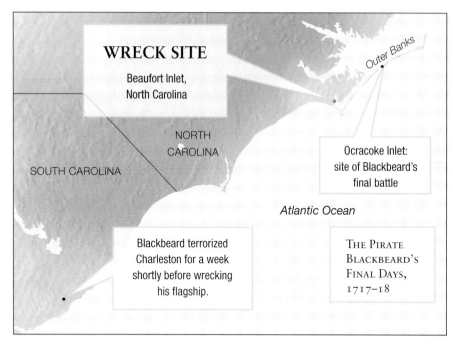

WRECK SITE
Beaufort Inlet,
North Carolina

Outer Banks

NORTH
CAROLINA

SOUTH CAROLINA

Ocracoke Inlet:
site of Blackbeard's
final battle

Atlantic Ocean

Blackbeard terrorized
Charleston for a week
shortly before wrecking
his flagship.

THE PIRATE
BLACKBEARD'S
FINAL DAYS,
1717–18

Some say Blackbeard wrecked his flagship deliberately to thin the ranks of his crew. Fewer men meant more loot for each.

Blackbeard escaped on the sloop *Adventure* but met his end on November 22, 1718. In Ocracoke Inlet on North Carolina's Outer Banks, Blackbeard engaged in battle with Lieutenant Robert Maynard of the Royal Navy, who had a commission to hunt down the brigand. In close, bloody combat, Maynard's sword lopped off Blackbeard's head, which he had displayed in victory, hanging from the naval ship's bowsprit.

REDISCOVERED

In 1996, Interstal, Inc., a private Florida company that researches and excavates shipwrecks, discovered the wreck of the *Queen Anne's Revenge* in the shallow Atlantic waters offshore from Fort Macon State Park, North Carolina. The excavation of the *Queen Anne's* wreck site is still ongoing. Recovered artifacts include firearms and ammunition, jewelry, gold, tableware, cuff links, and even leg irons used for discipline.

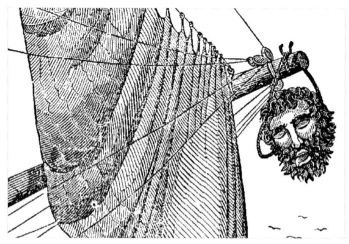

▲ The bowsprit, decorated here with Blackbeard's head, extends from the bow and is used to attach the forestay, which prevents the fore-mast from bending.

Pirates!

The popular image of a pirate as a swashbuckling, plundering outlaw loyal only to his Jolly Roger flag isn't entirely off the historical mark. But it refers to only one type of pirate—those who plied their trade during the so-called Golden Age of Piracy of the late seventeenth and early eighteenth centuries. Pirates operated all over the world long before this golden age, and they are still operating today. In fact, some experts fear that there has been an increase in piracy in the early years of the twenty-first century, as evidenced by the capture of the Saudi oil tanker *Sirius Star* by Somali pirates in 2008.

▲ A vessel captured by U.S. Navy ships for suspected piracy in the Indian Ocean, 2006. Piracy is an increasingly vexing issue in the waters between the Red Sea and Indian Ocean, off the Somali coast, and in the Strait of Malacca. More than 50,000 commercial ships use these busy waters every year.

◄ A classic image of a pirate captain from Howard Pyle's *Book of Pirates*

From the earliest history of maritime trade, ships have been vulnerable to criminal attack. Pirates flourished in the Mediterranean and Aegean Seas as early as the fourteenth century BCE. Scandinavian Vikings of the eighth to the tenth centuries were notorious pirates and raiders. In the nineteenth century, coastal India and the Persian Gulf were frequent targets for pirates after the spoils of the British and Dutch East India Companies. Pirates also patrolled the north coast of Africa, known as the Barbary Coast, waylaying Mediterranean vessels. Throughout history, pirates have captured not just loot, but also humans to sell into slavery.

As long as precious cargoes are shipped between ports, there will be brigands who hunt the seas. Maritime regulations and strict application of the law can only do so much to abate the lure of easy spoils, be they gold, oil, or human.

THE GOLDEN AGE OF PIRACY

Driven by the European colonial shipping trade with the New World, the Golden Age of Piracy flourished from about 1680 to 1730. Treasure ships regularly left the Caribbean for Europe—especially Spain—and pirates were poised to take their share. The pirates' aim was to capture the ship, not to sink it. The fate of those aboard often depended on the pirate captain's whim. Pirates might let the vanquished go free or join their crew, but murder was a distinct option. The captured captain had to rely on his crewmen's favor: a fair captain would survive, while a harsh one might not.

Despite the popular image of the pirate captain as a tyrant, pirates in fact operated democratically. Under a rigid pirate code, captains were elected, and all men aboard were entitled to an equal portion of the spoils. Offenses were met with any number of gruesome corporal punishments. Pirates sailed under no national flag, so their loyalty to their ship and comrades was serious business. These self-contained classless collectives attracted many who, for one reason or another, wished to escape more rigid societies.

▲ The Jolly Roger, a white skull and crossbones or crossed swords on a black field, is only one of a dozen or more pirate flag designs. Other distinctive pirate designs feature skeletons, hearts, or hourglasses to signify "your time is up."

▲ Two pirates duel over a treasure, while their comrades watch. Legends of buried treasure—and the bloodshed that accompanied its recovery—are popular remnants of the Golden Age of Piracy, but, on the whole, are greatly exaggerated.

PRIVATEERS

FROM THE SIXTEENTH CENTURY to the eighteenth century, many European colonial powers sanctioned privateering as a form of marine warfare. Privateers kept a portion of the spoils, while the remainder was turned over to the crown. Some privateers, such as William Kidd (c. 1645–1701), later became pirates. Privateering was internationally outlawed in 1856.

► Kidd was not only executed for piracy, but his body was hung in a gibbet over the River Thames as a deterrent for other pirates.

HMS *Bounty*

MUTINY IN THE SOUTH PACIFIC

In January 1790, the HMS *Bounty* burned and sank off remote Pitcairn Island in the South Pacific, an event far less famous than her storied 1789 mutiny. Indeed, it was the mutineers themselves who sank their ship, hoping to elude the pursuing Royal Navy. Thus ended the career of the compact, 90-foot (27 m) collier, which had sailed under the command of one of the Royal Navy's finest, William Bligh.

▲ A replica of the *Bounty*. As a collier, she had been designed to carry coal in bulk.

A BOUNTY OF BREADFRUIT

Commanding Lieutenant Bligh was entrusted with an important, if bizarre, mission: procure a cargo of live breadfruit trees from the South Pacific islands. The British crown intended to establish large breadfruit plantations in the Caribbean in order to feed the increasing number of slaves at work in British holdings there. For the purposes of this botanical experiment, the Royal Navy purchased the small collier *Bethia* and rechristened her the *Bounty*.

The journey went poorly nearly from the start. The *Bounty* spent almost a month attempting to round Cape Horn, finally giving up and turning east to the Indian Ocean. After 10 months' travel she attained Tahiti, to the vast relief of her officers and crew. It isn't hard to imagine why a filthy pack of Jack Tars cooped up on a tiny ship for 10 months might enjoy the Edenic delights of Tahiti. This they did, with great gusto, for five months, living ashore to harvest and package the precious breadfruit plants. After several desertions, dozens of tattoos, numerous amorous encounters with Tahitian women, and at least one marriage, the men of the *Bounty* installed their cargo of 1,015 potted breadfruit plants, reboarded the ship, and weighed anchor for the Caribbean.

CHRISTIAN'S MEN

Only three weeks into the journey, mutiny overtook the *Bounty*. The charismatic lieutenant, Fletcher Christian, incited roughly half the crew to join him in mutiny. Lieutenant

◀ Commanding Lieutenant William Bligh

▲ A contemporary engraving shows Fletcher Christian and the mutineers turning Lt. Bligh, along with other officers and crew members, adrift from HMS *Bounty*.

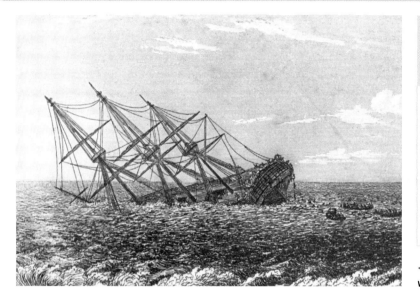

UNDER THE WATERS OF BOUNTY BAY

IN JANUARY 1957, photographer, writer, and polymath Luis Marden discovered the remains of the *Bounty* while diving in the eponymous Bounty Bay off Pitcairn Island on assignment for *National Geographic* magazine. To the present day, her ballast stones can still be seen from the surface of the gin-clear water.

◀ The HMS *Pandora*, sent to capture the HMS *Bounty* mutineers, was wrecked on the Great Barrier Reef, killing 31 crewmen and 4 mutineers.

Bligh and 18 loyalists were placed in the ship's longboat. Chartless, and with no more than a pocket watch and sextant for navigation, Bligh piloted the open boat more than 3,618 nautical miles (6,700 km) to safety in Timor. Along the way, he escaped cannibals, endured fierce storms, and navigated some of the world's most treacherous waters.

Fletcher Christian and the mutineers returned to Tahiti, but eventually took to the sea, hoping to find a more secure place to hide from the inevitable search by His Majesty's Navy. Mutiny was a grave charge indeed. The remainder of the band tried several islands over nine months' evasive sailing, only to be chased back to sea by fierce cannibalistic natives. Finally, they landed at Pitcairn Island. There in her bay, they burned and sank the *Bounty*. Several years of murder and mayhem plagued the islanders until there remained only two Englishmen and nine Tahitian women. The company restored some semblance of peace and became devout Christians. One of the men died of natural causes the next year, but after that, the Pitcairn Island band of mutiny survivors thrived, and their offspring live there to the present day.

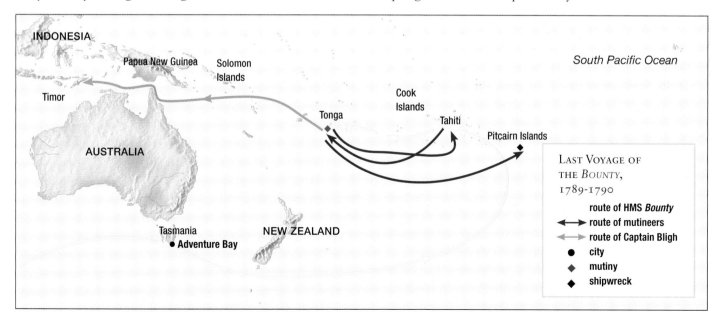

LAST VOYAGE OF THE *BOUNTY*, 1789-1790

→ route of HMS *Bounty*
↔ route of mutineers
→ route of Captain Bligh
● city
◆ mutiny
◆ shipwreck

SS *Tonquin*

FROM TRAPPING TO TERROR

In the early nineteenth century, the Pacific Northwest of the United States was still a great and terrifying wilderness for white explorers, trappers, and settlers. Navigation of locales like the Columbia River was made difficult by the paucity of maps and the hostility of various native peoples.

The captain and crew of the SS *Tonquin* sought beaver and otter pelts for John Jacob Astor's Pacific Fur Company. A fur transaction gone bad incited the natives and left nearly the entirety of the *Tonquin*'s crew dead. After luring numerous Indians onboard ship, the only remaining crewman lit the ship's gunpowder stores, destroying the ship, himself, and the raiders come to pillage.

A CAPTAIN'S FATAL ERROR

The 290-ton (260 metric tons), three-masted bark *Tonquin* sailed out of New York Harbor in spring 1810. Bound for the Pacific Northwest in search of animal pelts, she first had to round the treacherous Cape Horn on the tip of South America. During the arduous journey, Captain Jonathan Thorne proved himself a difficult and demanding taskmaster.

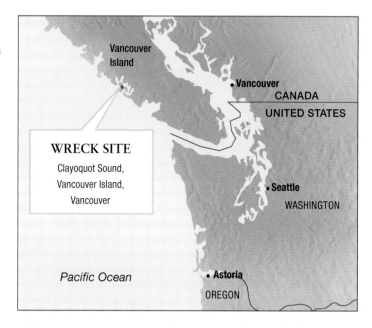

WRECK SITE
Clayoquot Sound, Vancouver Island, Vancouver

While not so unusual for a sea captain of the day, Thorne's threatening and bullying behavior would prove more problematic when he directed his barbs at native peoples.

Arriving at the mouth of the Columbia River, Thorne sent three successive boats to try to find the channel for the *Tonquin* to clear an infamous bar shoal. Each boat lost (only two men were eventually recovered) increased the bitterness of the sailors. The *Tonquin* was finally able to make her way upstream, and her crew spent more than two months building a fort and outbuildings, which would later become the town of Astoria—named for the sponsor of the expedition, John Jacob Astor.

▲ A bark, or barque, has at least three masts and square sails on all but the aftermost mast.

Having unloaded most of her cargo at Astoria by June 1811, the *Tonquin* then proceeded north to Clayoquot Sound, in the area around present-day Vancouver, in search of native trappers who would trade for pelts. The crew of the *Tonquin* found them in a Nuu-chah-nulth village, but tensions rose as natives and explorers failed to come to terms. Hotheaded Captain Thorne angrily threw a load of furs in the face of the village chief before ordering him off the ship—a fatal insult, as it turned out. The chief returned with a band of men and attacked the traders. The wild melee left only five crewmen alive onboard the *Tonquin*. Four of them attempted to escape in a canoe, only to be slaughtered ashore.

The sole remaining crewman, clerk James Lewis, hid overnight as he hatched plans for revenge. At dawn, he called out to the Nuu-chah-nulth on the shore to come aboard. As a band of Indians swarmed onto the ship, the duplicitous sailor lit the fuse that he had been concealing. Four and a half tons (4 metric tons) of gunpowder in the ship's stores exploded in a tremendous blast. This single blast destroyed the perpetrator, the Indians, and the *Tonquin*, leaving nothing but splinters floating on the waters of Clayoquot Sound.

CHRONICLE OF DECEIT

THE FATE OF THE *TONQUIN* would be unknown but for the sole survivor of the ship, one George Ramsey, also known as Lamazee. This son of a Chinook Indian mother and an English sailor managed to slip away during the height of the battle onboard and escape death by dint of his dark skin and ability to speak the native language.

▲ Built in 1926, the concrete-and-steel Astoria Column, located in Astoria, Oregon, depicts the adventures of the *Tonquin*, including her ignoble end at the top.

◄ The 125-foot (38 m)-tall Astoria Column chronicles the Lewis and Clark expedition of 1803–06 at the bottom, as well as other events in Astoria history.

▼ North America's largest rodent, the American beaver became such a favorite for the fur trade that it nearly went extinct by 1900. Its numbers have now recovered.

The *Golden Venture* | SMUGGLED HUMAN CARGO

▲ A contemporary painting of the *Golden Venture* and the desperate immigrants' final struggle to reach the shores of the United States. Weakened by their trials aboard ship, some unlucky souls never would.

For months, the 13 crew members of the *Golden Venture* had beaten and virtually imprisoned the 286 illegal immigrants crammed onto the tramp steamer. In scenes evocative of the barbaric slave ships of the African slave trade, the emigrants endured appalling conditions on the vermin-infested ship. Tensions were at the breaking point as the ship went aground on the sands off Rockaway Beach, New York, on June 6, 1993. In the mutinous scramble that followed, 10 refugees lost their lives. The rest were rescued and then incarcerated. Their plight elicited international attention.

WHAT PRICE AMERICA?

Desperate Chinese had paid up to $30,000 each to "snakeheads" (illegal immigrant smugglers) for the privilege of hiking from China through the mountains of Myanmar (Burma), and on to Thailand. From there, they packed onto the *Golden Venture*, a modern steel freighter rusting into a state of poor repair and dubious seaworthiness. Her overcrowded condition was commonplace and certainly did not hinder her departure. The *Golden Venture* stopped in Kenya for supplies before heading off on the long and dangerous transit around the Cape of Good Hope. The legendary troubled seas off the southern tip of Africa didn't fail to disappoint—*Golden Venture* and her much-abused human cargo confronted a hurricane while rounding the Cape.

As the crowded ship approached her destination, her passengers, treated as little more than captives, began to rebel. When the ship ran onto the sandbars of Rockaway

Beach at 2:00 AM on an unseasonably cold day, pandemonium ensued. With the desperately sought shores of America less than 100 yards (900 m) away, it is easy to understand why the frantic passengers went over the side of the ship in droves. The bitterly cold water killed 10 of them, but most managed to reach the shore.

THE AFTERMATH

The overwhelming odds the immigrants had overcome to get to the portal of freedom moved many, but other American arms were not as welcoming. The Immigration and Naturalization Service of the federal government rounded up the wreck survivors and immediately transferred them to a medium-security prison in York, Pennsylvania. Many were deported to various other countries, but a large number of the refugees languished in prison in York, until President Bill Clinton ordered the final 52 released on February 27, 1997, some four years after the wreck of the *Golden Venture*.

The *Golden Venture* itself was freed from Rockaway Beach and towed to the waters off Boca Raton, Florida. There she was sunk to serve as an artificial reef and destination for recreational divers. Rough seas during the hurricane season of 2005 reportedly broke up the wreck, leaving the memory of the *Golden Venture* to history.

WRECK SITE
Rockaway Beach,
Borough of Queens,
New York City

◀ A paper swan, constructed in the style now called *Golden Venture*

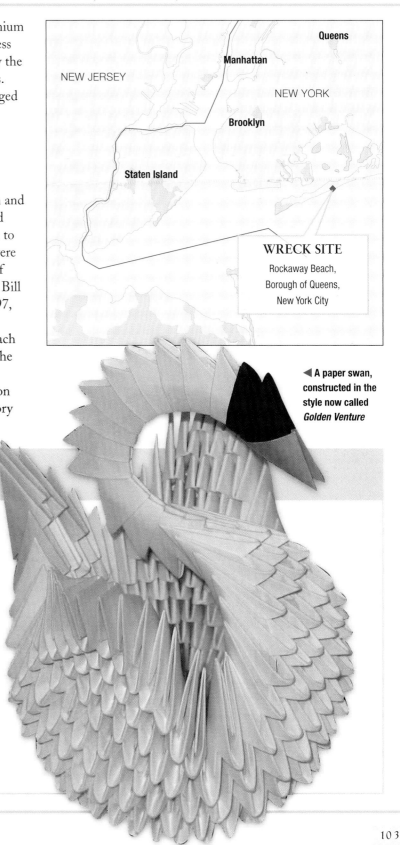

ANCIENT CRAFTS, NEW LAND

WHILE IMPRISONED IN YORK, PENNSYLVANIA, awaiting trial, the Chinese refugees practiced, refined, and publicized the ancient Chinese craft of paper folding. Tiny pieces of paper were folded into interlocking triangles in ever-increasing three-dimensional modular units. The *Golden Venture* refugees crafted more than 10,000 models of eagles, pineapples, swans, and more. These folk art sculptures charmed magazine editors and dignitaries as publicity for the refugees' cause. This modern three-dimensional style of paper craft became so popular, in fact, that it is now known as *Golden Venture* folding.

5 · CASUALTIES OF WAR

▲ *Battle of the Combined Venetian and Dutch Fleets Against the Turks in the Bay of Foja* by Abraham Beerstraaten, 1649

The *Mary Rose* GRAND WARSHIP OF HENRY VIII

When King Henry VIII ascended the English throne in 1509, war with France and enmity with Scotland had been ongoing for more than a century. The young king was determined to outdo both countries in naval might. Built by royal decree in 1509–10, the *Mary Rose* was by all accounts King Henry's favorite ship. Named for his sister Mary and for the Tudor rose, the stalwart four-masted carrack served her king for almost 40 years before sinking in 1545.

Equipped with 78 guns, the *Mary Rose* was fitted out for battle. She measured 125 feet (38 m) in length, with a beam of 38 feet (11.7 m). England went to war with France only a year after the *Mary Rose* was completed. She proved herself an able combatant, carrying 185 soldiers, a crew of 200 men, and 30 gunners. Refitted twice during her career, the *Mary Rose* boasted 91 guns when she sailed into battle for the last time.

Some reports maintain that this added load—she went from 500 to 700 tons (450–635 metric tons)—weighed her down, leaving her gun ports only 14 inches (36 cm) above the waterline. These measurements matter, for the causes of the *Mary Rose's* sinking are still disputed.

◀ Henry VIII is undoubtedly one of England's most famous monarchs, primarily for the dubious distinction of having broken with the Catholic Church because of his many matrimonies.

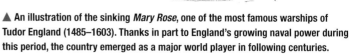

▲ An illustration of the sinking *Mary Rose*, one of the most famous warships of Tudor England (1485–1603). Thanks in part to England's growing naval power during this period, the country emerged as a major world player in following centuries.

◀ A conservationist sprays the hull of the *Mary Rose* with waxy polyethylene glycol to replace the water in the wood to prevent it from cracking as it dries out.

LOSS AND RECOVERY

A hostile French fleet, 225 ships strong, sailed on England in the summer of 1545. The *Mary Rose* was one of fewer than 100 English ships to meet it. The two forces met on July 19 in the Solent, a narrow channel of water between mainland England and the Isle of Wight. The *Mary Rose* survived the first day of battle but mysteriously sank on the second, even though all sailing ships were becalmed. King Henry himself witnessed the sinking of his beloved ship, and her complement of 400 men, as he stood watch from nearby Southsea Castle.

Nearly 300 years passed before a fisherman discovered the *Mary Rose* in 1836. It was not until 1979, though, that excavation to raise the *Mary Rose* began in earnest. Finally raised in 1983, she was nearly intact on her starboard side where she had lain in the silt of the Solent, but badly damaged on her port side. Like the wreck of the *Vasa*, recovered in Sweden two decades earlier, the *Mary Rose* was carefully treated to preserve her timber. She is now housed in a dedicated museum in Portsmouth, England, along with supplies and artifacts that went down with the magnificent Tudor warship.

WHO SANK THE *MARY ROSE*?

WHEN THE *MARY ROSE* went down in a dead calm, the French claimed that their cannons had done the fatal damage. The proud English navy disagreed. According to the English, she had probably heeled too far to starboard, coming about to fire a broadside. Either that, or Spanish mercenaries had misunderstood their English captain's orders and left the gun ports open to the waves.

Now that the *Mary Rose* has been raised, the mystery is gaining new scrutiny. The most recent theory holds that the day the *Mary Rose* sank, the French had sent out galleys, powered by oars rather than wind. The galleys advanced on the becalmed English fleet, fired their cannons, and struck the *Mary Rose* on her port side. A recent British Broadcasting Corporation (BBC) news report characterizes the long-held English view as Tudor-style "political spin."

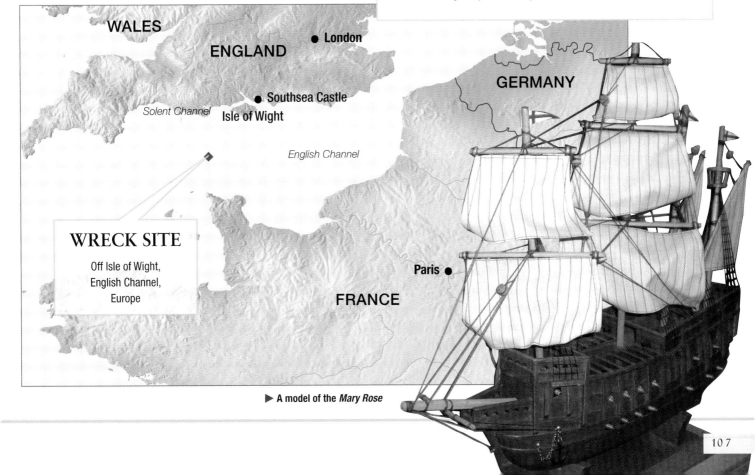

WALES

ENGLAND

● London

GERMANY

Solent Channel

● Southsea Castle
Isle of Wight

English Channel

WRECK SITE

Off Isle of Wight,
English Channel,
Europe

Paris ●

FRANCE

▶ A model of the *Mary Rose*

The Spanish Armada | MIGHT OF AN EMPIRE

The Spanish Armada was driven by three primary forces—politics, religion, and national wealth. In 1588, King Philip II of Spain planned what he hoped would be a definitive naval attack on England. With an unprecedented force of some 130 ships, he intended to eliminate the burgeoning Protestant faith and policies espoused by Queen Elizabeth I of England. This was a period of widespread religious strife between Catholics and Protestants through much of Europe. Philip also wanted to strike back at English interference with Spanish trade in the New World and shore up Spanish holdings in Flanders (present-day Belgium) and the Netherlands.

But things did not go as planned. Spain's decisive defeat at the hands of the English—aided by wind, weather, and luck—proved a turning point in the balance of world power. Protestant England superseded Catholic Spain in dominance of the seas. The shift had profound effects on trade, culture, and geopolitics that are evident even today.

PLAN OF ATTACK

King Philip of Spain and Queen Elizabeth of England were monarchs of the two most powerful naval empires of their time; Portugal—a major power in its own right—had recently come under Spanish dominance. But Philip and Elizabeth were also bitterly entangled through marriage. Philip was the former king consort of England; he had been married to Elizabeth's predecessor and half-sister, the Catholic Queen Mary I. The Protestant Elizabeth ascended the throne in 1558 after Mary's death, and she began persecuting Catholics.

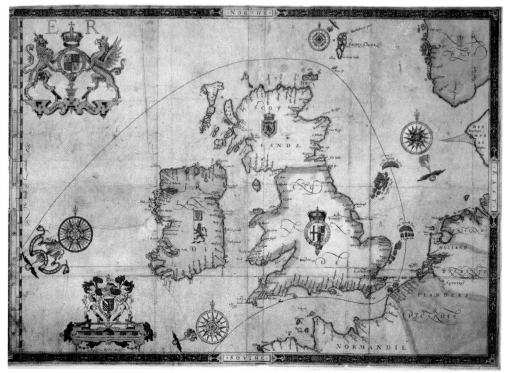

▲ A 1590 map showing the ill-fated route followed by King Philip's venerable Spanish Armada as it circled the British Isles

Philip conceived of his attack on his sister-in-law as a crusade and received papal aid and support.

The Spanish fleet was assembled and launched from Lisbon, Portugal, which Spain had controlled since 1580. Philip aimed to overwhelm the English with ships, firepower, and men. He ordered 28 new warships and converted scores of trade galleons for battle. Commanded by the Duke of Medina Sidonia, the spectacular fleet carried some 30,000 men. They sailed on May 28 for Dunkirk, where they were to rendezvous with a squadron of thousands more men commanded by the Duke of Parma. From this quarter, they would attack England.

Meanwhile, the English were making battle plans of their own. Privateers John Hawkins and Sir Francis Drake, together known as the "Sea Dogs," had plagued and plundered Spain's

New World treasure fleets for decades. Now they were put in command of Her Majesty's forces, reporting to the High Admiral, Lord Howard of Effingham. The English assembled a fleet of approximately 200 ships, including 25 "race ships." These purpose-built warships were faster, more maneuverable, and lower to the water, lacking the high stern- and forecastles that typified the Spanish-Portuguese fleet.

The chief differences between the two belligerents had more to do with tactics than with manpower. English troops consisted mostly of experienced sailors, while the Spanish troops were heavy on infantrymen. The Spanish planned to fire a rapid unison round and pull in close enough for the infantry to board the English ships, overpowering their crews in hand-to-hand combat. This strategy proved outmoded; the longer range and rapid reloading of English cannons shifted naval warfare to a new reliance on firepower.

▶ One of three so-called Armada Portraits of Queen Elizabeth I of England. The monarch is shown surrounded by allegories of power, with images of the Spanish Armada over her right shoulder and its defeat over her left.

▼ A contemporary image of the mighty Spanish Armada. The loss of its armada marked the beginning of the end for Spain's dominance of the seas.

FLOTSAM & JETSAM

Queen Elizabeth gave the most famous speech of her reign at Tilbury, England, following the defeat of the Armada. She declared, "I know I have the body of a weak and feeble woman. But I have the heart and stomach of a king."

The Spanish Armada CONTINUED

HELLBURNERS

ON THE EVE OF THE BATTLE OF GRAVELINES the English loaded eight ships with gunpowder, set them ablaze, and sent them toward the Armada. The Spanish troops panicked when they saw the fireships—such "hellburners" had done great damage three years earlier during the Siege of Antwerp. In fact, the English ships carried far less explosive power, but the so-called "Antwerp Fire" ships were so notorious that many Spanish ships cut their anchors and fled. Weeks later, these ships would be unable to drop anchor, and they would be dashed apart in the rocky, turbulent waters of the Scottish and Irish coastlines.

BATTLE, RETREAT, AND DEFEAT

Weather delayed the Spanish fleet's departure by several weeks and wrecked several ships before they even cleared Spanish waters. Arriving in July off the coast of Plymouth, in southwestern England, the Spanish met a well-prepared enemy. A series of beacons spread the news of the Armada's arrival, so English ships were battle-ready along the length of the English Channel. The fleets met in battle at Eddystone, Portland, the Isle of Wight, and off the coast of Calais before the definitive Battle of Gravelines on August 8, 1588.

▼ *Defeat of the Spanish Armada* by Philippe-Jaques de Loutherbourg, 1796, shows the desperation wrought by flames during the Battle of Gravelines.

By the time the Armada reached the coast of the Spanish-controlled Netherlands, the English had gained a tactical advantage, occupying the windward position. Near Gravelines, the two forces met in battle once more. The Spanish ships, downwind and outgunned, heeled far over to leeward, exposing their hulls to English cannon fire. Firing rapid-repeat volleys, the English overpowered the Spanish in broadside after broadside. The Spanish lost five ships and were forced to retreat into the North Sea. This course would spell doom for the Armada.

Wind and weather seemed to join forces with the English in the weeks following the Battle of Gravelines. By then,

▲ *The Spanish Armada off the English Coast* by Cornelis Claesz van Wieringen, 1620–25

the Spanish had no choice—gale winds from the south and an unrelenting English fleet forced them to continue north. English ships, joined by Dutch rebels, pursued the Armada until they neared the border of Scotland. The Spanish fleet rounded the tip of Scotland and proceeded south, along the west coast of Ireland. Ship after ship was wrecked along the rocky coastline in unusually ferocious Atlantic storms. Shipwrecked Spanish soldiers who made it ashore met with hostility or were murdered by the English in Ireland. By October, only half the Armada's ships straggled back to Spain, some foundering or even exploding on the return journey. Some 20,000 men died in the service of King Philip's extravagant, but failed, attack.

AFTERMATH

With all nature's forces appearing to turn against the Spanish Armada, it was easy for Queen Elizabeth to decree that God had been on the side of the English and, by extension, the Protestant faith. Indeed, England, along with the Protestant Netherlands, now entered a new era of naval power and colonial expansion, from South Asia to Africa to the Americas. The chastened Spanish, meanwhile, steered a different course in the New World, retreating from North America and concentrating their colonial power on Central and South America.

THE TOBERMORY GALLEON

ONE WRECKED SPANISH ARMADA SHIP has garnered more than her share of attention in the centuries following her wreck. The Tobermory Galleon, so called for the site of her wreck in Tobermory Bay on the Scottish Isle of Mull, was rumored to be holding treasure worth $45 million. The galleon has been the object of numerous diving expeditions over the centuries, which have turned up little more than the skull of a cabin boy—said to carry a curse. Recent scholarship has established that the galleon that blew up and sank in the remote Scottish harbor was actually the *San Juan de Sicilia* and was not, in fact, loaded with any treasure at all.

FLOTSAM & JETSAM

During his decades as a privateer, Sir Francis Drake earned the nickname *El Drago*, or "the dragon" from the Spanish sailors he terrorized.

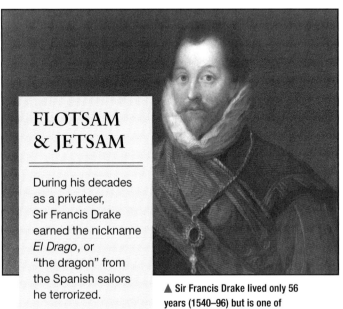

▲ Sir Francis Drake lived only 56 years (1540–96) but is one of England's most famous naval heroes.

L'Orient NAPOLEON'S FLAGSHIP

Napoleon Bonaparte's ambitions of capturing Egypt—and perhaps even proceeding on to India—ended early on the morning of August 2, 1798, with the destruction of the French flagship *Orient* in the Battle of the Nile. After searching all summer, Admiral Horatio Nelson's ships had cornered the French fleet at Abu Qir Bay, some 15 miles (25 km) off the coast of Alexandria, Egypt. The French had chained their ships together, with a shoal for protection on one side and the open sea on the other. And right in the center of the Gallic line was *L'Orient*, pride of Bonaparte's navy.

▲ George Arnald's painting *The Destruction of* L'Orient *at the Battle of the Nile* (1825–27) shows the ship at her moment of final destruction.

Such a coveted prize as *L'Orient* was naturally a prime target for the English gunners. Yet, this sitting duck had talons: the English ships *Bellerophon*, *Alexander*, and *Swiftsure* attacked, but the French ship's enormous firepower rebuffed all three. Nevertheless, an English shell had found its mark and set the seemingly indomitable *Orient* ablaze. Seven surrounding French ships cut their anchor lines in a desperate attempt to flee the impending violence of *L'Orient*'s exploding powder cache. All activity around the great ship ceased midbattle, as horrified sailors of both sides helplessly watched the fire grow. After 10 minutes of stillness—only the crackle of *L'Orient*'s burning timbers could be heard—the blaze reached the powder stores. Two nearly simultaneous explosions rocked the bay. In that one wrenching moment, both *L'Orient* and Napoleon's dreams of conquest disappeared into a thunderous cloud of smoke and debris.

THE BATTLE OF THE NILE

At a length of 214 feet (65.2 m), *L'Orient* carried 118 cannons on her three gun decks. Launched in 1791 as the *Dauphin-Royale*, she was rechristened *Sans-Culotte* during the French Revolution, finally taking on the name *L'Orient* in May 1795.

"THE BOY STOOD ON THE BURNING DECK . . ."

THOUGH MORE THAN 1,000 PEOPLE DIED when *L'Orient* exploded, one death in particular gained lasting renown. Captain Luc-Julien-Joseph Casabianca's 12-year-old son, Giocante, had accompanied his father aboard ship. The steadfast boy reputedly stayed at his post even while the ship burned, remaining on deck as the flames approached, and then detonated the powder stores. Giocante's heroism was commemorated in "Casabianca," a poem by Felicia Dorothea Hemans, first published in 1826.

▲ Napoleon Bonaparte, whose victories in Europe made him a legend, met with less success in Africa. His men did, however, discover the Rosetta Stone, which allowed translation of ancient Egyptian hieroglyphs into modern languages.

Mediterranean Sea

Abu Qir Bay

Alexandria

Nile River

WRECK SITE

Abu Qir Bay,
Alexandria,
Egypt

EGYPT

As the flagship of the French navy, she had borne the future emperor himself and more than a thousand sailors and soldiers to their conquest of Egypt. Her destruction at the hands of Nelson's armada left Napoleon and his armies stranded in North Africa.

The French fleet had evaded detection through subterfuge, keeping Nelson busy searching the Atlantic for a chimerical French attack on Ireland. They remained undetected at anchor in Abu Qir Bay for three weeks before their discovery by the British. Although Napoleon was not aboard *L'Orient* at the time of the battle, the loss of his flagship began the decimation of the French fleet by the British in one of the greatest and most decisive naval battles of all time. The Battle of the Nile was a resounding defeat for the French—and one with great geopolitical consequences. Napoleon's retreat from Egypt, leaving his troops stranded behind him, sounded the death knell for his dreams of an overseas empire.

▲ *The Battle of the Nile* by Thomas Luny (1759–1837) shows the line of ships standing helpless as their flagship burns. The French flag can be seen still flying above the doomed *Orient* in the middle.

WARSHIPS IN THE AGE OF SAIL

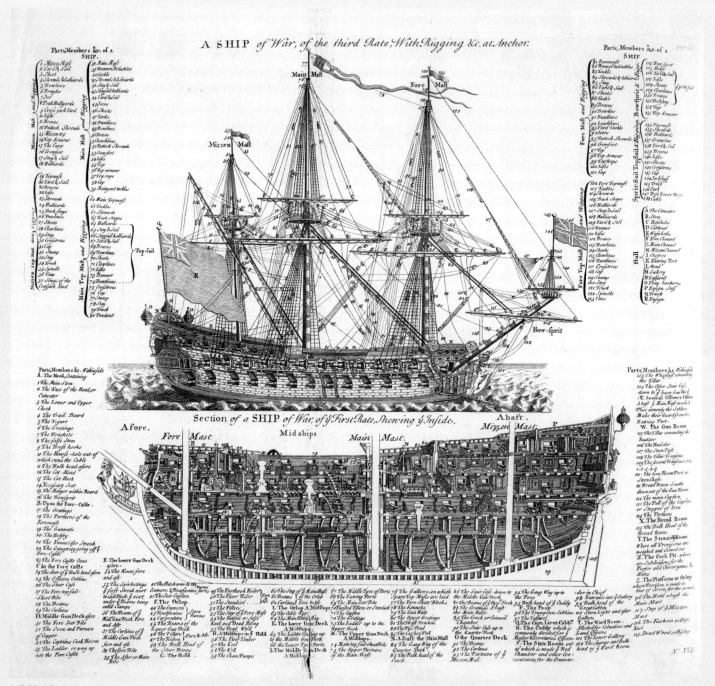

▲ British Royal Navy diagrams of a third-rate ship (top) and a cross-section of a first-rate ship (bottom) from 1828

Humans have been harnessing the power of the wind for millennia. The oldest-known sailing ships date from ancient Egypt—as long ago as 3500 BCE. The Age of Sail, however, generally refers to the golden age of European sailing ships from the late fifteenth to nineteenth centuries.

The Age of Sail was concurrent with European colonization in Africa, Asia, and the Americas, and ships grew to accommodate growing trade, exploration, and passenger transport. Naval might took on new urgency as Western powers battled for dominance of the seas and protection of their colonies and interests. The primary world powers during the Age of Sail were Britain, Spain, Portugal, France, the Netherlands, Russia, and later, the United States. Dominance—when achieved—proved fleeting, passing from power to power with the regularity of the tides.

FORM AND FUNCTION

The design, construction, and armament of sailing warships were all predicated on the way a ship handles when under sail. Square-rigged ships took on fore-and-aft or lateen rigging—principally on the aftermasts—to allow them to sail closer into the wind. The first European ships to feature this design were carracks, which appeared in the fifteenth century. Portuguese caravels and *naos*, Spanish galleons, and English galleys grew from this common ancestor ship.

Firearms became more advanced in the late sixteenth century, and naval battles shifted from onboard infantry engagement to long-distance firing. Deck-mounted cannons gave way to cannons carried belowdecks. Battleships expanded to include up to three dedicated lower decks for cannons, which fired through gun ports with hinged covers. The largest British man-o'-wars of the nineteenth century carried up to 120 cannons, divided between port and starboard. These huge ships, which reached over 2,500 tons (2,270 metric tons), were designated first-rate, while second-rate and third-rate ships carried up to 60 guns. Smaller armed ships, such as frigates, sloops, and brigs, which carried fewer than 40 guns, were fast and maneuverable, and supported these larger ships-of-the-line.

OWN THE WIND

NAVAL TACTICS, TOO, were contingent on the wind. A battleship would generally fire broadside on her enemies, but this was done most efficiently from upwind, or windward. Guns on a downwind ship—heeling far to leeward and exposing her hull—would fire too high, failing to strike the enemy's hull. The tactical advantage of an upwind position is known as the weather gage. Ships at a perpendicular angle—advancing or retreating, for example—could be fired upon as well. Raking fire, as this tactic is called, could damage the vulnerable stern or send shots the length of the enemy ship.

▲ The USS *Cumberland*, built as a 1,726-ton (1,566 metric ton) sailing frigate, became a sloop of war in 1855–56. In 1861, she served on Civil War blockading duty off the Confederacy's Atlantic coast and helped capture Forts Hatteras and Clark in late August of that year. On March 8, 1862, while she was anchored off Newport News, Virginia, the ironclad CSS *Virginia* came out to attack federal warships in Hampton Roads. The *Virginia* rammed the *Cumberland*, whose guns had been unable to hinder the Confederate ironclad. Unable to sail away, the *Cumberland* sank. This battle decisively demonstrated the power of the armored steam-powered warships against wooden sailing types.

RMS *Lusitania* | U-BOAT ATTACK

As the RMS *Lusitania*'s sleek hull smoothly cut the waters of New York Harbor on May 1, 1915, the war in Europe seemed far away. The United States had, as yet, no plan to join the fray. Aboard the *Lusitania*, bound for Liverpool, England, 1,959 passengers and crew enjoyed the British liner's famously luxurious trappings. Dubbed "The Greyhound of the Seas," her speed and status as a civilian liner was believed to be good protection against the German *Unterseeboots* ("undersea boats"), better known as U-boats, bedeviling the North Atlantic shipping lanes.

▲ The RMS *Lusitania* at dock in New York at the end of her 1907 maiden voyage

▶ An Irish recruitment poster from 1915. The sinking of the *Lusitania* became an international rallying point to secure the support of a war against imperial Germany.

The *Lusitania*'s captain, William Thomas Turner, had been instructed to keep his speed up and travel a zigzag course in order to evade the lurking undersea wolf pack. Unbeknownst to most of her crew and passengers, the *Lusitania* had recently been refitted as a ship of war, with ammunition magazines and gun mounts hidden under her teak decks. She also carried a secret cargo of ammunition and war contraband. *Lusitania* made good progress across the Atlantic, but lingering fog banks in the Celtic Sea caused her to slow down and hew a straight course.

Captain Walther Schwieger, in command of German submarine *U-20*, lay waiting some 15 miles (24 km) off the Irish town of Queenstown (present day Cobh). *U-20* had been harassing ships in the area, and had torpedoed several liners and merchant ships. The captain was thrilled to see the huge hull and distinctive four smokestacks of the *Lusitania* in his

▲ A 1915 cartoon published by the influential British satirical magazine *Punch*, showing the *Lusitania* in her final minutes. Negative press about the incident colored opinion against Germany, although the Imperial German Embassy had placed advertisements in 50 U.S. newspapers, including those in New York, that warned Americans to avoid crossing the Atlantic in ships flying British flags.

periscope. *U-20* fired one torpedo, which Schwieger watched all the way to a direct hit on *Lusitania*'s port side, below the waterline. He anticipated one explosion, but was astonished to see a second, bigger blast 15 seconds later. This blast devastated the great ship, and within 18 minutes the *Lusitania* had disappeared from sight beneath the frigid waters. The angle of the sinking prevented all lifeboats but one from launching, and this capsized immediately. Those passengers not trapped inside the ship were left floating amid the debris field, to die in the inescapable cold of the Celtic Sea.

THE INQUEST

Shortly after the tragic and devastating loss of 1,119 lives, authorities began piecing together what had happened. How had one torpedo caused such a large ship to sink so quickly? Most investigation and speculation centered on the mysterious second explosion. Suspicions quickly fell on the "secret cargo," which indeed turned out to be ammunition. Not only quite explosive, but—as prohibited war goods—a cargo that would have made *Lusitania* a fair target under the rules of war.

Though only a fairly small percentage of the dead were Americans (128), public opinion in the United States turned against Germany. Germany, in fact, agreed to give warning before firing upon civilian passenger liners in the future, but the die was cast. The *Lusitania* had awoken the slumbering lion of the United States, and within two years America would join Great Britain in the war against Germany.

▲ A *Lusitania* victim is carried away. The U.S. flag covering the body indicates the victim's nationality.

▶ The *Lusitania*'s builders published this diagram of her deck plans seven days after a U-boat sunk the liner. U-boats had already proved difficult to constrain under the rules of war. Legally, U-boats were required to breach the surface before attacking, in order to give enemy crews time to abandon ship—but following this rule put the U-boat crews at great risk, and so it usually went unheeded.

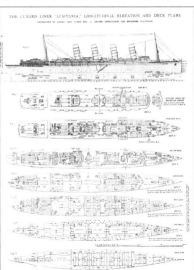

THE CUNARD LINER "LUSITANIA" LONGITUDINAL ELEVATION AND DECK PLANS.

SCOTLAND

North Sea

Atlantic Ocean

WRECK SITE

Off Irish coast, Celtic Sea, British Isles

NORTHERN IRELAND

Irish Sea

IRELAND

Dublin •

• Liverpool

UNITED KINGDOM

St George's Channel

ENGLAND

(Queenstown) Cobh •

WALES

London •

Celtic Sea

English Channel

COAL DUST

IT SEEMED QUITE LOGICAL that the second, fatal explosion had been caused by the detonation of *Lusitania*'s ammunition. Yet, when undersea explorer Robert Ballard dove the wreck of *Lusitania* in 1993, he determined that the hold carrying the ammunition was not the site of the second explosion. Instead, empty coal bunkers allowed coal dust to mix with air, creating an explosive aerosol mixture. When touched off by the fires ignited by the torpedo blast, the coal bunkers doomed the ship.

HMHS *Britannic*

THE *TITANIC'S* UNLUCKY SISTER

The *Titanic* had two sister ships. The *Olympic* was the second of the trio to be completed, and, although she encountered her share of accidents, she survived until her deliberate demolition in 1937. The third sister was the *Britannic*. The *Britannic* was to be the largest and most spectacular of the three, with a length of 1,000 feet (304 m). The White Star Line intended to christen her the *Gigantic*, and her launch was expected to guarantee the line's preeminence in transatlantic luxury service.

But two major events interceded. First, the sinking of the *Titanic* changed everything for her youngest sister. She shrank to a still-impressive 883 feet (269 m) in length, and her

▲ In 1976, famed marine explorer Jacques Cousteau (standing) dived the wreck of the *Britannic*, which lay on her starboard side in 375 feet (114 m) of water.

▲ The *Olympic*, sister ship to both the *Britannic* and the *Titanic*. The first to be built, she was the last to survive, and earned the nickname "Old Reliable."

name was changed from *Gigantic* to *Britannic*. The primary modifications, though, were for safety: the fore watertight bulkheads (which had been breached on the *Titanic*) now extended all the way up to the B-deck—three levels higher than the *Titanic*'s. Engineers also fitted *Britannic* with lifeboat davits, designed to launch lifeboats even in the event the ship was listing severely.

The second, and more fateful event, was the outbreak of World War I. Before the *Britannic* could enter passenger service, the British Admiralty requisitioned her as a hospital ship for service in the eastern Mediterranean Sea. Refitted with capacity for more than 3,000 wounded, close to 500 medical staff, and a crew of 860, she served her country well during wartime. But the *Britannic* never survived to make the glamorous transatlantic voyage she was designed for. A mine sunk the *Titanic*'s youngest sister off the coast of Greece on November 21, 1916.

ONE MORNING IN NOVEMBER

The *Britannic* had made five round-trips to the Mediterranean and was on her sixth in November 1916. As she entered the Kea Channel in the Aegean Sea, the crew heard a loud explosion at 8:12 on the morning of November 21. The ship had struck a mine on her starboard side. Many rushed for the lifeboats, but Captain Charles Bartlett decided he would attempt to beach the ship. Unfortunately, two lifeboats were launched anyway, while the three massive propellers were still turning. Crew members watched in horror as the propellers sucked the lifeboats into their churning vortex, tearing apart both the boats and their passengers. Captain Bartlett immediately ordered the engines cut, but within 15 minutes, the ship was listing severely, with water entering through the blast hole and also through open portholes in the lower decks. At 8:35 AM, the captain gave the order to abandon ship.

Rescue boats, from Greek fishermen to British destroyers, quickly arrived on the scene. But nothing could be done to salvage the massive Olympic-class ship. The great *Britannic* sank at 9:07 AM, less than an hour after the explosion, in spite of her lavish safety features. Although 1,036 people were saved, the gruesome lifeboat debacle claimed 30 lives.

▲ Lifeboats salvaged from the *Titanic*. Ultimately, the improved safety features on her sister ship the *Britannic* still didn't save the liner from destruction. Also complicating any hope of rescue from sinking early-twentieth-century ocean liners were the passengers' own clothes. Fashions of the day dictated heavy, constricting clothing. For women especially, enmeshed in cloth from head to toe, such styles contributed to a high death count. Even for those capable of swimming, cloth made heavy with water spelled death.

SURVIVOR!

ONE LUCKY WOMAN SURVIVED DISASTERS on all three Olympic-class ships. Violet Jessop worked as a stewardess onboard the *Olympic* when it sailed in 1911 and collided with the HMS *Hawke*. The following year, Jessop survived the wreck of the *Titanic*; employed as a crew member, she climbed aboard one of the first lifeboats. Undeterred, the brave woman signed on to serve as a Red Cross nurse and was assigned to HMHS *Britannic*. She survived this third disaster as well.

▲ Violet Jessop

WRECK SITE

Kea Channel,
Aegean Islands,
Greece

RMS *Laurentic* SECRET CARGO

▲ The *Megantic*, sister ship to the *Laurentic*. The ships were outfitted with experimental propulsion systems and tested against each other. The *Laurentic*'s, which proved most efficient, would later become a White Star Line standard, but the *Megantic* outlived her sister, surviving until sold for scrapping in 1933.

RMS *Laurentic* departed Buncrana, Ireland, through the picturesque Lough Swilly on January 25, 1917. She carried 475 passengers and crew for the transatlantic crossing to Halifax, Canada. In addition to the usual load of paying passengers, mail, and general freight, the *Laurentic* held a secret cargo in the second-class baggage room. No "second-class" cargo, it was gold bullion—3,211 bars worth 5 million pounds sterling (more than £250 million, or about $500 million today). This vast fortune was destined for the U.S. Treasury as payment for ammunition the United States had contributed to the British war effort.

Those aboard the *Laurentic* had no way of knowing that German submarine *U-80* had just completed a mine-laying mission attempting to block access to the northernmost Irish port. The *Laurentic* plowed right into the heart of the minefield and struck two mines in short succession, less than an hour after leaving port. Fifty minutes later, she lay at the bottom of the Lough, most of her passengers and crew drowned or killed by hypothermia in the frigid waters.

LOST AND FOUND

The *Laurentic* was built at the famous Harland and Wolff shipyard in Belfast, Northern Ireland, and was launched in 1908. She was one of a pair of liners built partly as prototypes for the *Titanic* and her sister ships, the *Britannic* and the *Olympic*. The *Laurentic* was equipped with three screws; a then-experimental low-pressure turbine engine powered one of them. Conventional engines drove the two outer props. This arrangement made the *Laurentic* one of the fastest ships afloat, an ability put to good use because the White Star Line used her to haul mail (hence the Royal Mail Ship designation) between Europe and North America.

Fortunately, the *Laurentic* was traveling with an unusually light load of passengers on her last journey. She sank rapidly, and although lifeboats were launched, the winter gale and frigid waters of North Ireland quickly took the lives of many of those who managed to escape the sinking ship.

The *Laurentic*'s vastly valuable cargo made salvage a priority for the British navy; within weeks the wreck had been located and teams of divers brought to bear. The *Laurentic* had sunk in fairly shallow water—only 130 feet (39 m)—which made her wreck accessible to divers of the era. Lieutenant-Commander Guyban C. C. Damant received the difficult and dangerous assignment of retrieving the *Laurentic*'s lost gold. Damant and his teams of divers mapped the wreck and gradually made their way to the second-class baggage room. The first year of diving (involving hundreds of dives) yielded a treasure trove of gold. Yet, even as Damant and his teams were retrieving gold bars, the Irish winter weather was pounding the wreck with swells off the North Atlantic.

The salvage divers had to stop work for the winter, and they returned the following year. Little did Damant and his teams know that they would be involved with the salvage operations for seven years, performing more than 5,000 dives. Eventually, they recovered all but 22 gold bars.

SWIFT JUSTICE

PRIOR TO HER SINKING, the *Laurentic* was one of the fastest ships on water. In 1910, Chief Inspector Walter Dew of Scotland Yard was hunting the notorious Dr. Hawley Harvey Crippen, who was fleeing murder charges in England. Dew used the *Laurentic*'s speed to his advantage, reaching Canada before his escaping quarry. There, Dew boarded the SS *Montrose* disguised as a pilot and arrested the astonished Crippen.

▲ Chief Inspector Dew escorts convicted wife-killer Dr. Crippen off the *Montrose*. The *Laurentic*'s speed advantage put the detective in Canada before his quarry.

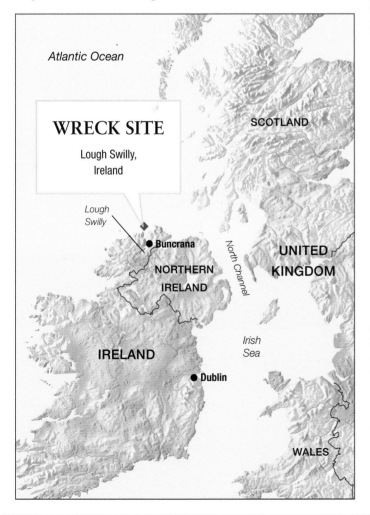

WRECK SITE

Lough Swilly, Ireland

Atlantic Ocean

SCOTLAND

Lough Swilly

● Buncrana

NORTHERN IRELAND

North Channel

UNITED KINGDOM

IRELAND

Irish Sea

● Dublin

WALES

▲ Reaching 164 feet (50 m) deep, Lough Swilly served as a major harbor for the British Royal Navy during World War I, and a boom protected it from U-boat attacks.

KMS *Bismarck*

THIRD REICH LEVIATHAN

The front view of the KMS *Bismarck* must have been a terrifying sight. The largest warship ever built (along with her sister ship, *Tirpitz*), she epitomized the naval component of Adolf Hitler's Third Reich. Measuring 118 feet (36 m) wide, the *Bismarck* bristled with armament, including eight enormous guns measuring 15 inches (380 mm). Her very first mission—and her last—would take her almost 4,000 miles (6,437 km) around the Atlantic. In a cat and mouse game involving aircraft, ships, and shore observers, the Allies tracked the *Bismarck* as she worked her way through fjords and up the coast of Norway before heading to the open Atlantic to attack Allied shipping.

The *Bismarck* and the German heavy cruiser *Prinz Eugen* fought in the Battle of the Denmark Strait on May 24, 1941. The two ships sank the pride of the British navy, the flagship HMS *Hood* in minutes. Another British ship, the *Prince of Wales*, was damaged so severely that she was forced to withdraw from battle. Upon hearing the news, British Prime Minister Winston Churchill channeled the rage of a nation when he famously bellowed, "Sink the Bismarck!"

AND SINK HER THEY DID

The *Bismarck* had received some battle damage from the *Hood* and headed back to Brest, France, for repairs. Two days later, on the night of May 25, the British caught up with her. Nearly antique Swordfish biplanes managed to drop torpedoes but wreaked only superficial damage. The next evening, another fleet of Swordfish from the aircraft carrier *Ark Royal* attacked the *Bismarck*—this time with success. A torpedo jammed the rudder, so the mighty warship could steam only in circles. Hasty repairs enabled the ship to sail straight, but not to turn. The most modern and terrifying ship afloat had been rendered a virtual sitting duck.

With her position known and her steering and propulsion crippled, the *Bismarck* steamed

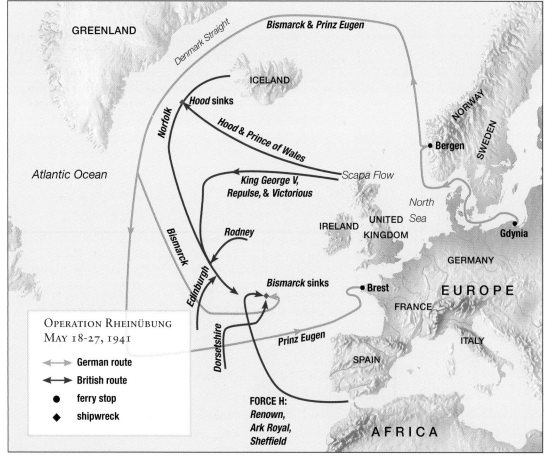

OPERATION RHEINÜBUNG
MAY 18-27, 1941

⟷ German route
⟷ British route
● ferry stop
◆ shipwreck

toward her fate. A flotilla of English battleships, including the HMS *Norfolk*, the *Dorsetshire*, the *King George V*, and the *Rodney* all converged on the *Bismarck*, barraging her with guns, bombs, and torpedoes. The German ship's armor was robust; several English ships used up their complement of torpedoes and shells and returned to port. The *Bismarck*'s superstructure had taken heavy damage, but her hull appeared relatively intact. Nevertheless, after nearly two hours of fighting, the *Bismarck* sank. Allied ships rescued a couple of hundred men but scattered when a German U-boat approached. Of the 2,200 men aboard, 1,995 perished in the sinking. Some reports claim that the *Bismarck*'s captain went down saluting, with the German colors still flying.

The British desperately wanted to believe that they had avenged the sinking of the HMS *Hood*, and the navy denied reports that the *Bismarck* had been scuttled. Decades later, underwater investigation revealed that the German crew had indeed scuttled their ship—her hatches had been opened from within. The *Bismarck*'s crew chose destruction at their own hands over defeat by the enemy.

▲ Two views of the *Bismarck*. The mighty warship was named after the famous nineteenth-century statesman Otto von Bismarck, known as the "Iron Chancellor," who was largely responsible for forging a unified German nation.

HMS *HOOD*

▲ HMS *Hood*, as she appeared in the mid-1920s

THE BRITISH FLAGSHIP HMS *HOOD* reigned as the largest warship in the world until the *Bismarck* dethroned her. Despite her massive hull, she had a weakness. The *Bismarck* gunners lobbed a fused shell so high that it came down almost vertically, piercing the relatively thin decks directly above the ship's ammunition stores. The shot penetrated the decks, entering and then detonating inside the ammunition magazine, sinking the steel behemoth within three minutes. Of the 1,418 crewmen aboard the HMS *Hood*, only 3 survived.

USS *Arizona* | FIRESTORM IN PARADISE

Sunday morning, December 7, 1941, dawned as a typically gorgeous day in Pearl Harbor, Hawaii. The sun rose over the USS *Arizona*, docked with the tender *Vestal* at Ford Island. Just as the sun was clearing the horizon, at 7:55 AM, air raid sirens, shortly followed by a call to General Quarters, pierced the Pacific calm. Moments later, planes from six Japanese aircraft carriers began their bombing runs.

The Japanese raid would soon precipitate the United States' entry into the Pacific Theater of World War II, but that morning in Pearl Harbor, American servicemen were more concerned with immediate survival. Japanese planes pummeled the *Arizona* with eight direct hits, the most devastating at 8:06. The bomb glanced off the second gun turret and detonated on armor that should have protected the ship. But an open hatch allowed the explosion to start a chain reaction that penetrated the black-powder magazine and then detonated the far more powerful smokeless powder supply. The resultant blast effectively destroyed the *Arizona*, pelted

▲ A Japanese photograph taken during the attack shows smoke already rising in what would become one of the most infamous days of American history.

▲ The USS *Arizona*, crippled by fire and sinking as she burned, after the Japanese bombing attack on the ships in the harbor

adjacent Ford Island with burning shrapnel, and launched a fireball high in the air. The fire burned for two days, sinking the great ship in her berth. Despite heroic fire-fighting and rescue efforts, 1,177 men lost their lives on the *Arizona* that beautiful Sunday morning in paradise.

A DATE THAT WILL LIVE IN INFAMY

The *Arizona* was built in the Brooklyn Navy Yards and commissioned in 1916. The massive super-dreadnought battleship began service just as the United States entered World War I. The scarcity of fuel oil in Europe kept the *Arizona* stateside during the war, but, over the next two decades, she patrolled Central and South America, transiting the newly constructed Panama Canal several times to cruise the Pacific. She became the flagship of Admiral Chester Nimitz (later to command the entire Pacific Fleet) and underwent several major overhauls during this period, acquiring modernized guns, communications, and fire control gear.

The Japanese raid on Pearl Harbor sank five battleships, two destroyers, and several support ships; many more were damaged. Scores of aircraft and vehicles burned or exploded, and more than 2,000 people perished.

LIFEBLOOD

AS THE REMAINING HULL OF THE *ARIZONA* sits on the harbor bottom, supporting only the chapel and memorial in lieu of a superstructure, both the ship and her surviving crew live on. Almst 70 years after her sinking, the great ship still emits oil—about 1 quart (1 liter) a year. Legend holds that this will continue as long as any of her crew still live. According to popular belief, the *Arizona* is showing her bond of solidarity with those who served her by oozing just a little bit of the ship's blood into the sea. To the chagrin of some, the U.S. Park Service, which oversees the wreck, is currently planning abatement measures to accommodate modern environmental sensibilities.

▶The USS *Arizona*, visible in the clear Hawaiian waters, now supports her own memorial, which tourists can only visit by boat.

After the USS *Arizona* sank onto the shallow, flat bottom of Pearl Harbor, her guns were transferred to shore emplacements. The sunken hulk was sheared off at the waterline, leaving only a single turret above water. The underwater hull sits in place as a memorial, visible through the clear water. A gleaming white chapel now straddles the sunken hull, giving visitors a place to remember and celebrate the sacrifice of so many sailors, airmen, and soldiers. Their names are engraved in marble above their grave, a rusting hull in the sparkling azure waters of Pearl Harbor.

▲ The USS *Arizona* burns. Reaction to the loss of ships and lives during the unprovoked attack on Pearl Harbor catapulted the United States into World War II.

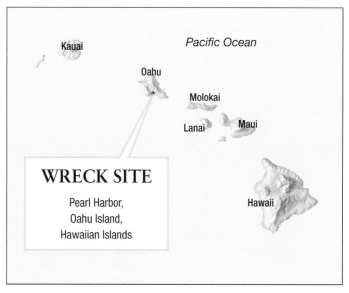

Pacific Ocean

Kauai

Oahu

Molokai

Lanai   Maui

Hawaii

WRECK SITE

Pearl Harbor,
Oahu Island,
Hawaiian Islands

MV *Wilhelm Gustloff* — THE WORLD'S DEADLIEST MARITIME DISASTER

▲ The *Wilhelm Gustloff*, serving as a hospital ship in 1939. In the confusion surrounding the end of World War II, the ship's demise went largely overlooked.

Refugee families huddled in the MV *Wilhelm Gustloff* as she pitched through the turbulent, icy Baltic in January 1945. Though the passage was sickening, the alternative was worse—mayhem or death at the hands of World War II Soviet troops, which had now overtaken all of East Prussia (present-day Poland and Lithuania). The sea promised the only hope of escape, so the refugees were grateful even for this poorly maintained, overcrowded hulk. Besides, the trip would be short, and the ethnic German families would soon be back in their homeland, war-torn though it was.

Tragically, most of the passengers and crew would never see dry land again, instead perishing in the worst maritime disaster in history—and one that remains largely unknown. The fog of war has obscured the fate of the approximately 9,500 men, women, and children who died in the wreck of the *Wilhelm Gustloff*. For in addition to the thousands of civilian refugees, the *Gustloff* was also carrying Nazi troops and wounded soldiers. She flew the colors of Hitler's Third Reich, and her military status made her fair game for the enemy—in this event the Soviet submarine *S-13*. Civilian families paid heavily for this association in what became history's deadliest shipwreck.

WHO'S IN CHARGE?

At 684 feet (209 m), the *Wilhelm Gustloff* was originally designed as a pleasure cruiser for only 1,500 passengers. But in wartime, and with such a pressing need for evacuation, the ship carried 10,582 passengers and crew when she departed Gotenhafen (present-day Gdynia, Poland) on January 30, 1945. Only one torpedo boat, the *Löwe*, escorted the *Gustloff*, after two other convoy boats encountered technical problems.

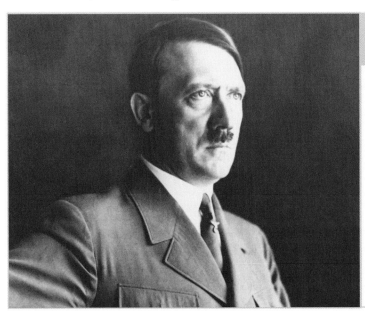

SWAN SONG FROM THE FÜHRER

WITH GERMANY'S POSITION on both Eastern and Western Fronts clearly crumbling, and Allied victory in Europe only months away, Adolf Hitler gave a radio address to his loyalists on the evening of January 30, 1945—the 12th anniversary of the Nazi Party's ascent to power. Aboard the *Wilhelm Gustloff*, the sound system broadcast the Führer's hour-long speech, which ended at 9:00 PM. Minutes later, the first Soviet torpedo struck the *Wilhelm Gustloff*.

◄ Adolf Hitler led the Nazi party to power and, subsequently, the world to war. He ruled Germany as a dictator from 1933 to 1945.

Onboard the *Wilhelm Gustloff,* the chain of command was unclear. Four captains were aboard—three civilian, one military. The passage along the southern coast of the Baltic was heavily mined, and Soviet subs were a prime threat. One shipping lane was supposed to be mine-free, and military Commander Wilhelm Zahn guided the ship into this lane. But Captain Friedrich Peterson feared a collision with minesweeper ships and gave a fatal command: he ordered the *Wilhelm Gustloff's* running lights illuminated.

Captain Alexander Marinesko of the Soviet submarine *S-13* had been tracking the *Wilhelm Gustloff* for hours; now he had his target in sight. Marinesko fired three successive torpedoes, striking the *Wilhelm Gustloff* on the portside fore, amidships, and aft—the final shot obliterating the engine room and the ship's power along with it. The overcrowded ship listed to starboard. Panic ensued as water rushed in; many passengers and crew were trapped belowdecks. Those above fared no better— the deck was iced over in the frigid weather, and passengers plunged to their deaths. Rescue boats arrived but were only able to save about 1,000 people—a large number by any measure, but only a fraction of the thousands of souls who perished in the Baltic Sea.

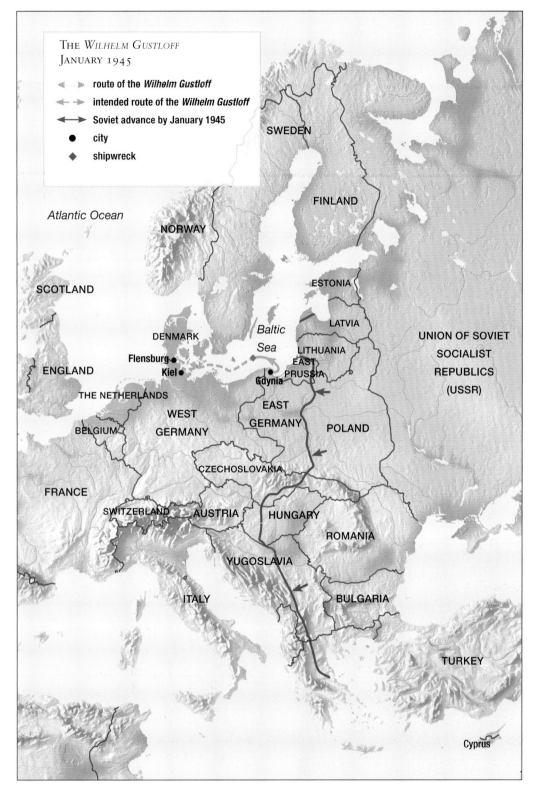

THE *WILHELM GUSTLOFF*
JANUARY 1945

◁ ▷   route of the *Wilhelm Gustloff*

◁-- --▷   intended route of the *Wilhelm Gustloff*

◀━━▶   Soviet advance by January 1945

●   city

◆   shipwreck

USS *Indianapolis*

SECRET MISSION, SILENT DEMISE

The heavy cruiser USS *Indianapolis* (CA-35) served her country like a prizefighter during World War II. She assisted at some of the most important battles and strategic operations in the Pacific, from the Battle of Iwo Jima to the capture of Okinawa. On March 31, 1945, during the assault on Okinawa, a Japanese fighter plane bombed the *Indianapolis*. The damage killed nine, but the cruiser pulled through, hobbling across the Pacific to San Francisco for repairs. The *Indianapolis* still had work to do, and she reported back for duty on what was to be her final mission: a top-secret delivery of uranium-235 and other parts for the atomic bomb "Little Boy," which would soon decimate Hiroshima.

Because of the secrecy of her mission, the *Indianapolis* traveled at top speed and without escort from Pearl Harbor to the island of Tinian, the site from which both atomic bombs would be carried and dropped on Japan. After delivering her cargo, the ship continued to Guam, and from there sailed for Leyte, in the Philippines. She was never to reach her destination. Just after midnight on July 30, 1945, two torpedoes from a Japanese submarine struck the USS *Indianapolis*. In just 12 minutes, she sank into the Pacific.

LEFT TO DIE

Three hundred men died in the initial blast onboard the *Indianapolis*, while some 900 were plunged into the dark Pacific Ocean. The men had no lifeboats, but many of them wore life jackets, and some had managed to cut loose rafts before their ship went down. Help, they expected, would soon

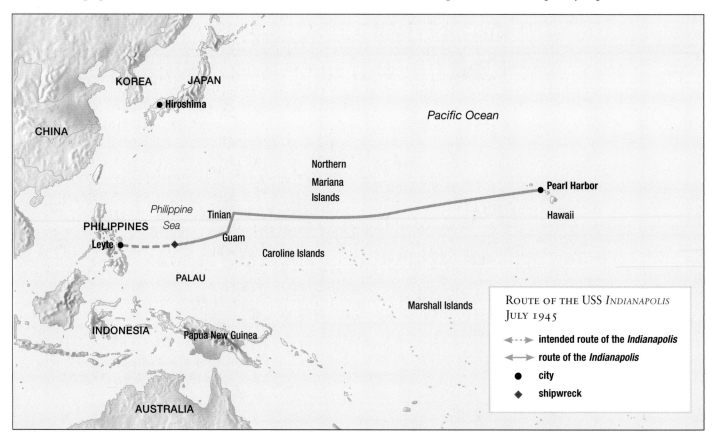

be on the way—operators on the cruiser had sent out three separate SOS calls from their sinking ship.

Help did not arrive, but sharks did. By daybreak the waters were teeming with them, and they attacked both the living and the dead. Still, the men expected rescue imminently.

FLOTSAM & JETSAM

On the morning of July 16, 1945—the same day the *Indianapolis* departed on her secret mission—scientists detonated the world's first atomic bomb outside Alamogordo, New Mexico.

After four and a half days, a U.S. patrol plane chanced to fly over the wreck site, and seeing the desperate men in the water, radioed a report. Finally, rescue boats and planes arrived, one plane even strapping survivors to its wings in a desperate rescue attempt. Of the 1,196 aboard the *Indianapolis*, only 316 survived. The rest were taken by sharks, starvation, or dehydration, or they died of their wounds as they waited in vain for their navy's response.

▲ Survivors, in Guam, are transported on stretchers to waiting ambulances.

THE *INDY*'S FINAL VICTIM

ON THE NIGHT THE *INDIANAPOLIS* SANK, American officials intercepted a Japanese report of an enemy ship sunk along the route of the cruiser. No action was taken. The SOS calls were reportedly received but ignored; one officer was drunk, one was indisposed, and the third wrote off the call as a prank. The officer tracking the *Indianapolis* in Leyte noted that the ship had failed to arrive, but he took no action. The navy initially claimed that a rescue mission would have compromised the ship's secret task, but later declassified documents revealed that the real failure was simply deadly neglect.

Instead, the blame fell on the ship's captain, Charles Butler McVay, who was court-martialed for "failing to zigzag"—a tactic used to elude submarines. Congress posthumously exonerated McVay in 2000; sadly, the weight of guilt had led him to commit suicide in 1968.

▲ The USS *Indianapolis* at Pearl Harbor, Hawaii, in a photograph taken around 1937

ARA *General Belgrano*

CONFLICT AT THE BOTTOM OF THE WORLD

The stormy waters of the Southern Atlantic tossed the ARA *General Belgrano* around on May 2, 1982—routine conditions for the Argentine navy cruiser. But this was wartime, when any routine patrol could end in violence. Earlier that year, on April 2, Argentina had invaded the remote Falkland Islands, considered British territory. Although neither Britain nor Argentina ever officially declared war, the Falklands Conflict was very serious business indeed for those involved.

A month into the conflict, the British submarine HMS *Conqueror* prowled the same stormy waters, in the stillness of the deep. Her captain, Chris Wreford-Brown, had been shadowing the *General Belgrano* for more than a day and had relayed his quarry's moves all the way up the command chain.

TIT FOR TAT

TWO DAYS AFTER the loss of *General Belgrano*, it was Argentina's turn to prevail. England lost the HMS *Sheffield* destroyer to an aerial attack. Though the Argentine Air Force only had five air-launched Exocet homing missiles, they used one to destroy the *Sheffield*. Twenty crew members were killed in the attack, though accompanying ships were able to rescue the bulk of the crew safely. As rescuers towed her to safety, the *Sheffield* burned and sank.

▲ The *General Belgrano* sinks in the South Atlantic Ocean surrounded by orange life rafts holding survivors.

On May 2, Prime Minister Margaret Thatcher herself ordered the *Conqueror* to fire upon *Belgrano*. Shunning the latest electronic torpedoes onboard for their reliability problems, Wreford-Brown fired three nearly antique mechanical Mk8 Mod4 torpedoes at the Argentinian cruiser. Two of them hit and detonated—one sheared off the bow of the *General Belgrano*, while the other pierced her hull and exploded in the engine room. This second blast was strong enough to blow a hole upward, clear through two mess halls filled with sailors and out the multiple decks above the engine room. A total of 275 men are thought to have died from the impact; eventually 323 would give their lives. With the ship filling with smoke and beginning to sink, Captain Hector Bonzo gave the command every sailor loathes: "Abandon ship!" The men began an orderly retreat to bright orange inflatable life rafts, which fanned out over the gray sea as the *General Belgrano* listed and sank beneath the stormy waters of the South Atlantic.

A LASTING IMPACT

The sinking of the *General Belgrano* had a number of effects on the Falklands Conflict. More than half of Argentina's eventual casualties occurred that day, and Argentina's navy lost its taste for the fight. Within a week, virtually the entire fleet put into harbor and stayed there for the remainder of the conflict, leaving the British navy to dominate the arena and operate without threat. The attack also had political ramifications because Argentina claimed that the *General Belgrano* had been retreating from the conflict area when attacked. The British chain of command insisted that the *Belgrano* was a legitimate target no matter what direction it was traveling. Nevertheless, the Argentinian government and public expressed outrage at the sinking, sparking a bout of nationalist fervor that continued for decades. Argentina's forces were compelled to retreat, and though hostilities ended and the British reasserted actual control of the islands, Argentina continues to claim the Falklands as its own.

▲ As the first woman to serve as prime minister, Margaret Thatcher guided Great Britain through the Falklands Conflict.

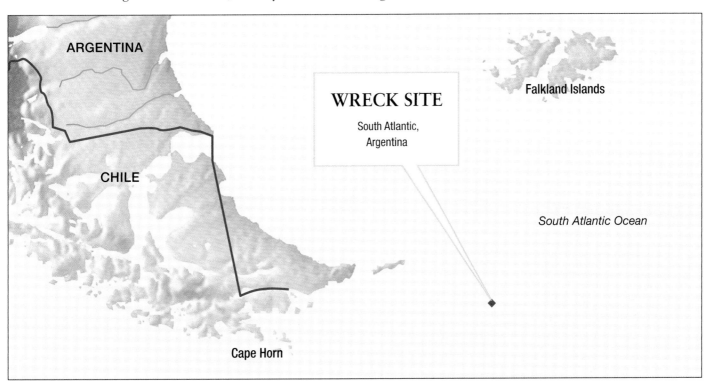

ARGENTINA

CHILE

WRECK SITE

South Atlantic, Argentina

Falkland Islands

South Atlantic Ocean

Cape Horn

6 · MYSTERY!

▲ *Dutch Boats in a Storm* by J. M. W. Turner, 1801

The *Santa Maria*

LOST SHIPS OF COLUMBUS

▲ A colored engraving depicts Columbus's 1492 departure for the New World. The explorer stands with one foot in a boat as he bids farewell to his benefactors, Queen Isabella and King Ferdinand of Spain. Beside them, a priest bequeaths his blessing to the endeavor.

most dedicated scholars and explorers have attempted to locate her remains, no one has ever identified the wreck site. The resting place of this most iconic of ships remains a mystery of the deep.

Of the three ships in Columbus's 1492 expedition (three more expeditions would follow), the *Santa Maria* was the largest, at approximately 70 feet (21 m) long, and carried square-rigged fore- and mainmasts and a lateen-rigged mizzenmast. A *nao* with a rounded hull, she was cumbersome and slow compared with the sprightlier carracks in her fleet of three. As the trio's flagship, the *Santa Maria* carried 40 of the 90 men in Columbus's first expedition.

Sailing south from Palos, Spain, and then

Every American schoolchild knows the year Columbus sailed the ocean blue. Each of them also know the names of the three ships that sailed in 1492—the *Niña*, the *Pinta*, and the *Santa Maria*. Less well known, however, is that *Santa Maria de la Immaculada Concepción*, as she was formally known, was shipwrecked off the coast of present-day Haiti. Though centuries of the best technology and the

west from the Canary Islands off the coast of Africa, Columbus was convinced he would eventually reach the east coast of Asia. Most educated people of the day believed that the world was round; they simply underestimated the size of the planet and overestimated the size of Eurasia. So Columbus promised his patrons, King Ferdinand and Queen Isabella of Spain, a speedy return, with his ships loaded with spices, silks, and gold.

THE NEW WORLD

After 33 days of sailing, Columbus's ships reached the Bahamas, then the north coast of Cuba, and proceeded to the island of Hispaniola (present-day Haiti and the Dominican Republic). There, according to Columbus's own journals, the crew engaged in several days of friendly interaction with the native Taíno people. On a calm Christmas Eve, the captain left a boy in charge of the tiller and turned in for the night. As the crew slept, the gentle swells drove the *Santa Maria* onto a reef, somewhere between present-day Cap-Haïtien and Caracol.

With his two remaining boats, and the help of Taíno people in dugout canoes, Columbus and his men salvaged a good portion of the timber from the *Santa Maria*. They constructed a fort on the shore and, because it was Christmas Day, named it *La Navidad*, or "The Nativity." There was not enough room on the remaining ships, so 39 men stayed behind. Columbus pledged to return, and the *Niña* and the *Pinta* sailed for Spain.

▲ Columbus claiming the New World for Spain

▶ An astrolabe from 1537. Mariners, geographers, and astronomers have used astrolabes since about the third century BCE. Although he relied chiefly on dead reckoning to plot his course, Columbus carried an astrolabe on his first voyage. The astrolabe was a complete circle of metal with a moving arm that a navigator would sight along to find a star's altitude. Bad weather thwarted Columbus's one attempt to use the astrolabe, and he never tried it again.

DEAD RECKONING

CHRISTOPHER COLUMBUS NAVIGATED HIS WAY across the Atlantic Ocean, through the West Indies, and back again using a combination of rudimentary tools—including a compass and a half-hour glass—and a hefty dose of intuition. Mostly, he plotted his course based on his speed and his estimated distance traveled from a known point, which was determined by the amount of time elapsed. Columbus plotted his course hourly and noted the findings in a detailed log. This method of navigation is known as dead reckoning. Some historians believe that Columbus used celestial navigation as well, with such tools as quadrants and astrolabes, which help determine latitude using the North Star as a guide.

The *Santa Maria* CONTINUED

WRECK OF THE FIRST TREASURE FLEET

IN 1502, AS COLUMBUS ARRIVED in the New World for the fourth time, he was denied entry to the port at Santo Domingo. The colonial governor of Hispaniola, Nicolás de Ovando, was preparing a fleet laden with gold and other treasures to depart for Spain. Ovando despised Columbus for political reasons and denied him entry into the port. Columbus took shelter in a nearby inlet, warning Ovando of an approaching storm, and counseling him to delay his fleet's sailing. The governor ignored Columbus, and the fleet of 30 ships set sail under darkening skies. All but one of the ships were destroyed.

SEARCHING THROUGH THE CENTURIES

When Columbus returned to Hispaniola in 1493, not a trace of the fort or his men was to be found. The structure had been burned and the men killed. Historians differ as to whether it was the Taíno themselves or the natives of other islands who turned against the Europeans. Columbus reportedly found one of the *Santa Maria*'s anchors, but neglected to make detailed notes as to its location. This oversight has baffled researchers, who, nevertheless, have made a near science of attempting to locate the wreck.

Several explorers made attempts to find the *Santa Maria* in the sixteenth century and again in the eighteenth century. But the search didn't really heat up until the twentieth century. Beginning in the 1930s, historian Samuel Eliot Morison retraced Columbus's four voyages and narrowed the possible wreck site down to a stretch of 14 miles (23 km). In 1962, Robert F. Marx, described by his peers as the "father of underwater archaeology," reenacted the journey of the *Niña*, a dramatic feat, but not one that yielded artifacts.

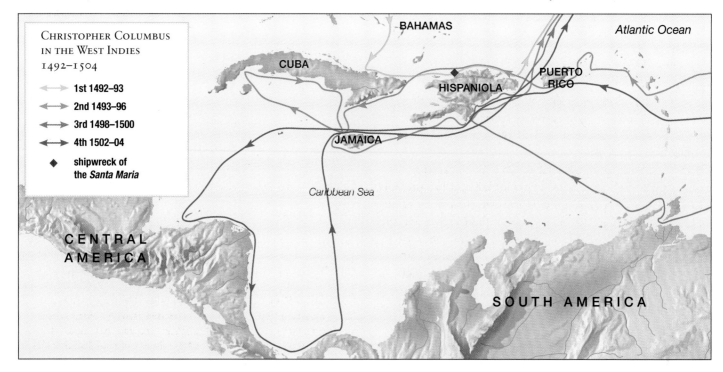

CHRISTOPHER COLUMBUS IN THE WEST INDIES
1492–1504

→ 1st 1492–93
↔ 2nd 1493–96
↔ 3rd 1498–1500
↔ 4th 1502–04
◆ shipwreck of the *Santa Maria*

BAHAMAS
Atlantic Ocean
CUBA
HISPANIOLA
PUERTO RICO
JAMAICA
Caribbean Sea
CENTRAL AMERICA
SOUTH AMERICA

From the 1960s until his death in 1972, explorer Fred Dickson found numerous artifacts on the coast of Haiti that date from the period of Columbus—including a tooth from a Spanish pig, a bone from an old-world rat, and shards of pottery that could have been Columbus's own. Ballast stones, timber, and metal hardware could have belonged to the *Santa Maria* (or to one of the many other ships known to have wrecked in the region). Finally, in 2004, noted underwater explorer Barry Clifford found what he believes to be timber from the *Santa Maria*. He describes the lost ship simply as "the Mount Everest of shipwrecks." The world still awaits positive identification. Until that time, the ruin of the *Santa Maria* remains undiscovered.

▲ Replicas of Christopher Columbus's most famous ships, with the *Santa Maria* in the middle. Although more than four centuries have passed, explorers still hope to find her remains, lost to history and the waters of the West Indies.

MORE JOURNEYS, MORE LOSSES

The *Santa Maria* may carry the most cachet of any undiscovered shipwreck, but she is not the only ship Columbus lost. Indeed, Columbus made a total of four journeys to the New World, and lost nine ships whose wrecks lie mostly undiscovered, dotted around the Caribbean waters of the West Indies.

On his second voyage, from 1493 to 1495, Columbus commanded 16 ships. While at port in Bahia Isabel, present-day Dominican Republic, fierce storms wrecked at least four of these—the *Gallega*, the *Maríagalante*, the *Cardera*, and the *San Juan*. On his disastrous fourth journey, Columbus lost two more ships, another *Gallega* and the *Vizcaína* in 1503 off the coast of Panama. Making his way back to Hispaniola, Columbus was stranded in St. Ann's Bay, Jamaica, for close to a year. Here he lost the *Capitana* and the *Santiago de Palos*. History's most famous explorer, now reviled by Spanish colonists, returned to Europe in a borrowed caravel on November 7, 1504, never to return to the New World.

▲ After months of sailing toward an unknown destination, the crystal waters and verdant shores of the Caribbean must have been more than welcome to world explorer Columbus and his crew. Today, the waters of the Caribbean hide several of Columbus's ships, whose wrecks draw explorers of a different type.

| The *Trinidad* | # CALIFORNIA'S MYSTERY CARAVEL |

▲ A working reconstruction of a square-rigged caravel. They are smaller than carracks, so explorers found them better suited to rivers and other difficult waters.

Legend has long held that an undiscovered sixteenth-century Spanish caravel was wrecked off the coast of Southern California, near San Diego. In the twentieth century, the legend gained new life when several local treasure hunters claimed to have proof of the caravel's remains. Scholars jumped into the fray, some intent on debunking, others hungry for a mystery solved. Although the debunkers seemed to carry the day, the legend of the *Trinidad*, the lost ship of Francisco de Ulloa, still persists.

The conquistador Hernán Cortés became famous as the prime architect of the Spanish conquest of Mexico in the sixteenth century. Explorer Francisco de Ulloa received a commission from Cortés to lead an expedition into the Gulf of California—also known as the Sea of Cortés. The Spanish hoped to discover the legendary Strait of Anián, which they believed led to a northern passage to the Atlantic. No such passage exists, as Ulloa was to discover. But what else did Ulloa discover, and how far north did he travel? Some claim that he turned back to Acapulco, some claim that he was killed in a sword fight, and others claim that he reached present-day San Diego. But none of these theories answers the persistent question: what became of the 35-ton (31 metric tons) caravel called the *Trinidad*, which was never seen again?

THE VOYAGE NORTH

Francisco de Ulloa departed Acapulco in July 1539 with three ships: the *Trinidad*, the *Santa Agueda*, and the *Santo Tomás*. The fate of the *Trinidad*'s sisters is clear—the *Santo Tomás* sank soon after setting off, and the *Santa Agueda* was sent back to Acapulco. Only the *Trinidad* sailed on. Perhaps.

Historians generally agree that Ulloa—who sent regular reports back to Cortés—traveled into the Gulf of California, reaching the mouth of the Colorado River. Failing to find the looked-for marine passage, however, Ulloa retreated along the east coast of Baja California. From there the *Trinidad* rounded the tip of Baja and headed north along the Pacific coast.

The story grows dim at Isla de Cedros, halfway up the coast of Baja. The pilot of the *Trinidad* returned to Acapulco in an open boat, swearing his ship had continued north until

▲ Hernán Cortés. Francisco de Ulloa sailed for Spain under the auspices of Cortés. Historians know little of Ulloa's life or career, which ended in circumstances as murky as those surrounding the loss of the *Trinidad*.

VOYAGE OF THE *TRINIDAD*
1539–1540

← → route of Francisco de Ulloa
● city
◆ *Trinidad* lost

Colorado Desert

Isla de Cedros

Baja Peninsula

Gulf of California

Rio Grande

NEW SPAIN (MEXICO)

Gulf of Mexico

Pacific Ocean

Acapulco

her crew was taken ill with dysentery in August 1540, and evacuated to shore, where most of the crew died. Meanwhile, a storm tore the *Trinidad* from her anchor, and she sank. Adherents to this story believe Ulloa perished with his crew. In 1952, an optometrist in Oceanside, California, discovered gold coins and skulls of European ancestry, allegedly confirmed by experts to date from the sixteenth century. The lost *Trinidad* became the buzz of the treasure-hunting set.

SAYS WHO?

After the 1952 discovery, the debunkers got right to work, quickly uncovering reports that Ulloa was present in Spain in 1543—three years after his supposed death. Other reports surfaced, claiming that Ulloa had been slain in 1540 by a disgruntled, sword-wielding former crew member. The famed treasure hunter Mel Fisher explored the *Trinidad*'s supposed wreck site in the 1980s and announced that he couldn't find anything. But clues continue to feed the legend: a Southern California surfer, for instance, reportedly broke his toe on a jewel-encrusted Spanish gold cross in the 1960s, and at least four groups have organized attempts to locate the wreck since 1968. Perhaps one day, someone will find the *Trinidad*. Or it may remain forever a mystery.

FLOTSAM & JETSAM

Rumors of an antiquated ship buried in the sands of Baja California's Colorado Desert have persisted since the 1860s. Some claim this is the lost *Trinidad*.

▲ The Colorado Desert. Ships wrecked on land are unusual, but not unheard of, as the USS *Wateree* shows (see pages 32–33). The same fate may have befallen the *Trinidad*.

The *Monongahela* | HERE BE DRAGONS

▲ Other sea serpent sightings have similarly captured the public imagination. The crew of the HMS *Daedalus* spotted one of the best-known serpents in 1868, illustrated here from first-hand accounts.

WHAT SORT OF BEAST?

Despite the detailed eyewitness accounts of the sighting, stalking, and killing of the *Monongahela*'s "serpent," it is still not clear what the creature might have been. Bowhead whales, giant squid, and manatees have all been posited as possible sources of sea monster sightings. But the men of the *Monongahela* and the *Rebecca Sims* were seasoned whalemen, unlikely to mistake any of those species for a monster. Jason Seabury, captain of the *Monongahela*, described the sighting thus:

> *The tail and head would occasionally appear in the surging bloody foam, and a sound was heard, so dead, unearthly, and expressive of acute agony, that a shrill of horror ran through our veins.*

Setting off from New Bedford, Massachusetts, on a whaling expedition in the nineteenth century could be compared with attempting a moon landing in the late twentieth. Sailors and astronauts alike would have had small doubt of running into unknown terrors as they headed off over the horizon to the ends of the known world.

When hunting the extremes of the planet in a tiny ship, companionship is a valuable commodity. Thus the whaleships *Monongahela* and *Rebecca Sims* found themselves sailing together mid-ocean in January 1851, having a "gam." This ritual performed between two whaleships of the same home port involved cruising together for a bit while officers dispatched boats to exchange mail, information, and crew members for short visits between the two ships. In the midst of this camaraderie, a lookout sighted the churning white water that marked whale activity. Not even a gam keeps a whaleship from whaling, so both the *Monongahela* and the *Rebecca Sims* launched whaleboats and gave chase.

But the brave boatmen soon realized that they weren't hunting a whale, but something else—something big, mysterious, and wholly dangerous. The *Rebecca Sims*'s whaleboats soon gave up the chase in the freshening squall. The *Monongahela*'s crews were more tenacious and pursued the creature, even as the storm grew into a full gale. After battling the beast for hours, they managed to slay it. It was clear that it wasn't a whale, but the captain knew the value of a genuine sea serpent, so he had it butchered, tried, and rendered. After all the adventure of the chase and kill, the two ships exchanged a final mail and news, and then went on their separate ways. The *Rebecca Sims* sailed home, and the *Monongahela* disappeared over the horizon, never to be seen again.

THE STUFF OF LEGEND

A whaleship vanishing into the arctic or Antarctic waters, where it plied its dangerous trade, isn't usually news. The disappearance of a ship bearing the confirmed and witnessed remains of an actual sea serpent is another story. Though the *Monongahela* never returned to port, the *Rebecca Sims* did. Numerous reliable witnesses aboard the *Rebecca Sims* told identical and plausible tales about the *Monongahela*'s long and dangerous stalking of the mysterious marine beast.

The consistency and detail of the sailors' stories gave them a patina of credibility. This intrigued newspaper and magazine writers and ensured that the tale of the lost sea serpent would spread far and wide. And spread it did, giving the *Monongahela* and her crew fame and admiration even as the ship itself disappeared into legend.

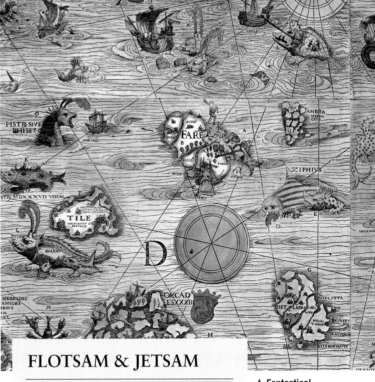

▲ A French ship called the *Alecton* attempted to capture a giant squid, at the time called a sea serpent, in 1861.

FLOTSAM & JETSAM

Maps from the Age of Sail often included images of sea serpents to connote unexplored regions, although the phrase "here be dragons" or similar warnings were actually quite rare.

▲ Fantastical creatures dot the oceans in a marine map of Scandinavia from 1539.

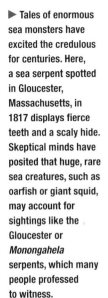

▶ Tales of enormous sea monsters have excited the credulous for centuries. Here, a sea serpent spotted in Gloucester, Massachusetts, in 1817 displays fierce teeth and a scaly hide. Skeptical minds have posited that huge, rare sea creatures, such as oarfish or giant squid, may account for sightings like the Gloucester or *Monongahela* serpents, which many people professed to witness.

The *Mary Celeste* — THE PHANTOM CREW

Ghost ships have long held a treasured place in every ship buff's imagination. These legendary hulks are found floating perfectly sound, with the conspicuous absence of a crew. Perhaps the archetype of all such ships was the *Mary Celeste*, found drifting in the Atlantic Ocean in December 1872. The English cargo ship *Dei Gratia* came upon the *Mary Celeste* in full sail, but on an erratic heading. Nobody was at the wheel.

After two hours of trying to hail the vessel, the *Dei Gratia*'s crew sent a party to board the *Mary Celeste*. What they found began a mystery that remains to this day. The *Mary Celeste*'s hull was sound, masts and sailing tackle in acceptable, if haphazard, condition, and stores properly stowed. She was reported as "a wet mess," with several hatches open to the sea, but she was certainly still seaworthy. The only

▲ Built in 1861 by Joshua Dewis in Nova Scotia, Canada, the *Mary Celeste* first bore the name *Amazon*. The ship immediately seemed cursed, with her first captain dying soon after she set off on her maiden voyage.

oddity was her lack of crew. Also missing were the ship's papers, excluding her log, which noted the last entry several weeks before. A skeleton crew from the *Dei Gratia* boarded and sailed her without incident to Gibraltar Harbor, where the investigation and speculation about the fate of the *Mary Celeste*'s crew began in earnest.

DEAD MEN TELL NO TALES

It was apparent to the bewildered boarding party that the crew of the *Mary Celeste* had left in a hurry, but perhaps not a panic. The yawl had been carefully launched, but not the lifeboat. Ship's papers were missing, but not the log. The rigging was in disarray, certainly not set by a crew intending to leave. And yet the sails were set, and the ship was pointed in the general direction of Gibraltar, her destination.

Theories as to what happened to her crew abounded. Some suspected murder by confederates of the captain of the *Dei Gratia*. But the captains of the two vessels were friends and

were seen dining with their wives in the weeks before their voyages. Others surmised that the crew feared their cargo of alcohol would explode. The images of the empty ship were freakish enough to guarantee the *Mary Celeste*'s place in history, while the literary enhancements over the years only burnished the picture.

Superstitious sailors had long considered the *Mary Celeste* unlucky. After the affair with her missing crew, the curse may as well have been carved in stone. She passed through the hands of no fewer than 17 owners over the course of 13 years after her mysterious discovery. Her last purchaser, one G. C. Parker, schemed to collect a payoff. He deliberately ran her aground on Rochelois Reef off the coast of Haiti and set her afire. Still, the *Mary Celeste* refused to sink, and Parker's fraud was revealed when he claimed the insurance on her non-existent cargo. The burned, wrecked hulk was left to rot. The *Mary Celeste* gradually succumbed to the sea and disappeared into the reef, taking her mystery with her.

A Brig's Officers Believed to Have Been Murdered at Sea.

From the Boston Post. Feb. 24.

It is now believed that the fine brig Mary Celeste, of about 236 tons, commanded by Capt. Benjamin Briggs, of Marion, Mass., was seized by pirates in the latter part of November, and that, after murdering the Captain, his wife, child, and officers, the vessel was abandoned near the Western Islands, where the miscreants are supposed to have landed. The brig left New-York on the 17th of November for Genoa, with a cargo of alcohol, and is said to have had a crew consisting mostly of foreigners. The theory now is, that some of the men probably obtained access to the cargo, and were thus stimulated to the desperate deed.

The Mary Celeste was fallen in with by the British brig Dei Gratia, Capt. Morehouse, who left New-York about the middle of November. The hull of the Celeste was found in good condition, and safely towed into Gibraltar, where she has since remained. The confusion in which many things were found on board, (including ladies' apparel, &c.,) led, with other circumstances, to suspicion of wrong and outrage, which has by no means died out. One of the latest letters from Gibraltar received in Boston says: The Vice-Admiralty Court sat yesterday, and will sit again to-morrow. The cargo of the brig has been claimed, and to-morrow the vessel will be claimed.

The general opinion is that there has been foul play on board, as spots of blood on the blade of

▲ A *New York Times* article from February 26, 1873, offers the theory that pirates slew the ship's crew, but fails to explain why they did not steal the cargo.

▲ The *Mary Celeste* may have run into a gale, but surely the crew would not have abandoned a seaworthy vessel.

◀ Benjamin Briggs, captain of the *Mary Celeste*, disappeared from his ill-fated vessel at the age of 37.

WHAT'S IN A NAME?

THE FATE OF THE *MARY CELESTE* understandably caught the attention of the world. An unknown young author named Arthur Conan Doyle found his interest piqued and penned a fictional tale for the January 1884 issue of *Cornhill Magazine*. Doyle's tale, "J. Habakuk Jephson's Statement," told of a ghost ship found drifting without a crew. As well as adding and enhancing terrifying details, Doyle's ship was known as the *Marie Celeste*, thus forever muddying the waters as to details of the real mystery.

SS *Waratah* | INTO THIN AIR

On her maiden voyage from London in November 1908, the Blue Anchor Line steamer SS *Waratah* made a safe and unremarkable crossing to Australia. Some of the approximately 700 passengers noted a bit too much rolling, but after all, that sort of action is certainly preferable to the jolting sort. In any case, the *Waratah*'s safe arrival soon erased any unpleasant memories. Besides, she was a lovely ship, with fine appointments and a delightful music lounge. She didn't have a wireless, but one can't expect everything.

The British liner's second sailing in April 1909, less than a year later, was equally uneventful. Disembarking her passengers at Melbourne, the *Waratah* proceeded to Durban, South Africa. From there, she would make a quick stop in Cape Town and then steam back to London. *Waratah* departed Durban on July 26, 1909, with 211 passengers and crew aboard. At around 4:00 the following morning, she passed the cargo ship *Clan McIntyre*. This was the *Waratah*'s last recorded contact with the world; she was never seen nor heard from again.

FLAMES, FLARES, AND FALSE LEADS

A number of ships reported seeing strange activity from passing liners shortly after the *Waratah* sailed from Durban. The British freighter *Harlow*'s crew reportedly saw two

FLOTSAM & JETSAM

The *Waratah* was named for the hardy, crimson-blooming shrub that is the state flower of New South Wales, Australia.

▲ A blood-red bloom from a waratah shrub, namesake of the doomed ship

▲ A popular theory explaining the disappearance of the *Waratah* also has some grounding in fact. Some researchers put forth the hypotheses that a rogue wave had overwhelmed the ship, either rolling her over outright or damaging her cargo hatches, allowing water to flood the holds and pull her down almost instantly. Later, a respected South African professor published a paper describing waves of up to 65 feet (20 m) high hitting the area in which the *Waratah* disappeared.

large rocket flares shoot up from a passing ship, followed by total darkness. Another ship, the liner *Guelph*, witnessed a passenger vessel near Durban the night of July 27. Under stormy skies, the *Guelph* used a signal lamp to contact the passing vessel. The reply was unclear, but the final letters seemed to spell out T-A-H.

On July 29, 1909, the *Waratah* was expected in Cape Town. The ship never arrived. Two ships were dispatched to search the surrounding waters for the missing liner, but came back empty-handed. In the year following the *Waratah*'s disappearance, numerous searches—including one that combed 14,000 square miles (36,260 sq. km) of water—returned with no clues. Reports and rumors ran wild. Paranormal explanations vied with the practical (a freak wave), the plausible (a whirlpool), the improbable (methane gas upwelling), and the grimly mundane: perhaps a storm-tossed, rudderless *Waratah* had drifted off into Antarctic waters, those aboard dying of cold and starvation.

A century of searches has turned up nothing conclusive. One team headed by Emlyn Brown searched for 22 years. In 1999, they located a likely wreck at the mouth of the Xora River, but a 2001 underwater search revealed that the wreck dated from World War II.

▲ The *Waratah* steams along the Indian Ocean.

EXPERT TESTIMONY?

BRITISH ENGINEER Claude Sawyer gained fame after the disappearance of the *Waratah* as the passenger who had disembarked the doomed ship. Upon arriving at Durban, he cabled home to his wife, "Thought *Waratah* top heavy, landed Durban."

Sawyer later testified at the inquest in London, recalling the nightmares and premonitions that had plagued him while aboard the ship. In one instance, he envisioned the steamer being struck by a huge wave, rolling to starboard (the actual direction of her customary list) and capsizing. Sawyer also described a vision of a man "in peculiar dress" brandishing a long, bloody sword. Whether such visions discredit Sawyer or bolster paranormal theories is a matter of personal opinion.

London

EUROPE

ASIA

AFRICA

Indian Ocean

Atlantic Ocean

Pacific Ocean

AUSTRALIA

Durban

Cape Town

Melbourne

ROUTE OF THE SS WARATAH, C. APRIL 1909

◀----▶ intended route of the SS *Waratah*

◀——▶ route of the SS *Waratah*

● city

◆ shipwreck

SS *Tubantia* SUNKEN TREASURE?

▲ The SS *Tubantia* was built as a fast mail and passenger steamer for service between the Netherlands and South America.

The Atlantic Ocean during World War I was a place of danger. When the SS *Tubantia*, a ship sailing under the neutral flag of the Netherlands, was torpedoed and sunk on March 16, 1915, the first mystery was who had hit her. Despite strenuous denials from the German government, the remnants of a German torpedo from U-Boat *UB-13* embedded in one of the *Tubantia*'s lifeboats solved that question quickly. Further efforts of the Germans to distance themselves from the sinking of a neutral vessel failed; the condition of the wreck and eyewitness reports contradicted the Germans' story. (Their far-fetched claim was that the torpedo had been fired weeks before and merely drifted into *Tubantia*'s path.)

Astonishingly, there had been no loss of life in the sinking, and after much politically charged diplomacy, the German government took responsibility for the loss of *Tubantia* and paid reparations to the Dutch. And here is where the story might have ended, if not for the oddly extensive attention paid the wreck. Over a period of months, which then turned into years, a series of multinational dive teams made repeated and intensive dives on the wreck of the *Tubantia*. What could possibly have prompted such interest?

GOLD IN THE CHEESE

The Dutch liner *Tubantia* was constructed in 1913 as a fast and luxurious liner, able to deliver mail with the utmost speed and passengers with the utmost comfort. Early adoption of electricity for everything onboard, from lighting and ventilation to personal cigar lighters in every stateroom,

LET THERE BE LIGHT

AT ANCHOR 58 MILES (93 km) from the Dutch coast, the *Tubantia* illuminated nearly every light she had, relying on her blazing presence to inform even the most ardent submarine attackers of her identity. When the tactic failed and a German torpedo struck the *Tubantia*, three ships in the vicinity—the *Breda*, the *Krakstau*, and *La Campine*—immediately interceded. Thanks to the alert crews of these ships, there were no casualties.

heralded the state-of-the-art character of *Tubantia*. Her electric lights, including an enormous illuminated sign spelling out her name, were touted as an additional safety feature. It was thought that by highlighting the ship and her flag, both German and Allied attackers would see her neutral status and eschew attacks. The attempt to attract passengers during those dark days of underwater wolf packs largely failed; one reason *Tubantia*'s sinking avoided casualties is that there were so few passengers onboard. Fear of wartime attacks, neutrality notwithstanding, kept most people away—wisely, as it turned out in the *Tubantia*'s case.

In 1922, mere weeks after the Dutch government had given up salvage rights to the *Tubantia*, a multinational group of divers began to investigate the wreck. The mystery began to intrigue observers as the dive team stayed on site from May until stormy seas and weather shut down operations in November. As soon as the weather eased the following spring, the dive operation began again. All its strenuous underwater labor, including underwater demolition, merely yielded a hold full of Dutch cheese. Rumors immediately began that the cheese somehow concealed gold bullion, being hidden from the prying eyes of German and Allied customs inspectors. These rumors proved false, however, because both the original multinational dive team and subsequent Italian teams all failed to salvage much of value. Though the pull of Edam or Gouda can be strong, it seems safe to say that the mystery of the *Tubantia*'s cheese may never be solved.

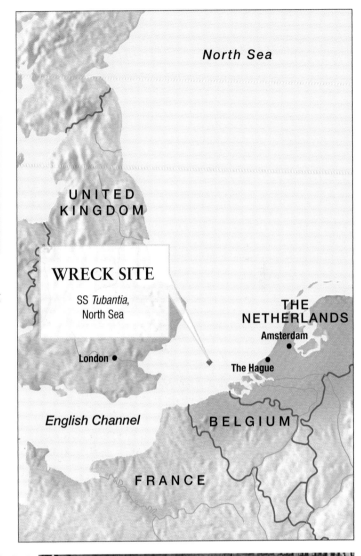

WRECK SITE

SS *Tubantia*,
North Sea

North Sea

UNITED KINGDOM

THE NETHERLANDS

Amsterdam

London

The Hague

English Channel

BELGIUM

FRANCE

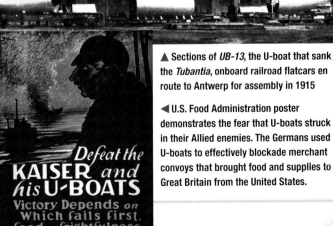

▲ Sections of *UB-13*, the U-boat that sank the *Tubantia*, onboard railroad flatcars en route to Antwerp for assembly in 1915

◄ U.S. Food Administration poster demonstrates the fear that U-boats struck in their Allied enemies. The Germans used U-boats to effectively blockade merchant convoys that brought food and supplies to Great Britain from the United States.

Defeat the KAISER *and his* U-BOATS
Victory Depends on Which fails first, food or frightfulness

SS *Carroll A. Deering* | MYSTERY SHIP

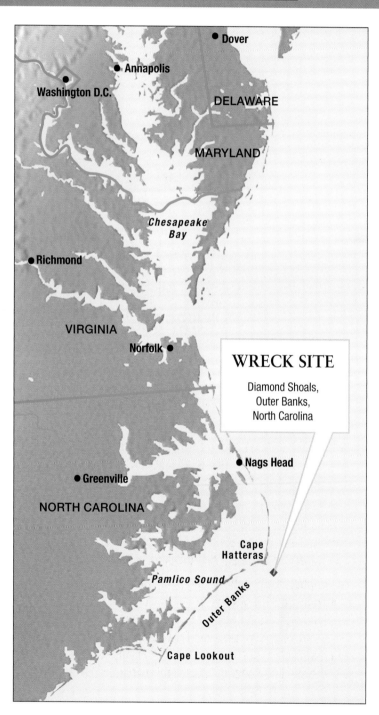

WRECK SITE

Diamond Shoals,
Outer Banks,
North Carolina

The five-masted schooner *Carroll A. Deering* turned south out of Norfolk, Virginia, on September 8, 1920, bound for Rio de Janeiro with a load of coal. Veteran Captain W. B. Wormell had been recruited at the last minute when the regular captain of the *Deering* fell ill. Wormell's first mate, Charles B. McLellan, had also just joined the ship. Together, they commanded a crew of 10 men, mostly Danes, on a routine commercial run down the east coasts of North and South America and then back up.

Routine it seemed, until the *Carroll A. Deering* hailed the *Cape Lookout* lightship off the coast of North Carolina on January 28, 1921. A "thin red-haired man with a foreign accent" reported that the *Deering* had lost both her anchors, but was otherwise in good shape. The lightship's radio was out, so there was nothing her crew could do but note it in the log and wish the *Deering* good luck. The lightship's log also noted the unusual sight of the crew milling around the foredeck. Nothing else seemed amiss, though, until three days later, on January 31, when C. P. Brady of the Cape Hatteras Coast Guard Station spotted a five-masted schooner, run aground on the Diamond Shoals off Cape Hatteras, North Carolina. Heavy seas prevented surf boats from reaching the helpless ship, but four days later, the wrecker *Rescue* arrived, followed soon after by the cutter *Manning*. The *Rescue*'s captain, James Carlson, boarded the ship and confirmed its identity: it was the *Carroll A. Deering*. Her hull and five masts were in good working order, her sails were set, and mealtime preparations were underway in the galley. But all was silent, the wind and waves the only sound. The *Carroll A. Deering* sat eerily empty, her crew having apparently vanished into thin air.

THE CASE OF THE DISAPPEARING CREW

What had happened? Here was a ghost ship in plain sight, with no literary conceits to abate the shock. Investigation into the *Carroll A. Deering*'s condition indicated that the crew had left with some planning. The ship's compass and sextant were missing, along with charts, the log, the anchors, and both lifeboats. All personal belongings had been removed. But where had the crew gone? And why?

The disappearance of the *Deering*'s crew is often lumped in with otherworldly Bermuda Triangle events, but no UFOs are needed to come up with credible theories on the fate of the missing men. Piracy, smuggling, and even communists from New York City were blamed, but mutiny may be the most plausible explanation. First mate McLellan had been overheard discussing mutiny in a sailor's bar in Rio. And it was apparent to the crew of the *Cape Lookout* lightship that no officers had hailed them; the Scandinavian crew appeared to be the only ones onboard. If they had mutinied, retribution came brutally: starvation and death aboard a drifting lifeboat.

Until 1921, the wrecked hull of the *Carroll A. Deering* remained where she had run aground on the shoals. That March, what was left of her was towed away and dynamited. No trace of the ship now survives. And with no one left to tell the tale, the fate of the *Deering* and her crew remains, ultimately, an enigma. The *Deering*'s proximity to the infamous Bermuda Triangle contributed to her mystique. Rum runners, smugglers, pirates, aliens—romantic characters all, but the truth of the *Carroll A. Deering*'s fate is probably much more mundane. With no proof, however, she is sure to keep her place in the annals of famous maritime mysteries.

▲ The *Carroll A. Deering*

▲ The enigmatic *Carroll A. Deering* ran hard aground on the Diamond Shoals. This infamous stretch of water extends many miles out from Cape Hatteras. Although lighthouses and lightships have guarded the shoals since the early nineteenth century, the area is still one of the most dangerous on the Atlantic Seaboard.

MUDDY WATERS

CHRISTOPHER COLUMBUS GRAY, a colorfully named Hatteras local, claimed to have found a message in a bottle on a North Carolina beach:

Deering captured by oil burning boat something like chaser. Taking off everything handcuffing crew. Crew hiding all over ship no chance to make escape. Finder please notify headquarters deering.

The improbable and confusing note was given greater credence when Captain Wormell's wife identified the handwriting as that of the chief engineer on the *Deering*. Eventually, however, Gray admitted the fraud, and the mystery of the *Carroll A. Deering* plunged again into the swirling opaque waters of the Atlantic Ocean.

THE BERMUDA TRIANGLE

NORTH
AMERICA

*Atlantic
Ocean*

Bermuda

FLORIDA

*Gulf of
Mexico*

Cuba

Haiti

Dominican
Republic

Jamaica

Puerto Rico

Caribbean Sea

CENTRAL
AMERICA

THE BERMUDA TRIANGLE

Triangle's boundaries

It was Christopher Columbus himself who penned the first record of odd goings-on off the coast of Florida. The very night before his historic landfall in the New World, the explorer noted abnormal compass variations in his ship's log, and "strange dancing lights on the horizon." Ever since, the triangle of ocean with vertices at Bermuda, Miami, and Puerto Rico has birthed more than its fair share of strange phenomena and bizarre events.

More colorfully known as the Devil's Triangle, this patch of sea has become firmly entrenched in popular culture. Lloyd's of London and the United States Coast Guard both aver that not only is there nothing supernatural about the area, but also that it's not even particularly dangerous. Dozens of books, movies, and magazines would have us believe otherwise. To them and their rapt readers it is a place of bizarre, unexplained, and dangerous phenomena.

FORSAKEN FLIGHT 19

Perhaps the most famous and mysterious occurrence in the Bermuda Triangle was the disappearance of Flight 19, a training flight of five U.S. Navy TBM Avenger torpedo bombers lost in 1945. The pilots were inexperienced, and the weather off the coast of Florida can be unpredictable. Shore listeners picked up odd radio messages, and it did not take long for authors to embellish the tale with supernatural explanations. Still, the fate of Flight 19 has never been satisfactorily determined.

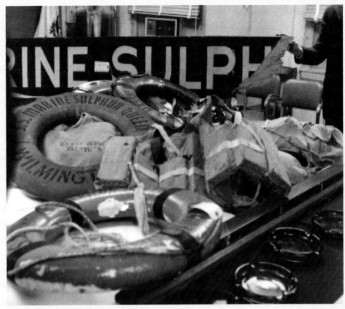

▲ A pile of life jackets, preservers, ash trays, and other odds and ends: the only remains of the *Marine Sulphur Queen* that the Coast Guard could recover

LOST SHIPS OF THE TRIANGLE

Besides the strange condition of the *Carroll A. Deering*, a number of ships have gone mysteriously missing in the Bermuda Triangle. One of them, the USS *Cyclops*, cost 306 lives. A collier leaving Barbados on March 3, 1918, she disappeared without a trace into the mists of the Bermuda Triangle. In February 1963, the *Marine Sulphur Queen* sailed out of Beaumont, Texas, set her course for Norfolk, Virginia, and vanished near the Florida Keys. Disappearances have occurred as recently as 1995, when the *Jamanic K* sailed out of Cap-Haïtien, never to be seen again, and in 2000, when the *Tropic Bird* was found deserted off the West Indies with a log book onboard that cuts off mid-entry. Explanations for these losses range from UFOs to the dangerous currents and whims of the Caribbean Sea. Although there is little agreement about the details, clearly the Bermuda Triangle attracts believers and skeptics alike.

▲ The USS *Cyclops* served as a navy cargo ship during World War I. In January 1918, as part of the war effort, she sailed to Rio de Janeiro, Brazil, to fuel British ships. On her return voyage, she was last seen at Barbados on March 3 and 4. Shortly after that, she disappeared into the Bermuda Triangle, leaving no trace of her 306-member crew or her cargo of heavy manganese. The loss of the *Cyclops* remains the worst noncombat disaster in U.S. naval history.

SS *Andaste*

THE LAKE NEVER GIVES UP HER DEAD

The Great Lakes of North America contain some of the most dangerous waters in the world. Due to particular variations of weather and topology, waves there are more violent and unpredictable than those on the oceans. Lakers that transport bulk cargo have always been at the forefront of marine design, because they cope with the difficult local conditions. During the last decades of the nineteenth century, the vogue focused on "whalebacks." These featured gunwales that curved inward at the top, giving a fully loaded ship the profile of a whale. This design was thought to allow the steep-sided waves common to the Great Lakes to sweep past a ship, rolling gently over the sloping surface rather than slamming into a traditionally vertical face.

A raw materials carrier of semi-whaleback design, the *Andaste* carried up to 3,000 tons (2,720 metric tons) of ore and stone on the Great Lakes. Built in 1892, she had served ably for more than 30 years when new owners installed large cranes atop her decks, enabling her to load and unload cargo at any dock, thus increasing her profitability. These construction changes may well have had the unfortunate effect of unbalancing the ship, making it more prone to roll in the choppy, windy seas of the Lakes.

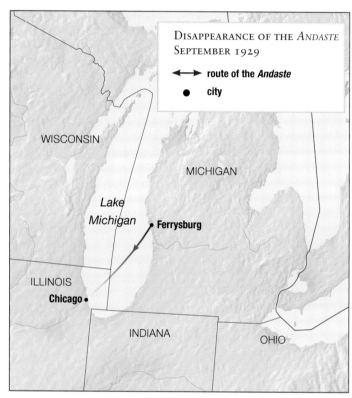

DISAPPEARANCE OF THE *ANDASTE*
SEPTEMBER 1929

⟷ route of the *Andaste*
● city

WISCONSIN

MICHIGAN

Lake Michigan ● Ferrysburg

ILLINOIS
Chicago ●

INDIANA

OHIO

▲ A postcard published in 1900 shows the stately *I. W. Nicholas* passing between its docked compatriots, the squat whaleback *Andaste* (at left) and the schooner *B. L. Pennington* (right). The *Andaste* and the *Pennington* sank in the same year.

The *Andaste* took on a load of gravel the afternoon of September 9, 1929, at Ferrysburg, Michigan, and departed in a freshening gale for Chicago. Overdue by the morning of September 10, the first wreckage began to appear a day later. Sometime in the night, the *Andaste* had sunk in Lake Michigan with the loss of all 25 hands, from 62-year-old Captain Albert L. Anderson to 14-year-old cabin boy Earl Zietlow, on his first Lake voyage. The *Andaste*'s wreck was never found; her fate was never determined.

THE WHY AND THE WHEREFORE

Where and how the *Andaste* wrecked may never be known. Tantalizing clues remain. Fellow ship captains suggest she may have gone down 25 to 30 miles (40–48 km) offshore, which would indicate either inundation by a rogue wave or mechanical trouble. Yet, several local farmers awakened by

RADIO, RADIO

AFTER THE SINKING OF THE *ANDASTE* and loss of all hands without a trace, officials began a blue-ribbon inquest. Though no blame was ascribed to the owners of the *Andaste*, the inquest did result in three far-reaching recommendations for the future. First, all ships would be required to install wireless gear and maintain radio contact with shore stations. Second, a central reporting agency was instituted to receive and act on reports of missing ships. And, finally, a series of rescue stations was established on all of the Great Lakes to attempt to save victims of the deadly local weather conditions.

▲ A whaleback ship, once a common Great Lakes freighter, featured a unique design with a distinctively round hull. This allowed waves to wash over the ship.

▲ The *Andaste* operated on the Great Lakes for the Cleveland Cliffs Iron Company.

▲ Lake Michigan covers 22,300 square miles (57,757 sq km) and reaches a depth of 923 feet (281 m). Its sheer size makes discovering the *Andaste*'s fate unlikely.

the storm in the early hours of September 10 reported seeing ship's lights far too close to shore. In this case, navigation errors or storm winds blowing the ship off course may have caused her to founder on the rocks. The small amount of wreckage, and the bodies that drifted ashore days later, would seem to argue for the former. But Lake Michigan doesn't often give up her secrets, and the fate of the *Andaste* may never be known.

7 · BLAZE OF GLORY

▲ *The Bombardment of Algiers* by Martinus Schouman, 1823

USS *Princeton*

EXPLOSION ON THE POTOMAC

▲ A colored lithograph, published in 1844, depicts the explosion aboard the USS *Princeton*, when the ironically named "Peacemaker" shattered the peace of the Potomac River cruise. The blast killed or mortally wounded 7 and injured about 20 people. Shown at the center of the blast are Representative Virgil Maxcy of Maryland; Secretary of State Abel P. Upshur; Captain Beverly Kennon, Chief of the Bureau of Construction, Equipment and Repair; Secretary of the Navy Thomas Gilmer; and Captain Robert F. Stockton. Maxcy, Upshur, Kennon, and Gilmer were among those killed.

EXPLOSION SITE

USS *Princeton*,
Potomac River,
Maryland

Washington, D.C.

VIRGINIA

Potomac River

MARYLAND

There is a certain point at which making a bigger gun requires more than just making a bigger gun. As the explosive force becomes more powerful, it will eventually surpass the ability of iron to contain it, even if the size of the barrel grows. Captain Robert F. Stockton of the USS *Princeton* learned this lesson at the cost of six lives.

Marine architect John Ericsson designed the *Princeton* as a state-of-the-art test platform. The first warship outfitted with a propeller and coal-fired engine to supplement her three masts, she handily won speed races during her first week of sea trials in autumn 1843.

The *Princeton* had two enormous experimental guns mounted on her deck: the "Oregon" and the "Peacemaker." The Mersey Iron Works of England had designed and built the Oregon by using an untested, but promising, technology of binding the breech of the gun in iron rings. Her 12-inch (300 mm) barrel could project 50 pounds (23 kg) of explosive power 5 miles (8 km) over the horizon.

Hogg and Delamater built the Peacemaker in New York City under the guidance of Captain Stockton, who, perhaps, misunderstood gun-making techniques. Stockton ordered the Peacemaker built with a breech as thick as the Oregon's—but without the strengthening iron bands. This flaw would turn fatal on February 28, 1844, when the Peacemaker exploded in a fireball of molten iron and lead that killed seven people and injured a score more.

MISFORTUNE STRIKES

Captain Stockton had shepherded the construction of the *Princeton* through the labyrinthine congressional and military consignment process, and then through its design and construction. Keen to promote the wonders of his new ship, Stockton showed her off to various denizens of the Green Book of Washington society on a series of lunchtime cruises on the Potomac River. Wednesday saw the culmination of Stockton's publicity tour as he hosted a picnic cruise for some 200 guests, including the president of the United States, John Tyler, and numerous dignitaries.

Whether overtaken by the excitement of the moment or out of hubris, Stockton gave in to entreaties from the gathered luminaries to fire his gun one last time, even as it still glowed hot from the previous blast. The gun exploded as it fired, and the 25-pound (11 kg) charge blasted its fury in all directions. Seven people were killed instantly, among them former New York state senator David Gardiner, Secretary of State Abel Upshur, and Secretary of the Navy Thomas Walker Gilmer.

Astonishingly, Captain Stockton escaped blame for the accident and later went on to be elected senator. The *Princeton* herself served American interests in Europe for five years after the accident on the Potomac. She was scrapped upon the discovery of worms infesting her hull on July 17, 1849.

▲ The USS *Princeton*. Her new design and state-of-the art guns attracted the curiosity of many Washingtonians during the winter of 1844. So high was their interest that the ship made three trial trips with passengers onboard down the Potomac River. During these excursions, the Peacemaker gun was fired several times.

◀ Swedish inventor John Ericsson later designed the USS *Monitor*.

CUPID'S ARROW

ALTHOUGH THE EXPLOSION of the Peacemaker had certainly jarred lovely young Julia Gardiner, her sister, and the other guests belowdecks, it was apparently nothing compared to the announcement of the death of her father, former New York state senator David Gardiner. Upon hearing the grim news, the fetching Miss Gardiner fainted dead away into the arms of the nearest male. Said male happened to be John Tyler, president of the United States—and eligible widower. Kismet struck as Julia awoke to gaze back into the concerned eyes of the shocked president. Four months later, the 24-year-old Julia Gardiner became Julia Tyler when she and the 54-year-old president married in a White House ceremony.

▲ First Lady Julia Tyler. Her father lost his life aboard the USS *Princeton*.

SS *Sultana*

AMERICA'S WORST SHIPWRECK

The waning weeks of the Civil War did not want for drama. Sandwiched between the assassination of President Abraham Lincoln and Confederate General Robert E. Lee's surrender at Appomattox, the fate of the SS *Sultana* never got the notice it deserved. In retrospect, we can now recognize the tragedy for what it was: the worst marine disaster ever to occur in the United States.

The *Sultana* was a side-wheel steam paddleboat that plied the Mississippi River, carrying loads of cotton and livestock between New Orleans and St. Louis. Launched in 1863, the *Sultana* was often put to military use; at 1,720 tons (1,560 metric tons), the ship was large enough to carry troops and supplies when unladen with goods. On her final trip, she carried some 2,400 passengers. When a boiler exploded in the wee hours of April 27, 1865, at least 1,700 people perished. Exact numbers are hard to ascertain, but some historians think as many as 2,000 may have died on the dark Mississippi River.

▲ The *Sultana* aflame. Weakened by their ordeal in prisoner-of-war camps, thousands of Union soldiers died.

MISSISSIPPI BURNING

The SS *Sultana* could officially carry 376 people, including her crew. The day of her sinking, thousands of jubilant, recently liberated Union soldiers from Confederate prisoner-of-war camps celebrated onboard. The extra load of passengers and an unusually strong spring current combined to put extra strain on the boilers. If they had been in good working order, the extra load might not have been a problem. The boilers, however, had undergone hasty and insufficient repairs in Vicksburg, Mississippi, where the *Sultana* had taken on her crush of passengers.

For two days, the *Sultana* continued upriver with her load of livestock, sugar, and boisterous ex-prisoners. So crowded was the ship that Captain J. C. Mason feared for her stability. When she docked at Memphis, Tennessee, on April 26, he gratefully unloaded her cargo and several hundred passengers mercifully disembarked. Another patch job on the leaky boiler satisfied the captain enough that he pushed off from Memphis

▲ A photo taken just a day before the explosion shows the overloaded *Sultana*.

around midnight, leaving behind a handful of lucky soldiers who had missed the boat.

It happened at 2:00 AM. The boiler exploded with a fury, sending men, machinery, furniture, and flaming debris flying into the dark river. When the two funnels crashed into the water, along with the ship's superstructure, even those who could swim were crushed into the deep. Many died of hypothermia in the Mississippi River, made frigid by the spring snowmelt. Icy water and searing flames claimed more than 1,000 lives. The conflagration was so enormous that it could clearly be seen in Memphis, some 12 miles (19 km) downriver.

It was not until an hour after the initial explosion went off that the first rescue boat, the steamer *Bostonia II,* arrived. She managed to pick up scores of survivors from the wreck. Still, bodies of victims continued to be found downriver for months, some as far as Vicksburg. Others were gone without a trace. Other vessels soon joined the *Bostonia II* in its rescue attempt, including the steamer *Arkansas,* the *Jenny Lind,* the *Essex,* and the USS *Tyler.* The ships transported about 500 survivors, many of them severely burned or in hypothermic shock, to hospitals in Memphis. Although these Union soldiers had been enemies of the South just weeks earlier, the citizens of the city opened their hearts to the wounded and dying.

THE FORGOTTEN DEAD

RELEASED UNION WAR PRISONERS practically stampeded the USS *Sultana* at Vicksburg. So great were the numbers that the officers delayed taking roll until the *Sultana* was underway. Even then, no one ever made an exact record of passenger names. When the ship caught fire, the hundreds of men cast into the river were largely weak, malnourished, or sick ex-prisoners who had little chance of surviving the strong, icy current. Many who had served their country bravely died anonymously in the Mississippi River.

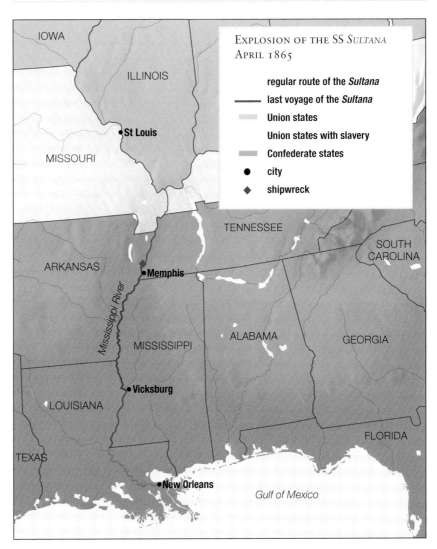

▲ The gunboat USS *Tyler.* During the rescue attempt, volunteers manned the *Tyler.* The U.S. Navy had discharged the ship's regular crew just days before the *Sultana* disaster.

USS *Maine* | "REMEMBER THE *MAINE*!"

The armored cruiser USS *Maine* had been designed and constructed as a test platform for a number of different technologies. When commissioned in September 1895 she and her sister ship, the *Texas*, each incorporated various design differences to test new ideas in nautical architecture. Not all new ideas are good ones, and the *Maine* turned out to be rather bad at both of her assigned tasks: she was too small and lightly armored to compete with battleships, and she was too heavy, slow, and hard to refuel to function as a cruiser. Her experimental arrangement of guns, each offset from the ship's centerline, meant that she was particularly poor at firing both sets of guns broadside, a fundamental flaw in a battleship.

▲ The USS *Maine* steams into Havana Harbor on January 25, 1898, after being dispatched from Key West, Florida. The U.S. government felt that her presence would protect American interests at a time when Cuba was beset by civil disturbances.

▲ The USS *Maine* in Havana Harbor. At the time, tensions not only ran hot between the United States and Spain, but also between Spain and Cuba, which was agitating for independence. In the end, Cuba traded one Western power for another: Spain ceded Cuba to the United States at the end of the Spanish-American War. President Theodore Roosevelt, however, granted Cuba some measure of independence in 1902.

So the *Maine* found herself serving ceremonial roles, such as showing the colors and demonstrating American might in the harbor at Havana, Cuba, as frictions with Spain were increasing at the turn of the twentieth century. At 9:40, on the night of February 15, 1898, two gargantuan blasts shattered the peaceful tropical harbor. The blasts nearly blew off the front third of the *Maine*, and she quickly sank amid further explosions and fire. The timing of the explosions saw most of the *Maine*'s crew either asleep or relaxing, and, despite immediate rescue attempts by nearby vessels and onlookers, 288 sailors and officers died that night in Havana Harbor.

THE MYSTERY OF THE *MAINE*

The explosion of the *Maine* set off parallel blasts in U.S. foreign policy. Immediate blame for the disaster fell to the Spanish. The hawkish cry "Remember the *Maine!*" inflamed public opinion and helped push the country into the Spanish–American War, which began several months after the sinking.

Investigators began trying to determine the cause of the explosion even while the wreck still burned. Though a definitive cause was never pinpointed, two main theories were cited to explain the tragedy: a contact mine explosion, or spontaneous combustion of coal stores, which then ignited the ship's cache of ammunition. Underwater surveys showing a hole in the *Maine*'s hull deformed inward, as if hit by an external force, bolstered the former theory. Details arguing against this explanation include the lack of a waterspout and the dearth of dead fish (both of which commonly appear after an underwater mine explosion) in the harbor. The second, less politically fraught possibility, is that coal in the *Maine*'s fuel bunkers spontaneously ignited, which in turn set off the ammunition stored one uninsulated bulkhead away. Although explosions like this did occur occasionally, both the age and type of the *Maine*'s coal supply argue against the possibility of spontaneous combustion.

Ultimately, what or who sank the *Maine* will probably never be known. But there is no doubt of the results of that tragedy: the loss of 288 sailors' lives that balmy night in the tropics and one brief, but violent, war.

THE LONGEST SHIP

BEFORE THE BULK OF THE *MAINE* was refloated and buried at sea, parts of her were salvaged and mounted ashore as memorials to the men who served and died aboard her. Her foremast is installed in a monument at the U.S. Naval Academy in Annapolis, Maryland, while her mainmast is located 35 miles (56 km) away at Arlington National Cemetery, Virginia. Midshipmen at the Naval Academy joke that this makes the *Maine* the navy's longest ship.

► The mast of the *Maine* crowns her memorial at Arlington National Cemetery.

▲ A Washington, D.C., memorial parade down Pennsylvania Avenue in honor of the victims of the USS *Maine* drew huge crowds of spectators outraged by the tragedy.

▲ A U.S. flag hangs from the mast of the wrecked *Maine*. Sensationalist newspaper coverage of the disaster led to accusations of yellow journalism—a name for the kind of biased reporting that pushes scandals and juicy headlines over evenhanded reporting of issues. Several prominent newspapers took a portion of the blame for inflaming public opinion and pushing the United States into a war with Spain.

The *General Slocum*

INFERNO ON THE EAST RIVER

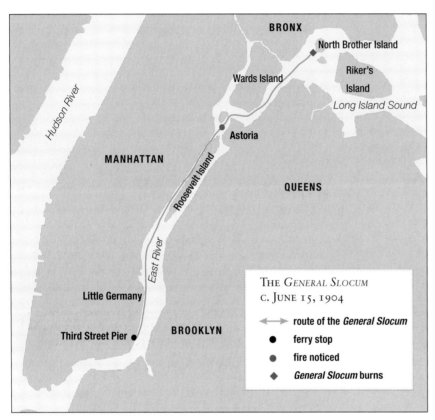

BRONX

North Brother Island

Riker's Island

Wards Island

Long Island Sound

Hudson River

Astoria

MANHATTAN

Roosevelt Island

QUEENS

East River

Little Germany

Third Street Pier

BROOKLYN

THE *GENERAL SLOCUM*
C. JUNE 15, 1904

⟷ route of the *General Slocum*

● ferry stop

● fire noticed

◆ *General Slocum* burns

The day of the annual church picnic was always a festive one for the hardworking immigrants of New York's Little Germany district in Lower Manhattan. In 1904, St. Mark's Evangelical Lutheran Church chartered a ferry for the day of the picnic, June 15. Hundreds of families eagerly boarded the *General Slocum* for a cruise to park grounds on Long Island. China and glassware were carefully packed in straw inside several large barrels. This same straw would later ignite, causing the worst disaster to befall New York City until the terrorist attacks of September 11, 2001.

The morning was fine as the three-deck side-wheel steamer left the East River pier with some 1,400 aboard. Passengers waved to other boats and people on the shore, who gaily waved back. According to historian Claude Rust, whose grandmother perished in the disaster, the mood on shore began to change as the ferry neared Astoria, Queens. Passersby were no longer waving: they were signaling danger, their terrified faces reflecting the knowledge of what few onboard knew: the *General Slocum* was on fire.

THE END OF LITTLE GERMANY

Captain William Van Schaick commanded the *General Slocum* on her final outing. At 30 minutes out, a 12-year-old

▲ A fireboat tries to douse the flames onboard the *General Slocum*, but is too late to save the ship, its passengers, or the neighborhood from which they hailed.

▶ A monument to the *General Slocum* disaster in New York City's Tompkins Square Park. Little Germany once surrounded this Lower East Side park.

boy approached him, shouting, "Hey, mister, the ship's on fire!" Instead of investigating, the captain dismissed the observant lad as a pesky prankster. But soon it was clear—the forward portions of the ferry were ablaze. Passengers panicked, and many jumped overboard as soon as the blaze began to spread.

Captain Van Schaick had to make a decision: steer his burning ship toward the nearby Bronx, landing near an oil refinery in a heavily populated area, or make for North Brother Island, close to Riker's Island. Van Schaick opted for the sparsely populated North Brother Island. His choice only compounded the disaster: winds fanned the flames of the fire during the three-minute passage. The *General Slocum* ran aground bow first, while passengers crowded toward the still-intact bow. Many jumped to their deaths, the majority of these women and children who either could not swim or were drowned by the weight of their heavy clothing. Others were fatally pulled into the still-rotating paddlewheels or were crushed when the three decks collapsed. In all, 1,021 people perished in the *General Slocum* disaster.

Captain Van Schaick was convicted of poor oversight and served several years in prison. The community of Little Germany was shattered by the disaster. Its bonds unraveled, as survivors largely moved to other neighborhoods. The once-vibrant community of immigrants was no more.

▲ Nineteenth-century magazine illustration of emigrants boarding a New York–bound steamer from Hamburg, Germany. German immigration to the United States peaked in the last third of the nineteenth century. Many of them—as with other immigrant groups—settled in ethnically exclusive neighborhoods in New York City.

▲ A contemporary illustration of the *General Slocum*

LIFESAVERS

THE CREW OF THE *GENERAL SLOCUM* could do little to save their ship or her passengers. Through years of neglect, fire hoses simply fell to bits when uncoiled. The lifeboats fared no better; several indifferently applied coats of paint had sealed them onto the ship. The life preservers also proved to be in an unforgivable state of disrepair, their rotted canvas splitting to reveal crumbled cork inside. A few preservers held, and panicked parents strapped these onto their children, throwing them overboard to escape the flames. Relief turned to horror, though, as their children sank beneath the waves; it was later revealed that the life-preserver manufacturers had inserted iron bars to bring the devices up to standard weight.

FIREBOATS

"Water, water, everywhere, nor any drop to drink," reads the classic poem "The Rime of the Ancient Mariner," by Samuel Taylor Coleridge. A boat ablaze faces a similar conundrum—the very thing that will help quell the fire is largely inaccessible. How to press that vast quantity of water into service? Enter the fireboat, a specialized vessel that can pump thousands of gallons of seawater per minute. Firefighters can aim nozzles on deck manually at a burning target.

The first fireboats appeared in the late nineteenth century. Originally built along the tugboat model, fireboats usually span from 80 to 120 feet (24–30 m) in length, with about a 20-foot (6 m) beam. Most have raised control towers, and some feature cranes to aid rescues. In colder climates, these workhorse vessels often do double duty as icebreakers.

SMOKE ON THE WATER

Most fireboats around the world are owned and operated by a maritime branch of a metropolitan fire department. Nearly every major port city employs at least one fireboat, which is used to battle blazes both on ship and on shore. Often, fireboats have the advantage over land-based firefighting equipment. With an unlimited supply of water and a clear vantage point, fireboats can easily extinguish a burning building near a waterfront.

In addition to their firefighting, emergency, and rescue duties, fireboats sometimes perform civilian service as well, participating in municipal celebrations and holidays. With powerful jets of water arcing in spectacular plumes, a fireboat demonstrating its skills is as glorious a sight for onlookers as it is a welcome one for a ship in distress.

▲ Firefighters test out the crane on the *William Lyon MacKenzie*, one of Toronto Fire Services' two fireboats. The *William Lyon MacKenzie* also features an aerial tower, two diesel-driven water pumps, and five nozzles. Toronto Fire Services is Canada's largest fire department.

▲ Rotterdam fireboats display their pumping prowess.

▼ A Dutch fireboat extinguishes the flames on a burning ship in Velsen-Noord.

A HEROIC ENCORE

The *John J. Harvey* was the largest fireboat in the New York City Fire Department (FDNY) and in the world when she was launched in 1931. Named for a fallen hero of the FDNY fireboat fleet, the *Harvey* boasted a length of 130 feet (39.6 m) and a capacity to pump nearly 20,000 gallons (75,690 liters) per minute. She served her city well for six decades under the designation Marine Two, battling such major fires as the 1942 wreck of the grand SS *Normandie.* When she retired from active service in 1995, the *Harvey* would have been sold for scrap had a group of preservationists not stepped in. In 1999, after preliminary restoration, she sailed again. In 2000, the *John J. Harvey* was placed on the National Register of Historic Places.

Then came the events of September 11, 2001. Responding quickly to the terrorist attacks, a small group of the *Harvey's* owners and volunteers spontaneously converged at

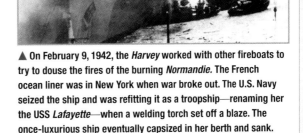

▲ On February 9, 1942, the *Harvey* worked with other fireboats to try to douse the fires of the burning *Normandie.* The French ocean liner was in New York when war broke out. The U.S. Navy seized the ship and was refitting it as a troopship—renaming her the USS *Lafayette*—when a welding torch set off a blaze. The once-luxurious ship eventually capsized in her berth and sank.

their ship and speeded to the fallen World Trade Center. As the old fireboat was evacuating some 150 survivors, the FDNY called her back into service. Reclaiming her old Marine Two moniker, the *John J. Harvey* spent 80 hours pumping water onto the smoldering wreck at Ground Zero. Her heroism, and the dedication of her volunteer crew, earned her an Honor Award from the National Trust for Historic Preservation.

▲ The fireboat *John J. Harvey* salutes the MV *Norwegian Spirit* as the massive cruise ship enters New York Harbor. The *Harvey* served as a New York City Fire Department fireboat from 1931 to 1995. Her owners, who bought her at auction in 1999, restored her and now use her for day trips on the Hudson. She briefly, and brilliantly, returned to service for the FDNY on 9-11, when her owners stepped up to aid in evacuating people from Ground Zero. But she soon got called up for official active service. So many water lines were damaged that day that the FDNY needed her to pump water at the disaster site.

8 · LEGENDS OF THE DEEP

▲ *The Ninth Wave* by Ivan Aivazovsky, 1850

Noah's Ark

WRECKS OF THE OLD TESTAMENT

▲ *Animals Boarding the Ark* by Jacopo Bassano, c. 1579. According to tradition, Noah took two of every species.

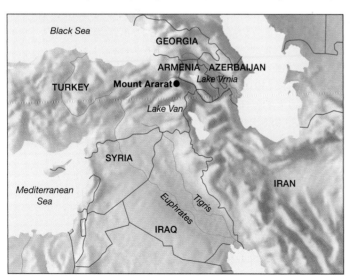

According to Genesis, the first book of the Bible, Noah built an ark as God told him, so that all God's creatures could survive the coming flood. Noah's was the mother of all arks, big enough to hold two of every single species living upon the earth. At 450 feet long, 75 feet wide, and 45 feet high (137 m by 23 m by 14 m), the ark was large enough for three stories of cages, stalls, and stores. The bilges carried food and supplies; the next level up held humans and "clean" animals. "Dirty" animals, along with insects and birds, completed the scene on the top deck (Jewish tradition deemed animals clean or unclean according to dietary laws). All went as God had planned: while he washed the earth clean in a 150-day-long flood, the ark kept the seeds for a new generation of life alive.

None of the beasts starved, reproduced, or ate each other. The number of passengers aboard after six months of floating the desolate aquatic wasteland equaled the number Noah had started with. This, however, was no pleasure cruise for Noah and his family. God's appointed caretaker went without sleep for nearly a year while he tended to the myriad beasts of field and forest. And so it was sweet relief indeed when a dove returned with an olive branch in its mouth, and the ark could at last come aground on Mount Ararat, in present-day Turkey.

LOOKING FOR THE ARK

Jewish and Christian scholars, religious leaders, and adventurers have been trying to verify the story of Noah's ark for thousands of years. Is the tale of Noah's ark a myth—a sacred tale whose truth is not necessarily historical in value—or could it possibly have been true in a more prosaic sense? Several television programs produced in the 1980s used newly developed satellite imaging technology to "find" suspiciously rectangular shapes on Turkey's Mount Ararat. These ostensible photos of shipwrecked remains led researchers to the spot, where they purported to find actual wood and remnants of a stablelike structure. Unfortunately, all of these searches were later revealed to be hoaxes (one hoaxer had cooked wood in a mixture of teriyaki sauce and iodine to achieve that perfect "ancient" patina).

FLOTSAM & JETSAM

The word *antediluvian*, used to describe something very old, literally means "from before the flood." The flood in question, of course, is the one described in Genesis.

▲ The dove flies away from the beached ark, before returning with an olive branch.

BIG FISH STORY

ANOTHER MAJOR NAUTICAL ADVENTURE chronicled in the Christian Bible's Old Testament (the Hebrew Torah) is the story of Jonah and the Whale. While battling a gale on the trip from Nineveh to Jaffa, Jonah's shipmates determined that Jonah himself was the reason for the storm. When Jonah admitted that they were right, they promptly tossed him overboard to appease an angry God. Their action seemed to work, because the storm ceased. But a giant fish (often translated as a "whale") overtook Jonah and swallowed him. During his three days inside the belly of the beast, Jonah prayed and repented for his wickedness. God was pleased, forgave Jonah, and ordered the fish to release the wretched man. Returning to Nineveh a changed man, Jonah became a prophet, as God had previously commanded, exhorting the townspeople to repent.

◀ Jonah's shipmates toss him into the stormy seas.

169

| Ship of Faith | # SHIPWRECK OF THE APOSTLE PAUL |

Few shipwrecks have had as far-reaching effects as the wreck of the Apostle Paul. The first Christian nation was established around 60 CE on Malta after the ship carrying Paul was wrecked on the island's shores. A vivid description of the incident appears in the fifth book of the Christian Bible's New Testament, Acts of the Apostles (often simply called Acts). Scholars largely agree that the chapters describing the wreck (Acts 27–28) have a solid historical foundation.

In the years following his conversion to Christianity, Paul undertook a series of three missions to spread his faith throughout West Asia. In 58 CE, shortly after his third mission, Paul was arrested in Judea by Roman authorities. After being held without trial for two years, Paul pleaded to

be heard by Julius Caesar himself. His request granted, Paul departed Caesarea for Rome in the fall of 60 CE, accompanied by Luke the Evangelist, author of Acts and of the third Gospel of the New Testament. Paul was one of several prisoners the Roman centurion Julius escorted aboard an Egyptian grain ship, which they boarded in early October at Myra (present-day Demre, Turkey).

THE STORM-TOSSED SEA

With fall well underway, travel in the Mediterranean could be unpredictable and dangerous. The prevailing westerlies forced westbound ships to zigzag or tack to their destinations. The captain of Paul's ship accordingly headed southwest

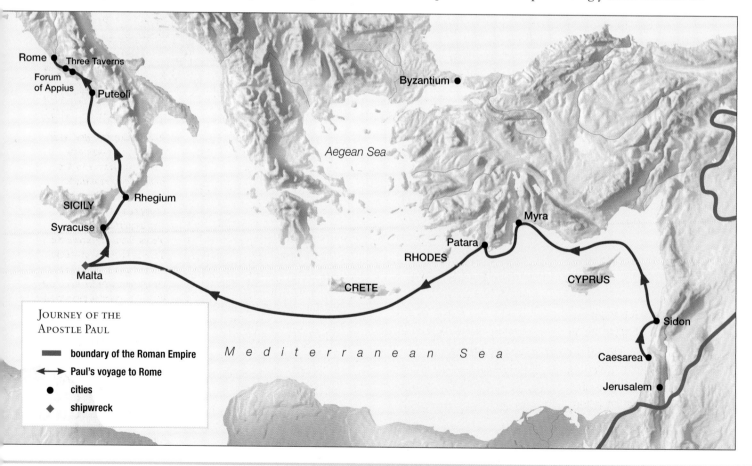

JOURNEY OF THE APOSTLE PAUL

━━ boundary of the Roman Empire
→ Paul's voyage to Rome
● cities
◆ shipwreck

from Myra, which took them along the southern shore of Crete. The ship put in at Fair Havens (present-day Kali-Limones), where those aboard could observe Yom Kippur, the Jewish day of atonement.

Here the weather began to turn bad. According to Luke, Paul counseled the captain to remain in a safe harbor, warning of "injury and much loss, not only of the lading and the ship, but of our lives." (Acts 27:10) But the captain pressed on, hoping to reach a larger port in Crete and overwinter there. A gentle southerly wind beckoned, and Paul's ship set off.

Soon the storm Paul had predicted struck with a vengeance. The gale is described in Acts as *Euraquilo*, a Greek-Latin compound that roughly translates as a nor'easter. The captain decided to allow the ship to drift rather than run ahead of the wind. After three days, the crew began throwing the ship's tackle overboard, terrified of imminent demise. Paul told the 276 men aboard the ship that an angel had assured him that none on board would be harmed—only the ship would be destroyed. According to Paul's vision, the ship would run aground on an island.

On the fourteenth day of the storm, Paul's vision was borne out. The ship was driven to the island of Malta, and ran aground bow first on a sandy beach—present day St. Paul's Bay. The violence of the waves soon broke apart the stern, but all aboard made it safely to shore, either by swimming or by clutching on to the wreckage of the ship.

GOOD GRACES

Paul is said to have performed several miracles on Malta, including healing the father of the local governor, Publius. Malta became the first Christian nation when Publius converted to Paul's faith.

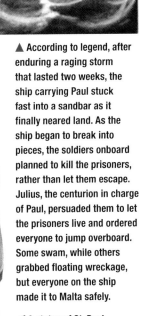

▲ According to legend, after enduring a raging storm that lasted two weeks, the ship carrying Paul stuck fast into a sandbar as it finally neared land. As the ship began to break into pieces, the soldiers onboard planned to kill the prisoners, rather than let them escape. Julius, the centurion in charge of Paul, persuaded them to let the prisoners live and ordered everyone to jump overboard. Some swam, while others grabbed floating wreckage, but everyone on the ship made it to Malta safely.

◄ A statue of St. Paul stands outside St. Peter's Basilica in Rome.

Skuldelev Ships | SECRETS OF THE FJORD

▲ *Havhingsten fra Glendalough* in dock. The *Havhingsten* is a faithful reconstruction of *Skuldelev 2*, the second longest Viking longship ever found.

▶ All five of the Skuldelev ships are on display at the Viking Ship Museum in Roskilde, Denmark. *Skuldelev 2* is an oak-built, sea-going longship, built for war. At about 100 feet (30 m) long and 12.5 feet (3.8 m) wide, she held a crew of 70 to 80 men. This long, slim ship was built for speed and probably reached speeds of up to 15 knots (28 km/h) with a rowing crew of 60. Under sail she could probably move even faster.

At the dawn of the second millennium, Scandinavia was the site of protracted Viking raids—largely the result of conflict between Denmark and Norway. The Danish capital, Roskilde, was particularly vulnerable to attack by sea. Sometime around the year 1050, five Viking ships, constructed by boatyards as far away as Dublin, maneuvered deftly into position. Their owners began filling them with stones until they sunk into the dark waters of Roskilde Fjord, near Skuldelev. The Peberrenden, a narrow neck of the fjord, presented a natural barrier, defending Skuldelev and Roskilde. The five ships sunk there would have neatly prevented any attack by sea when they were scuttled, and they endured nearly a thousand years, long after anyone remembered that they were there. Fisherman cut a channel through them sometime in the ensuing centuries, and recalled the wrecks merely as underwater navigational landmarks.

And there they lay, five anonymous hulks lying in the silt of a northern fjord, until archaeologists

located them in 1962. The shallowest of them lay in only 6 feet (2 m) of water, the others barely deeper. A coffer damn was constructed around the wrecks to allow archaeologists to properly excavate them, board by board. What had originally appeared to be six ships were revealed as five when two of the ships turned out to be fore and aft of the same enormous vessel. The fine silt had perfectly preserved all five ships so well that a window was opened onto the legendary, long-vanished world of the Vikings.

MASTER BUILDERS

Even as archaeologists worked under sprinklers to keep the wood wet, it was becoming clear what a spectacular and valuable find the Skuldelev ships represented. Each of the five ships hailed from a different boatyard, built to varied designs for entirely different uses. *Skuldelev 1* was a stout, oceangoing vessel of pine, meant for a crew of eight. The biggest wreck, *Skuldelev 2*, revealed a warship capable of carrying a crew of 60 or more, propelled by oar, sail, or both. *Skuldelev 3* was a smaller cargo ship, and *Skuldelev 5* was smaller warship, while *Skuldelev 6* completed the catalog of types as a fishing boat. These vessels revealed a treasure trove of information on ship construction, commerce, and politics of the time.

All of the ships showed evidence of multiple repairs, indicating that (quite sensibly) old, well-used ships were put to service for the barricade in their final mission. The widely varying woods and construction techniques displayed on the five ships presented historians with new data, enriching modern views of the lives of Scandinavians some thousand years ago. The Skuldelev ships serve as both grave marker and guidebook to the culture that created and sank them in those cold waters so long ago.

WRECK SITE

Skuldelev Ships,
Roskilde Fjord,
Denmark

THEORY VS. PRACTICE

THE EXCAVATION OF THE SKULDELEV SHIPS piqued the interest of shipbuilders, who used the detailed plans of the wrecks to construct replicas. The *Sebbe Als*, one replica of *Skuldelev 5*, managed to make 5 knots under oar alone and reached up to 12 knots under sail, nearly twice what nautical theorists had predicted. Though it was still difficult to conceive of the bravery of those who would challenge the northern oceans in an open boat, actually building one left no doubt as to the possibilities these sturdy craft presented to their original owners.

▲ The *Sebbe Als*, launched in 1969, is a replica of *Skuldelev 5*. She was built with copies of the original Viking tools. She is still used for day trips, and every summer, she takes a one-to-three-week summer cruise. The *Sebbe Als* has traveled along most of the Danish and north German coasts.

◄ The *Skuldelev 5*

The Lost Fleet | KUBLAI KHAN'S NAVY

▲ Kublai Khan

Japan is an island nation, situated only 124 miles (200 km) from mainland Asia at its closest point. Yet over the millennia it has remained culturally distinct from and politically independent of its large and powerful neighbors to the west. This is due in part to two failed invasion attempts in the thirteenth century, which proved so disastrous that Japan has remained independent to this day. The wrecked fleets were the work of Kublai Khan, ruler of the largest superpower of his time.

Grandson of Mongol conqueror Genghis Khan, Kublai Khan founded the Yuan Dynasty and commanded a vast empire at the height of his rule. By the late thirteenth century, the Mongol empire stretched from the east coast of China through all of Central Asia, and as far west as present-day Hungary. After conquering Goryeo (present-day Korea) in 1270 after a series of bloody campaigns, Kublai Khan looked farther east still, toward Japan.

At first, Kublai Khan attempted a kind of bullying diplomacy, sending envoys to request "friendly relations" from the Japanese emperor. During this period, however, Japan was dominated by the powerful shoguns—military commanders of large regions of the country. By the time the message reached the emperor in Kyoto, military officers had already rebuffed the Mongol emissary. After numerous such attempts, Kublai Khan settled on a show of force. From newly subjugated Goryeo, Khan assembled a fleet of about 900 ships, which would carry approximately 23,000 Mongol, Korean, and Chinese soldiers.

▲ Kublai Khan ruled the world's largest empire and commanded the world's largest navy, boasting more than 700 ships. Yet, within 15 years, Kublai had squandered his massive fleet launching audacious attacks on Japan, Vietnam, and Java.

ILL WINDS

Kublai Khan's fleet sailed in November 1274 and overtook several of Japan's smaller islands before landing on Kyushu, the southernmost of Japan's four principle islands. By order of Japan's shogunate leader, Hojo Tokimune, a force of some 10,000 gathered to meet the Mongol fleet. The Japanese samurai were skilled hand-to-hand combatants, but the invaders brought with them sophisticated battle tactics and weaponry. But weather was on the side of the Japanese; a heavy storm blew in, and the Mongol leaders ordered their troops back to their ships. Hundreds of Mongol ships were lost, and Japanese warriors boarded the others; now their infantry combat skills served them well. The remaining Mongol invaders limped back to the mainland.

▲ Detail of a Japanese painting scroll depicting the Mongol invasions

Undeterred, Kublai Khan launched a second invasion seven years later, in 1281. In the intervening years, the Japanese had built fortresses and a long, fortified wall at Hakata, in present-day Fukuoka Prefecture. Meanwhile, Khan had assembled an armada of more than 4,000 ships and at least 100,000 men. The odds were against the Japanese, but, once again, nature came to the rescue. This time a massive typhoon swept in and destroyed Kublai Khan's fleet, reducing it by at least half, and securing Japan for a second time.

The pair of samurai victories not only ensured Japanese independence but helped generate a sense of nationality that has endured to this day. Usually, samurai fought amongst themselves in unending feudal wars, but, united against a common enemy, their victories over the Mongols gained legendary status.

THE WAY OF THE WARRIOR

THE VICTORY OF THE SHOGUN leader Hojo Tokimune over the Mongol invaders helped cement Buddhism's importance in Japanese culture. Tokimune's spiritual leader was the influential Zen master Bukko, whose thinking contributed to the samurai code called Bushido, or the Way of the Warrior. Bushido combined elements of native Japanese Shinto with Buddhist, Confucian, and Daoist influences. The rigid samurai code of moral and physical conduct is an integral part of Japanese culture.

▶ A Japanese samurai

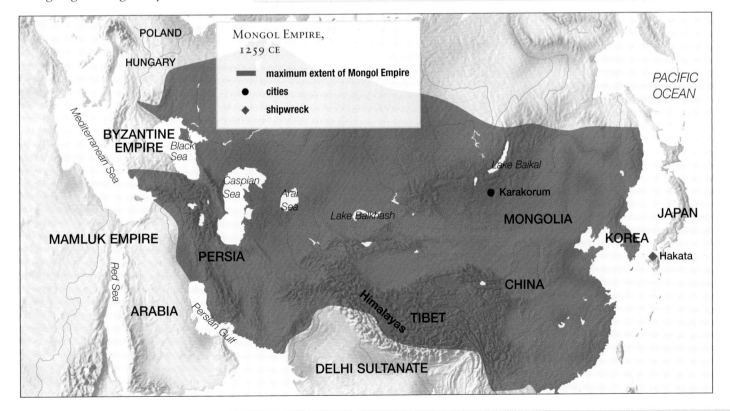

MONGOL EMPIRE, 1259 CE

■ maximum extent of Mongol Empire
● cities
◆ shipwreck

POLAND

HUNGARY

PACIFIC OCEAN

Mediterranean Sea

BYZANTINE EMPIRE *Black Sea*

Caspian Sea

Aral Sea

Lake Baikal

● Karakorum

Lake Balkhash

MONGOLIA

JAPAN

KOREA

MAMLUK EMPIRE

PERSIA

Red Sea

Persian Gulf

ARABIA

Himalayas

TIBET

CHINA

◆ Hakata

DELHI SULTANATE

| Ship of Air | THE PHANTOM WRECK OF NEW HAVEN |

The Puritans of seventeenth-century New England were not a frivolous lot. Piety and sobriety were their daily bread, and wild-eyed fancy was roundly shunned. So it is uncharacteristic indeed that hundreds of otherwise levelheaded people should all witness a phantom ship that seemed to melt into the air. Yet such was the case in 1647 in the New Haven Colony, when men, women, and children by the hundreds attested to an eerie apparition that has come to be known as the phantom ship of New Haven.

When a ship is lost at sea, it leaves behind a void, as loved ones, property, and hopes disappear into the deep. In the case of the New Haven Colony, the void was large and terrifying. In this smallest of independent New England colonies—New Haven wouldn't be incorporated into Connecticut Colony until 1665—trade wasn't going so well. The struggling settlers had to filter all their trade with England through the ports of their wealthier neighbor to the north, the Massachusetts Bay Colony. In 1646, the people of New Haven pooled their meager resources and contracted a 150-ton (136 metric ton) cargo vessel from a Rhode Island shipyard to carry a load of goods to England.

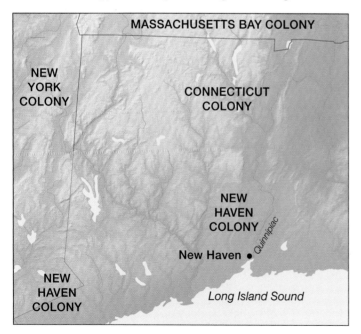

▲ The Puritans who settled the New Haven Colony faced many hardships and had placed a great deal of hope in the successful journey of the "Great Shippe."

UNDER FULL SAIL

On an icy January day in 1647, the "Great Shippe" finally departed New Haven. The ship was towed out into open water with great effort; men had to manually break the ice for a three-mile stretch. Finally she got underway, loaded with animal pelts and hides, wheat, peas, important documents, and some of the highest-ranking citizens of the community—the colonists' last great hope.

Spring arrived, but without any word of the ship from any quarter. Weeks turned to months, and all began to despair. The colony's spiritual leader, Reverend John Davenport, prayed for a sign from God. Six months after her departure, in June 1647, a great thunderstorm blew in from the northwest.

Before the air cleared, a mysterious sight appeared at the mouth of the Quinnipiac River—a ship half there and half not there. With all sails set, she proceeded upriver, sailing directly into the wind as if under full sail. Crowds gathered to watch her ghostly progress. According to a contemporary report, the ship was "of like dimensions" to their own, leading all to surmise that their ship had met a tragic end. As spectators watched in awe, the ship's sails appeared to shred and dissipate, her masts toppled, and finally she heeled over and "vanished into a smoky cloud." Here at last was the closure they desired, even if otherworldly.

The legend of New Haven's ghost ship has lived on through the centuries. In 1858, Henry Wadsworth Longfellow captured the story in his poem "The Phantom Ship," which ends: "And the pastor of the village / Gave thanks to God in prayer, / That, to quiet their troubled spirits, / He had sent this Ship of Air."

ye Ghoft Ship

▲ Woodcut of New Haven colonists watching in awe as the phantom ship evaporates in the fog. Thirty minutes had passed from the time the ship first appeared on the horizon to its seeming disintegration before their eyes.

ON GOOD AUTHORITY

THE REDOUBTABLE PURITAN MINISTER Cotton Mather (1663–1728) had no truck with the supernatural. Witches, ghosts, and apparitions were the work of the devil, as Mather repeatedly asserted during the Salem Witch Trials. Yet in his *Magnalia Christi Americana*, Mather reprinted a glowing account of the New Haven phantom ship, exhorting the reader to believe the story word for word. He pointed to the "many credible gentlemen that were eyewitnesses of this wonderful thing," and called the account "as undoubted as 'tis wonderful."

▶ Cotton Mather: an unlikely supporter of the ghostly vision of the "Great Shippe"

The *Flying Dutchman* GHOST SHIP

The *Flying Dutchman* is perhaps the most famous of history's many spectral vessels, and the most terrifying. As early as 1795 the *Dutchman* appears in print, and sightings of her have continued up to the present day. The ghost ship is said to sail forever with a crew of dead men. Their captain is a wraith who made the mistake of cursing the winds that beset his ship. Thus our piteous captain (variously known as van der Decken, van Dam, or van Straaten) was in return cursed to roam the seas for all eternity.

The legend tells of an unfortunate ship, plagued by an all too common storm while trying to get around the Cape of Good Hope, the treacherous point of land on the farthest southern tip of Africa. The passengers and crew pleaded with the captain to turn the ship around. As the crew came to mutiny, the captain shot and killed the ringleader of the rebellion, tossed his body overboard, and continued his mad journey into the maw of the storm. Just as all appeared lost, the captain cursed the storm, the winds, and the very sea, and swore to continue to sail around the Cape until judgment day.

Suddenly the sea calmed and a ghostly figure appeared on the deck. With a withering glare, the ominous spirit damned the captain and his crew for all eternity to ride the stormy seas off the Cape. Furthermore, the spirit continued, "gall shall be your drink, and red-hot iron your meat." And so the *Flying Dutchman* (it's not clear whether the name refers to the ship itself or the Dutch captain) is said to haunt the stormy seas off the Cape of Good Hope. Woe betide any who spy her— a glimpse of her is enough to curse a hapless sailor to death.

TRADE ROUTE

From Europe to the Indian Ocean, around the Cape of Good Hope

EUROPE

ASIA

AFRICA

Cape of
Good Hope

▲ George V

◄ The HMS *Bacchante*. For three years, Prince George and his brother Albert served as midshipmen aboard the *Bacchante*. In July 1881, George noted in his diary: "At 4 AM the *Flying Dutchman* crossed our bows."

FLYING THROUGH FICTION

The *Flying Dutchman* legend has inspired artists and has appeared in many fictional forms. It was captured in a painting by Albert Pinkham Ryder, now in the Smithsonian American Art Museum in Washington, D.C., and in a painting by Howard Pyle, known for illustrations of pirates. Richard Wagner's 1843 opera, *The Flying Dutchman*, was the most famous fictional adaptation of the tale until 2006, when the legend was given modern prominence when it appeared as a central plot element in the immensely popular Pirates of the Caribbean film series.

▶ The *Flying Dutchman* makes an appearance in the film *Pirates of the Caribbean: At World's End.*

APPARITIONS ON THE HIGH SEAS

The roll of witnesses to the *Flying Dutchman* includes a king of England, who saw the ghost ship in 1881 while serving aboard the HMS *Bacchante* as midshipman. While coming around Cape Horn, the future King George V stood on watch as the *Dutchman* crossed ahead of their bows. The poor soul who first spotted the ghostly ship fell from the rigging and died hours later. George never forgot the sight, and wrote of the "strange red light, as of a phantom ship all aglow." As recently as March 1939 the *Dutchman* was sighted from land, fighting a gale off the Cape of Good Horn. When the ship turned to seek the shelter of Table Bay, it is said to have sailed into a cloud bank and vanished.

Scientists have offered a plausible explanation for the legend, positing that the apparition is an artifact of light and water. Those who have seen her eerily glowing rigging and ghostly full sails bearing down upon them in a storm off the tumultuous tip of Africa, however, will tell a very different tale.

▲ The *Flying Dutchman* by Albert Pinkham Ryder. In ocean lore, the sight of this ship spells doom.

SUPERNATURAL AT SEA

The sea can be one of the most terrifying places on earth. Thus it comes as little surprise that it has inspired a long and colorful history of supernatural events and tales. Men—and, historically, nearly all sailors were men, because women were once considered bad luck on ships—who braved the daunting mountains of wind and water in tiny wooden vessels can perhaps be forgiven for ascribing supernatural causes and motivations to natural events.

When confronted by an eerie glow in the rigging, miles from nowhere, on the dark and lonely dog watch, who wouldn't think first of St. Elmo's Fire? Sitting in our comfortable, dry chairs ashore it is easy to talk of static electricity, relative humidity, and atmospheric anomalies. But when glowing balls of light creep down the rigging, and then detach themselves to bob about the deck, emitting naught but a slight buzzing, well, it takes a strong and emotionless man to remain calm in such straits. Combine the wondrous mysteries of the sea with the imagination of men cooped up in a cramped ship for months on end and one is bound to encounter the supernatural.

VISIONS IN THE WAVES

St. Elmo's Fire is a well-known example of a natural phenomenon with supernatural elements ascribed to it. Other common nautical legends, including sea serpents and mermaids, may also have natural antecedents. Giant squid or oarfish may have supported tales of ocean monsters, while manatees may have done the same for mermaids—although anyone who has seen the fat, wrinkly, porcine mammals must wonder just how desperate these sailors were. Confronted by scurvy, hot days in a tropical sun, and months of a monotonous landscape, however, imaginations might well run wild. Whatever factors combined to push sailors' visions into the fantastic, it is probably not surprising that those who ply the seas construct and reinforce a belief structure that makes sense of the events they witness.

▲ An illustration of a ship beset by St. Elmo's Fire. The phenomenon is unusual but natural, caused by a grounded object (like a ship) entering an electric field, such as those that thunder storms can create.

▲ The manatee, a large, herbivorous marine mammal that favors shallow, tropical waters, is a far cry from the stereotypical image of the lithe and lovely mermaid.

▲ Mermaid legends usually describe the creatures as beautiful but deadly, enchanting sailors with loveliness or with song in order to drown them.

VERY SUPERSTITIOUS

A COROLLARY OF SUPERNATURAL BELIEF is superstition. Sailors might be the most superstitious lot ever to walk (or rather, sail) the earth. If one chooses to violate a set of seemly random proscriptions, one should be prepared to endure the wrath of one's shipmates, if not Mother Nature herself. Bad luck might be the most feared phenomenon aboard ship. The following (partial) list delineates some of the most popular omens of such a catastrophe: sighting a cormorant or curlew, killing an albatross, starting a voyage on Friday, carrying a black sea bag, stepping aboard left foot first, and, finally, and perhaps most perilously: allowing a woman or a banana onboard.

▲ Northern royal albatross

THE FINAL WORD: LOST AT SEA

Widow's walks were a prominent feature of coastal New England architecture during the Age of Sail. This small deck, often precariously perched on the highest point of a house's roof, afforded a view of the harbor and the sea. Here, those with loved ones at sea could scan the horizon for a glimpse of a returning ship, hoping that it carried beloved seafarers safely home. As the previous pages attest, many watched in vain.

Although the term *widow's walk* may give the impression that only men died at sea, this is certainly not the case. It is true that in ancient and early modern times, most seafaring identities—fisherman, sailor, or explorer, for example—were the province of men. During the Age of Sail, though, when many European powers established colonies all over the globe, and the transatlantic slave trade was a harsh and flourishing business, increasing numbers of women and children joined the ranks of those lost at sea. The great passenger liner disasters claimed the lives of thousands of families collectively. As these losses remind us, the sea is a vast and dangerous place. It has carried men and women to the farthest corners of their known worlds, but it has also claimed its share of life.

▲ We may admire the stark beauty of a stormy sea, knowing full well of its awesome power. Throughout history, the sea has claimed untold lives.

A legend persists that on the night of the *Titanic*'s sinking, the ship's orchestra played the hymn "Nearer My God to Thee." This is, in fact, not true, but it points to a common response across cultures to loss at sea—grief commingled with faith. Against such an inexorable foe as the sea, our schemes and dreams can seem but small and insignificant. And yet, undaunted, we continue to take to the sea.

THE SEA GIVETH

Shipwrecks destroy lives and property, but they give back as well. In many coastal areas, from Southeast Asia to North Carolina's Outer Banks, the detritus of wrecked ships is turned into building supplies for locals. It is not uncommon to see houses constructed entirely of shipwreck timber in some parts of the world, sometimes incorporating porthole windows and pieces of rigging. The landlocked wreck of the USS *Wateree* in Peru became an inn.

◄ A widow's walk. Many houses in old seafaring and coastal towns still feature these seemingly quaint additions. But, far from quaint, they are reminders of the anxiety felt by many families as they waited for the return of a loved one at sea.

A MILLION UNTOLD WRECKS

These pages have focused on grand and glorious ships and disasters of great magnitude, but there are untold numbers of those lost at sea in small boats. In every ocean, river, and lake of the world, the fisherfolk, the casual sailor, the worker on a coal barge, the couple out for a paddle—these too have lost their lives. It happens every day and goes largely unnoticed. Statistics are hard to come by, but it is a safe bet that the numbers of small or single losses around the world and throughout the years add up to a larger number than all the dramatic disasters combined. Each of these small tragedies leaves behind a circle of mourners for whom the scope is irrelevant. Whether lost on a *Waratah* or a *Wee Lass*, such a death still leaves an irreparable hole in the lives of those left behind.

Underwater, wrecks often become rich habitats for wildlife, and those in shallow water are favorite dive spots. Sunken ships can be well preserved when they are finally located, sometimes emerging nearly intact from the undersea silt, as was the case of the *Mary Rose* and the *Vasa*. Such discoveries rank with the best archaeological finds on terra firma, offering a window into a vanished world.

▲ Shipwreck on a beach in Norway. Often, locals will make good use of timber salvaged from a beached wreck, using it to build houses and other structures.

▲ Lionfish swim around a submerged shipwreck in Egypt. Wrecked ships often form artificial reefs that form thriving habitats for marine plants and animals.

FURTHER READING

BOOKS

Ballard, Robert D. *Ghost Liners: Exploring the World's Greatest Lost Ships.* Boston: Little, Brown, 1998.

Ballard, Robert D., with Malcolm McConnell. *Adventures in Ocean Exploration : From the Discovery of the Titanic to the Search for Noah's Flood.* Des Moines, IA: National Geographic Books, 2001.

Bass, George F. *Ships and Shipwrecks of the Americas: A History Based on Underwater Archaeology.* New York: Thames & Hudson, 1996.

Bonansinga, Jay. *The Sinking of the Eastland: America's Forgotten Tragedy.* New York: Citadel, 2005.

Bonsall, Thomas E. *Great Shipwrecks of the Twentieth Century.* Baltimore: Bookman Publishing, 1988.

Bound, Mensun. *Lost Ships: The Discovery and Exploration of the Ocean's Sunken Treasures.* New York: Simon & Schuster, 1998.

de Kerbrech, Richard. *Ships of the White Star Line.* Hersham, UK: Ian Allan Publishing, 2009.

Field, Greg. *Great Ship Disasters.* Osceola, WI: Motorbooks, 2003.

Fine, John Christopher. *Treasures of the Spanish Main: Shipwrecked Galleons in the New World.* Guilford, CT: The Lyons Press, 2006.

Flayhart, William Henry III. *Disaster at Sea: Shipwrecks, Storms and Collisions on the Atlantic.* New York: W. W. Norton, 2003.

Hoehling, A. A. *Lost at Sea: The Truth Behind Eight of History's Most Mysterious Ship Disasters.* Nashville: Thomas Nelson, 1999.

Horner, Dave. *Shipwreck: A Saga of Sea Tragedy and Sunken Treasure.* New York: Sheridan House, 1999.

Kinder, Gary. *Ship of Gold in the Deep Blue Sea.* New York: Vintage, 1999.

Konstam, Angus. *Ghost Ships: Tales of Abandoned, Haunted, and Doomed Vessels.* London: PRC Publishing, 2005.

Konstam, Angus, and Pennington, Claudia. *The History of Shipwrecks.* New York: The Lyons Press, 2002.

Lansing, Alfred. Endurance: *Shackleton's Incredible Voyage.* New York, Basic Books, 1999.

Lee, Robert E. *Blackbeard the Pirate: A Reappraisal of His Life and Times.* Winston-Salem, NC: John F. Blair, 1984.

Lord, Walter. *Day of Infamy, Sixtieth Anniversary: The Classic Account of the Bombing of Pearl Harbor.* New York: Holt, 2001.

Lyon, Eugene. *Search for the Motherlode of the* Atocha. Florida: Florida Classics Library, 1989.

Marx, Robert, and Jennifer Marx. *New World Shipwrecks 1492–1825: A Comprehensive Guide.* Garland, TX: Ram Pub Co., 1994.

Marx, Robert F. *In the Wake of Galleons.* Flagstaff, AZ: Best Publishing Company, 2001.

———. *Shipwrecks in the Americas.* New York: Dover, 1987.

McKee, Alexander. *Wreck of the* Medusa: *The Tragic Story of the Death Raft.* New York: Signet, 2000.

Miller Jr., William H. *Doomed Ships: Great Ocean Liner Disasters.* Mineola, NY: Dover, 2006.

Pelta, Kathy. *Discovering Christopher Columbus: How History Is Invented.* Minneapolis: Lerner Publications, 1991.

Philbrick, Nathaniel. *In the Heart of the Sea: The Tragedy of the Whaleship* Essex. New York: Viking Penguin, 2000.

Pickford, Nigel. *The Atlas of Shipwrecks and Treasure*. New York: Dorling Kindersley, 1994.

Platt, Richard. *Eyewitness Shipwrecks*. New York: Dorling Kindersley, 2005.

Quinn, William P. *Shipwrecks Along the Atlantic Coast: A Remarkable Collection of Photographs of Maritime Accidents from Maine to Florida*. Orleans, MA: Commonwealth Editions, 2004.

Ratigan, William. *Great Lakes Shipwrecks and Survivals*. Grand Rapids, MI: Wm. B. Eerdmans Publishing Company, 1960.

Ritchie, David. *Shipwrecks: An Encyclopedia of the World's Worst Disasters at Sea*. New York: Checkmark Books/ Facts on File, 1999.

Seibold, David J., and Adams, Charles J. III. *Shipwrecks and Legends 'Round Cape May*. Reading, PA: Exeter House Books, 1987.

Spignesi, Stephen J. *The 100 Greatest Disasters of All Time*. Secaucus, New Jersey: Citadel Press, 2002.

Stick, David. *Graveyard of the Atlantic: Shipwrecks of the North Carolina Coast*. Chapel Hill, NC: UNC Press, 1985.

Ulloa, Francisco de. *The Voyage of Francisco Ulloa, 1539*. Madison: Wisconsin Historical Society, 2003.

Walton, Timothy R. *The Spanish Treasure Fleets*. Sarastoa, FL: Pineapple Press, 2002.

White, Jefferson. *Evidence and Paul's Journeys*. Hilliard, OH: Parsagard Press, 2001.

Wilson, Neil. *Great Sea Disasters: The World's Worst Sea Accidents*. Bristol, UK: Paragon, 1998.

WEB SITES

DEATH ON THE DARK RIVER: THE STORY OF THE *SULTANA* DISASTER
www.rootsweb.ancestry.com/~genepool/sultana.htm

E-ADVENTURE.NET: THE WRECK OF THE *SAN AGUSTIN*
www.e-adventure.net/sea/shipwrecks/sanagustin.html

MARINER'S MUSEUM
www.monitorcenter.org/

THE MEL FISHER MARITIME MUSEUM
www.melfisher.org/1622.htm

NORTH CAROLINA MARITIME MUSEUM
www.ncmaritime.org/Blackbeard/qar.htm

STORY OF THE *ATOCHA*
www.atocha1622.com/Atocha

A SLAVE SHIP SPEAKS: THE WRECK OF THE *HENRIETTA MARIE*
www.melfisher.org/exhibitions/henriettamarie/overview.htm

THE WRECK OF THE MANILA GALLEON *SAN AGUSTIN*
www.caribbeanarchaeology.com/SanAgustin.htm

INDEX

Clayoquot Sound, Canada, 100
Cleveland Cliffs Iron Company,
Clifford, Barry, 93, 137
Clinton, Bill, president of the
    United States, 103
clipper ship, 28
coal barge, 26
coal ship, 76
Cobh, Ireland, 116
Coffin, Owen, 22
Coleridge, Samuel Taylor, 164
collier, 77, 98
Colorado Desert, 139
Colorado River, 100, 138
Columbus, Christopher, 10,
    134–135, 151
Concord, 94
Concorde, La, 94
Confucianism, 175
Connecticut Colony, 176
Conqueror, HMS, 130–131
Conrad, Joseph, 63
Conway, RMS, 30, 31
copper, 16
Cornelisz, Jeronimus, 88–89
Cornhill magazine, 143
Cortés, Hernán, 138–139
Cousteau, Jacques, 74, 118
Crete, 171–172
Crippen, Dr. Hawley Harvey, 121
Cristoforo Colombo, the, 80
cruiser, 128
Currituck Beach, North Carolina,
    48, 49
Currituck Lifesaving Station, 48,
    49
Cyclops, USS, 151

D

Daedalus, HMS, 140
Daedalus sea serpent, 140
Dahlgren smoothbore cannon, 24
Dakar, Senegal, 56
Dakar-Ziguinchor ferry route, 57
Damant, Guyban C. C., 121
Danger Point, 68

Daoism, 175
Dauphin-Royale, the, 112
Davenport, John, 176
Dead Chest Island, British Virgin
    Islands, 31
dead reckoning, 135
de Chaumareys, Hugues Duroy, 47
Dei Gratia, the, 142
de Loutherbourg, Philippe-Jaques,
    110
Demre, Turkey, 170
Devil's Triangle. *See* Bermuda
    Triangle
Dewis, Joshua, 142
Dew, Walter, 121
Diamond Shoals, 26, 148–149
Dickson, Fred, 137
diving bell, 45, 74
diving suits, 74
Djula people, 57
Djurgården, Sweden, 44
dolphin, 60
Doña Paz, MV, 56, 84–85
Doria, Andrea, 81
Dorsetshire, the, 123
Doyle, Arthur Conan, 143
Drake, Sir Francis, 15, 108, 111
Drake's Bay, 14, 15
dredger, 59
Dry Tortugas, 16, 17
Duba, Saudi Arabia, 62
Dublin, Ireland, 172
Duke of Medina Sidonia, 108
Duke of Parma, 108
Duke University, 27
Dumali Point, 84
Dunkirk, 108
Dunraven, the, 74
Durban, South Africa, 144–145
Dutch East India Company
    (VOC), 88–89, 96

E

earthquake, 32
East Asia
    trade with, 14, 15

East Coast, United States, 49, 80
Eastland, SS, 10, 50–51
East River, 162
Eddystone, England, 110
Edmund Fitzgerald, SS, 40–41
Elephant Island, 37
Elizabeth I, queen of England,
    108–109
Empress of Ireland, RMS, 76–77
Endurance, HMS, 10, 36
English Channel, 107, 110
Erebus and *Terror* expedition, 38
Erebus, HMS, 10, 34–35
Ericsson, John, 24, 156, 157
Ernest McSorley, Captain, 40
Escheverz y Zubiza, Antonio
    de, 18
Essex, the (whaleship), 22–23, 159
Estonia, MS, 54
Euraquilo, 171
Exxon Valdez, the, 61

F

Fair Havens. *See* Kali-Limones
Falkland Islands, 130–131
Falklands Conflict, 130–131
Ferdinand II, king of Aragon, 134,
    135
ferry, 56, 84
    coastal, 52
    cruise, 54
    overcrowding, 56, 57, 62
    roll-on/roll-off (RO/RO), 62–63
Ferrysburg, Michigan, 152
fireboat, 162, 164–165
Fisher, Mel, 16, 17, 20, 91, 139
fishing boat, 173
Fishing Rip Shoal, 81
Fleet, Frederick, 71
Flight 19, 151
Florida Keys, 151
Florida Straits, 90
Flying Dutchman, the, 178–179,
    179
Ford Island, Hawaii, 124
Fort Clark, 115

Fort Hatteras, North Carolina, 115
Fort Macon State Park, North
    Carolina, 95
Fort Resolution, 34
forward-slanting bow, 76
Franklin, Jane (Lady Franklin), 35
Franklin, Sir John, 34
French navy, 56
Friedrich, Caspar David, 38
frigate, 46, 115
    sailing, 68
Fukuoka Prefecture, Japan, 175

G

Galician coast, Spain, 58, 59
Gallega, the, 137
galleon, 26, 115
    Manila, 14, 15
    Spanish, 16, 18, 21, 26
galley, 115
gam, 140
Gambia, 56, 57
Gardiner, David, 157
Gaspar Strait, 66
Gdynia, Poland, 126
General Belgrano, ARA, 130–131
General Grant, the 28–29
General Slocum, the, 162–163
Genesis, 168–169
Genghis Khan, 174
Genoa, Italy, 80
George V, king of England, 179
Géricault, Théodore, 46
ghost pipe fish, 74
giant squid, 180
Gibraltar Harbor, 142
Gigantic, the, 118
Gillis, James H., 32
Gilmer, Thomas Walker, 156, 157
Gloucester sea serpent, 141
gold, 16, 18, 19, 20, 28, 29
gold bullion, 120
Golden Age of Piracy, 94, 96–97
Golden Venture folding, 103
Golden Venture, the, 102–103
Gorée Island, Senegal, 90

ACKNOWLEDGMENTS AND CREDITS

Many thanks to my husband, Chris Carroll, who contributed to many sections of the book.

I would also like to thank Sophia, Lucinda, and Marea Carroll for their patience, assistance, and forbearance.

CREDITS

ABBREVIATIONS USED

iSP = *iStockphotos.com;* JI = *JupiterImages;* LoC = *Library of Congress;* NARA = *National Archives and Records Administration;* NASA = *National Aeronautics and Space Administration;* NOAA = *National Oceanic and Atmospheric Administration;* PD = *Public Domain;* SS = *Shutterstock;* USCG = *U.S. Coast Guard;* USN = *U.S. Naval Historical Center;* Wi = *Wikimedia*

l = left; *r* = right; *t* = top; *b* = bottom; *m* = middle

6 PD/John Willima Waterhouse 10*tl* PD/Ludolf Backhuysen 10*br* LoC 11*tr* NOAA 11*bl* NOAA 12–13 PD/Hendrik Kobell 14*tr* Wi/PD 14*bl* SS/Steffen Foerster Photography 15*tl* Wi/Myriam Thyes 15*tr* JI 15*br* Wi/PD 16*bl* PD/Willem van de Velde the Younger 16*mr* SS/scol22 17*tl* SS/Jack Weichen 17*bl* Wi/Marc Averette 17*br* NOAA 18*tr* JI 18 inset JI 19*tr* Wi/PD 20 PD 21*ml* Wi/PD 21*m* Wi/PD 21*tr* SS/Roxana Gonzalez 21*br* SS/1971yes 22 JI 23*t* JI 24*mr* NOAA 25*tl* LoC 25*tr* LoC 25*br* LoC 27*tr* NOAA 27*br* NOAA 28*tr* NOOA 29*tr* SS/Pichugin Dmitry 29*bl* NOOA 29*br* SS/Chris Gin 30*bl* NOAA 31*tr* NOAA 31*bl* Wi/Legis 32 JI 33*tl* USN 33*br* Wi/PD 34 NOAA 35*bl* JI 37*tr* NLOA 37*bl* NOAA 37*br* Wi/PD 38*ml* Wi/Caspar David Friedrich 38*br* NASA 40 Wi/PD 41*mr* SS/Michael Coddington 41*br* Wi/Annebethmi

42–43 PD/Wijnand Nuijen 44*tl* JI 44*tr* Flickr/Piero Sierra 45*bl* Wi/Peter Isotalo 45*tr* Wi/Henrik Sendelbach 45*br* Wi/Chris 73 46*tl* Wi/Théodore Géricault 46*br* Wi/PD 47*br* Wi/Pinpin 48*ml* SS/Keith Murphy 49*tr* LoC 49*bl* PD 50*tr* LoC 50*b* LoC 51*mr* LoC 51*bl* LoC 51*br* LoC 52 NOAA 53*br* LoC 54*ml* Wi/Stan Shebs 54*br* Wi/Kalle Id 55*tr* Wi/Tage Olsin 55*mr* Wi 56 AP/French Navy 57*ml* Wi/Rignese 57*br* Wi/Ji-Elle 58*tr* Wi/Luis Miguel Bugallo Sánchez 58*bl* AP 59*tr* Flickr/Colin Brace 59*bl* Wi/Mila Zinkova 60 NOAA 61*tr* NOAA 61*bl* Flickr/Jim Brickett 62 Wi/Amr Fayez 63*tr* Flickr/Nataraj Metz 64–65 PD/Carl Wilhelm Barth 66*tl* LoC 67 AP/Roland Weihrauch 68*ml* USN 69*tr* JI 69*bl* Wi/Dewet 70 JI 71*tr* JI 71*br* JI 72*ml* LoC 72*bl* LoC 73tm LoC 73*tr* LoC 73*mr* Wi/Looi 73*bl* NOAA 74*tl* SS/Stephan Kerkhofs 74*bm* Wi 75*tl* NOAA 75*br* USN 75*bl* SS/Khoroshunova Olga 76*tr* LoC 76*bl* Library and Archives Canada 77*tr* SS/Ronen 77*br* LoC 78*l* Wi/PD 79*tr* Wi/PD 79*m* LoC 79*br* Library and Archives Canada 80 USCG/Harry Ahysen 81*tl* USCG/Karen Smith 81*br* Wi/Agnolo Bronzino 82*tl* AP 83 AP/USCG 84 AP 85*tr* NOAA 85*bl* AP/Joseph Capellan 86–87 PD/Willem van der Velde the Younger 88*tl* Wi/PD 88*br* Wi/Roo72 89*mr* Wi/svdmolen 89*br* Wi/svdmolen 89*bl* Wi 90*bl* LoC 90*br* LoC 91*mr* Wi/Rémi Kaupp 92 Wi/PD 93*tr* Wi/Willem van der Velde the Younger 93*br* Barry L. Clifford 94 Wi/Jean Leon Gerome Ferris 95*br* Wi/PD 96*l* Wi/PD 96*r* Wi 97*l* Wi/PD 97*mr* SS/Margo Harrison 97*br* Wi/PD 98*ml* Wi/Pete Carney 98*m* PD 98*br* LoC 99*tl* Wi/PD 100*l* Wi/superbfc 101*l* Wi/cacophony 101*tr* SS/Thomas Barrat 101*br* JI 102 USCG/Mei Ki Kam 103*br* Wi/Archivaldo 104–105 PD/Abraham Beerstraaten 106*t* JI 106*l* NOAA 106*r* JI 107*r* Flickr/Ben Sutherland 108 Wi/PD 109*tr* Wi/PD 109*b* JI 110 Wi/PD 111*l* Wi/Cornelis Claesz. van Wieringen 111*r* LoC 112 Wi/Arnald George 113*tl* Wi/

Jacques-Louis David 113*br* Wi/Luny Tho 114 LoC 115 LoC 116*t* LoC 116*r* LoC 1 JI 117*tr* LoC 117*mr* Wi/PD 118*r* NASA 118*l* LoC 119*tr* Wi/PD 119*bl* Wi/PD 120 LoC 121*mr* LoC 121*br* Wi/wildwords 12 USN 123*mr* USN 123*bl* USN 124*r* NARA 124l NARA 125*tr* USN/Jayme Pastoric 1 LoC 126*tl* Wi/PD 126*bl* JI 129*tr* USN 12 USN 130 AP 131*tr* LoC 132–133 PD/J. N W. Turner 134 LoC 135*tr* LoC 135*m* Wi ragesoss 137*t* Flickr/Larry Wentzel 137*b* S Ramunas Bruzas 138 SS/Ricardo Manuel Silva de Sousa 139*tl* PD 139*br* SS/Brian V 140 LoC 141*tr* Wi/Olaus Magnus 141*m* 141*b* PD 142 Wi/PD 143*tl* iSP/Stanislav Pobytov 143*bl* Wi/PD 144*tr* SS/Gail John 144*bl* SS/Ilya Genkin 145*tl* PD 146 Wi/P 147*mr* PD 147*b* LoC 149*l* SS/Doug Lem 149*r* PD 151*tr* USCG/PD 151*bl* LoC 152 PD 153*tr* LoC 153*br* SS/Doug Lemke 15 PD 154–155 PD/Martinus Schouman 156 LoC 157*tr* USN 157*m* LoC 157*br* LoC 1 LoC 158*bl* LoC 159*bl* USN 160*tr* USN 1 Wi/PD 161*tr* SS/Cynthia Farmer 161*br* LoC 161*bl* LoC 162*br* Wi/Erik Edson 16 Wi/PD 163*tr* LoC 163*bl* Wi/Samuel War Stanton 164*bl* Wi/Joshua Sherurcij 164*mr* Gaby Kooijman 164*br* SS/Gertjan Hooijer 165*t* Flickr/Vidiot 165*m* LoC 166–167 Po Ivan Aivazovsky 168*tl* Wi/Jacopo Bassano 169*tr* Wi/Gustave Doré 169*bl* PD 171*bm* SS/Massimo Merlini 171*tr* PD 172*tl* Wi/Christian Bickel 172*bl* Wi/Casiopeia 173*b* Wi/Steen Weile 173*bm* Flickr/Val Buzeta 174*tr* Wi/Anige 174*ml* Wi/PD 174*bl* Wi/PD 175*tr* Wi/PD 176*tl* LoC 177*mr* LoC 177*br* LoC 178 inset LoC 178*br* National Maritime Museum 179*tr* Photofest 179*br* W Albert Pinkham Ryder 180 NOAA 181*tr* J 181*br* U.S. Fish and Wildlife Service 181/V Frederic Leighton 182*bl* SS/bierchen 182*tr* Chee-Onn Leong 183*tl* SS/Pinosub 183*br* Rich Carey 183*bl* SS/Marek Slusarczyk